PRACTICE MAKES PERFECT™

Intermediate French Grammar

Eliane Kurbegov

New York Chicago San Francisco Lisbon London Madrid Mexico City
Milan New Delhi San Juan Seoul Singapore Sydney Toronto

The McGraw·Hill Companies

Copyright © 2013 by The McGraw-Hill Companies, Inc. All rights reserved. Printed in
the United States of America. Except as permitted under the United States Copyright
Act of 1976, no part of this publication may be reproduced or distributed in any form
or by any means, or stored in a database or retrieval system, without the prior written
permission of the publisher.

2 3 4 5 6 7 8 9 10 11 12 13 14 15 16 17   QVS/QVS   1 9 8 7 6 5

ISBN   978-0-07-177538-0
MHID   0-07-177538-2

e-ISBN   978-0-07-177539-7
e-MHID   0-07-177539-0

Library of Congress Control Number 2012933504

McGraw-Hill, the McGraw-Hill Publishing logo, Practice Makes Perfect, and related
trade dress are trademarks or registered trademarks of The McGraw-Hill Companies
and/or its affiliates in the United States and other countries and may not be used
without written permission. All other trademarks are the property of their respective
owners. The McGraw-Hill Companies is not associated with any product or vendor
mentioned in this book.

Interior design by Village Bookworks, Inc.

McGraw-Hill products are available at special quantity discounts to use as premiums and
sales promotions or for use in corporate training programs. To contact a representative,
please e-mail us at bulksales@mcgraw-hill.com.

This book is printed on acid-free paper.

Contents

Introduction

You have a good understanding of French and feel you are ready to move on. You want to progress toward a higher level of proficiency in the French language, but advanced grammar books still look overwhelming. Then this book is for you.

This highly useful book is well suited for the student who has mastered the basics of French grammar. It can also be used as a review book at the end of a second- or third-year course or as a supplement to an online French course. *Intermediate French Grammar* aims at expanding your knowledge and usage of verb tenses as well as your knowledge and usage of syntactical structures. It also aims to familiarize you with function words (such as relative pronouns), which make sentences richer and more detailed.

Each unit in the book is self-contained and therefore can be studied independently. A total of 18 lessons follow a simple and progressive format designed to help you learn, review, and retain knowledge of intermediate grammatical forms and structures. User-friendly charts serve as preparation for exercises, and an Answer key at the end of the book will help you verify your mastery of the material. You will practice present, past, and future tenses in addition to commonly used *present and past conditional* as well as *present and past subjunctive mood* verb forms. Adjectives, adverbs, prepositions, and pronouns are also important parts of this book.

As the focus of the book is grammar, vocabulary will be presented as a context in which to review and practice grammatical and syntactical forms. Each new concept or structure is introduced with explanations, followed by highlighted examples illustrating and clarifying the new grammatical points, and a variety of exercises for practice. Among those exercises, some are designed to test your writing skills and some are embedded in contextualized reading material designed to help you review and practice essential structures and concepts in an interesting and fun manner. These exercises allow you to practice what you are learning and assess your understanding of concepts as well as put your knowledge into real-world tasks such as reading about the Olympic Games and writing about what the world will look like in 50 years.

À vous la parole! Amusez-vous bien tout en apprenant!

Present tense and uses of regular and stem-changing verbs

Uses of the present tense

In French, the present tense is used to indicate that an action or a situation takes place at the very moment when one is speaking or that it takes place routinely.

Mes parents **travaillent** aujourd'hui.	*My parents are working today.*
Je **glande** dans ma chambre en ce moment.	*I loaf/hang out in my room at the moment.*
Mon grand-père **n'entend** pas bien.	*My grandfather does not hear well.*
Tu **arrives** toujours en retard.	*You always arrive late.*

Note that there is no direct equivalent of the English progressive present tense in French. To state that something *is happening*, simply state that it *happens*.

Tes amis **attendent** en bas.	*Your friends are waiting downstairs.*
Tu **descends**?	*Are you coming down?*

You may also use the idiomatic expression **être en train de** (*to be in the middle of*) followed by an infinitive verb to stress the progressive present.

Je **suis en train de** choisir un cadeau.	*I'm (in the middle of) choosing a gift.*
Paul **est en train de** cuisiner.	*Paul is (in the middle of) cooking.*
Nous **sommes en train de** rêver.	*We are (in the middle of) dreaming.*
Son père **est en train de** travailler.	*His father is (in the middle of) working.*

The present tense is sometimes used for future actions.

J'arrive tout de suite.	*I'll be right there.*
Tu rappelles demain?	*Will you call back tomorrow?*
Nous restons en France cet été.	*We'll stay in France this summer.*
Vous passez ce weekend?	*Will you stop by this weekend?*

The present tense is used after **depuis** to indicate that the action started in the past is still going on in the present.

Depuis que **tu habites** ici, je ne suis plus seule.	*Since you have been living here, I'm no longer alone.*
Depuis que **tu as** cet iPad, tu es constamment occupé.	*Since you got this iPad, you are constantly occupied.*

The present tense of regular verbs

Remember that the first step in conjugating a regular -**er**, -**ir**, or -**re** verb in the present tense consists of identifying the stem or root of the verb by dropping its infinitive ending.

INFINITIVE FORM:	jouer	finir	répondre
STEM:	jou-	fin-	répond-

The second step consists of adding the appropriate endings for that category of verbs and for the subject of the verb.

	-er jouer	-ir finir	-re répondre
je	joue	finis	réponds
tu	joues	finis	réponds
il, elle, on	joue	finit	répond
nous	jouons	finissons	répondons
vous	jouez	finissez	répondez
ils, elles	jouent	finissent	répondent

Je joue au Monopoly avec mes copains.
Marc et Luc gagnent le plus souvent.
Quelquefois, **nous finissons** très tard.
Sabine perd souvent car elle ne fait pas attention.

I play Monopoly with my friends.
Marc and Luc win the most often.
Sometimes we finish very late.
Sabine often loses because she does not pay attention.

Here are some commonly used regular -**er**, -**ir**, and -**re** verbs in their infinitive forms, which you may use in exercises found in this chapter.

-er		-ir		-re	
accompagner	*to accompany*	choisir	*to choose*	attendre	*to wait for*
adorer	*to love, adore*	éblouir	*to dazzle*	défendre	*to defend*
annoncer	*to announce*	finir	*to finish*	descendre	*to go down*
arriver	*to arrive*	grandir	*to grow*	entendre	*to hear*
bavarder	*to chat*	réussir	*to succeed*	perdre	*to lose*
cuisiner	*to cook*	saisir	*to seize*	répondre	*to answer*
débarrasser	*to clean up*				
écouter	*to listen to*				
étouffer	*to suffocate*				
éviter	*to avoid*				
glander	*to loaf*				
laver	*to wash*				
partager	*to share*				
passer	*to spend (time)*				
plaisanter	*to joke*				
raccrocher	*to hang up*				
raconter	*to tell (stories)*				
rentrer	*to go back*				
rester	*to stay*				
travailler	*to work*				
tromper	*to fool*				

Ces lumières m'**éblouissent**.
Vous **choisissez** toujours les plus jolies serviettes.

These lights dazzle me.
You always choose the prettiest napkins.

Nous **passons** beaucoup de bons moments dans ce café.	*We spend many good moments in this café.*
Tu **entends** la question?	*Do you hear the question?*
Le vendredi, je **rentre** tôt du travail.	*On Fridays, I come home from work early.*
Les activités sportives **rendent** les gens énergiques.	*Sports activities make people energetic.*

Remember that the verbs **ouvrir** (*to open*), **couvrir** (*to cover*), **découvrir** (*to discover*), and **offrir** (*to offer*) are conjugated like regular **-er** verbs.

Tu **ouvres** la fenêtre, s'il te plaît? On étouffe dans cette chambre.	*Can you open the window, please? We are suffocating in this room.*
Elle **couvre** ses sofas avec des coussins.	*She covers her sofas with pillows.*
Les enfants **découvrent** tôt ou tard qu'il y a des règles à suivre.	*Children discover sooner or later that there are rules to follow.*
J'offre toujours un joli cadeau à maman pour la Fête des Mères.	*I always offer a pretty gift to Mom for Mother's Day.*

Note that a verb remains in the infinitive form when it appears after a preposition such as **de**, **avant de**, or **pour**.

Il saisit toujours l'occasion **de me défendre**.	*He always seizes the opportunity to defend me.*
Je prépare le dîner **avant de téléphoner** aux copains.	*I prepare dinner before calling friends.*
Elle descend l'escalier **pour ouvrir** la porte.	*She comes down the stairs to open the door.*

DU VOCABULAIRE UTILE. *Useful vocabulary.*

Examine this vocabulary list before doing the next exercises.

amusant	*funny*	le dîner	*the dinner*
au téléphone	*on the phone*	l'e-mail	*the e-mail*
avoir envie de	*to feel like*	patiemment	*patiently*
bref	*in short*	pendant	*during*
faire/laver la vaisselle	*to do/wash the dishes*	peut-être	*maybe*
heureusement	*fortunately*	tout le temps	*all the time*
la coquette	*the flirt* (f.)		

EXERCICE
1·1

Ma famille et moi. *My family and I.* Write the correct present tense form of each verb in parentheses on the line provided.

Dans ma famille, on 1. _cuisine_ (cuisiner) et on

2. _mange_ (manger) ensemble tous les soirs. Après le dîner, les enfants

3. _débarrassent_ (débarrasser) la table et 4. _lavent_ (laver) la

vaisselle. Maman et papa 5. _regardent_ (regarder) le journal télévisé et moi, je

6. __réponds__ (répondre) aux e-mails de mes copains ou à leurs questions sur Facebook. Quelquefois je 7. __téléphone__ (téléphoner) à ma copine Chloé. Elle 8. __adore__ (adorer) qu'on 9. __bavarde__ (bavarder) toute la soirée. Le problème, c'est qu'elle n'a jamais envie de 10. __raccrocher__ (raccrocher).

EXERCICE
1·2

Mes frères, ma sœur et moi. *My brothers, my sister, and I. Write the correct present tense form of each verb in parentheses on the line provided.*

Mon frère aîné Jérôme 1. __plaisante__ (plaisanter) tout le temps. Il
2. __raconte__ (raconter) des histoires vraiment amusantes. Pendant les soirées,
tout le monde 3. __écoute__ (écouter) Jérôme et nous, nous
4. __attendons__ (attendre) patiemment la fin de l'histoire. Patrick, mon autre frère,
5. __réussit__ (réussir) toujours à 6. __éviter__ (éviter) les
préparations. Il 7. __travaille__ (travailler) tard au bureau ou il
8. __accompagne__ (accompagner) une copine chez elle avant de
9. __rentre__ (rentrer) chez nous. Bref! Il 10. __choisit__ (choisir)
le moment quand tout est prêt pour 11. __arriver__ (arriver). Nadine, ma sœur
12. __prétend__ (prétendre) ne pas être intéressée par les garçons, mais elle
13. __passe__ (passer) beaucoup de temps devant le miroir de la salle de bain
quand j' 14. __annonce__ (annoncer) l'arrivée de mes copains. Quelle coquette!
Elle 15. __trompe__ (tromper) peut-être les autres, mais pas moi! Quand elle
16. __descend__ (descendre) finalement l'escalier, elle
17. __éblouit__ (éblouir) tous mes copains. Nadine 18. __saisit__
(saisir) généralement toutes les occasions de parler à mes copains. Moi, heureusement j'
19. __entends__ (entendre) tout. Elle 20. __grandit__ (grandir) trop
vite, ma petite sœur.

À vous d'écrire! *Your turn to write! Write this paragraph in French, remembering to conjugate all verbs appropriately.*

I have a small family: a mom, a dad, one brother, and one sister. We eat dinner together every night. My mom and my sister Nina cook. During dinner, Dad talks a lot and we listen. He is very funny and loves to tell jokes.

After dinner, I clean up the table; my dad and my brother wash the dishes. My sister who has many friends spends a lot of time on the phone. My mom stays in her room and answers e-mails.

J'ai une petite famille : une mère, un père, un frère et une soeur. Nous mangeons ensemble chaque soir. Ma mère et ma soeur cuisinent. Pendant souper, mon père parle beaucoup et nous écoutons. Il est très drôle et adore racontrer des blagues. Après le souper, je nettoie la table ; mon père et mon frère font le vaisselle. Ma soeur qui a beaucoup d'amis passe beaucoup de temps au téléphone. Ma mère reste dans sa chambre et répond aux emails.

The present tense of stem-changing -er verbs

Remember that some regular -er verbs have a slight stem change as they are conjugated in the present tense.

♦ **-Er** verbs that have a **g** in the stem will end in **-eons** in their **nous** form. Similarly, if an -er verb has a **c** in the stem, it will become **ç** in the **nous** form.

Nous **mangeons** tard le samedi soir.	*We eat late on Saturday nights.*
Nous **avançons** vraiment doucement.	*We progress really slowly.*

♦ **l → ll:** The verbs **appeler** (*to call*) and **rappeler** (*to call back*) double the **l** in the stem in all forms except for the **nous** and **vous** forms.

Tu **appelles** encore ta copine?	*Are you still calling your girlfriend?*
Vous **rappelez** ce soir, d'accord?	*You'll call back tonight, OK?*

♦ **t → tt:** The verb **jeter** doubles the **t** in the stem in all forms except for the **nous** and **vous** forms.

Je **jette** les vieux journaux dans le container du recyclage.	*I'm throwing the old newspapers into the recycling bin.*
Nous **jetons** nos chaussures quand elles sont démodées.	*We throw away our shoes when they are out of style.*

♦ **é → è:** The **é** in the following verbs becomes **è** in all forms except for the **nous** and **vous** forms.

céder	*to give up/in*	protéger	*to protect*
décéder	*to pass away*	répéter	*to repeat*
espérer	*to hope*	révéler	*to reveal*
posséder	*to possess*	rouspéter	*to complain*
préférer	*to prefer*	tolérer	*to tolerate*

Les enfants **rouspètent** quand ils ont trop de devoirs.
The children complain when they have too much homework.
Le plus faible **cède** au plus fort.
The weakest gives in to the strongest.
Nous **espérons** avoir raison.
We hope to be right.
Vous **tolérez** beaucoup de choses.
You tolerate many things.

♦ **e → è:** The **e** in the following verbs becomes **è** in all forms except for the **nous** and **vous** forms.

acheter	*to buy*	enlever	*to take/put away*
amener	*to bring along*	lever (une chose)	*to raise/lift (a thing)*
élever (les enfants)	*to raise (children)*	semer	*to sow*
emmener	*to take along*		

Ces parents **élèvent** bien leurs enfants.
These parents raise their children well.
Nous **achetons** tous nos fruits au marché.
We buy all our fruit at the market.
Mon frère nous **emmène** au cinéma ce soir.
My brother is taking us to the movies tonight.
Tu **enlèves** ton livre? Nous mangeons.
Will you put away your book? We're eating.

♦ **y → i:** The **y** in the following verbs becomes **i** in all forms except for the **nous** and **vous** forms.

envoyer	*to send*
essayer	*to try*
essuyer	*to wipe (dry)*
nettoyer	*to clean*
payer	*to pay*
tutoyer	*to use the familiar **tu** address*
vouvoyer	*to use the formal **vous** address*

VOCABULAIRE UTILE. *Useful vocabulary.*

Examine the following vocabulary before doing the following exercises.

à la fin	*at the end*	cela	*this, that*
chaque	*each*	d'abord	*first (of all)*
l'amoureux (m)	*lover*	la pagaille	*disarray*
la paix	*peace*	la prière	*prayer*
le champ de bataille	*battlefield*	le couvent	*convent*
le mousquetaire	*musketeer*	le sorcier	*sorcerer*
les lunettes	*glasses*	malheureusement	*unfortunately*
personne	*nobody*		

La famille des Schtroumpf. *The Smurf family.*

Chaque Schtroumpf 1. __possède__ (posséder) un trait de personnalité distinct. Par exemple, le Schtroumpf à lunettes 2. __porte__ (porter) des lunettes. Le Schtroumpf paresseux 3. __rouspète__ (rouspéter) avant de 4. __travailler__ (travailler). Tous les Schtroumpfs 5. __respectent__ (respecter) le Grand Schtroumpf, mais ils le 6. __tutoient__ (tutoyer). Dans cette famille, on ne 7. __vouvoie__ (vouvoyer) personne. Les Schtroumpfs 8. __habitent__ (habiter) en paix et en harmonie dans un joli petit village.

Mais un jour le sorcier Gargamel 9. __envoie__ (envoyer) une Schtroumpfette au village. D'abord la Schtroumpfette 10. __sème__ (semer) la pagaille dans la famille Schtroumpf. Mais à la fin, les Schtroumpfs 11. __cèdent__ (céder) à son charme et tout le monde 12. __aiment__ (aimer) la Schtroumpfette.

Des cousins célèbres. *Famous cousins.* *Write each one of the following -er verbs in the appropriate present tense form.*

Le personnage principal du célèbre film *Roxane* est un mousquetaire et il s'

1. __appelle__ (appeler) Cyrano. Beaucoup de gens se

2. __moquent__ (moquer) de lui parce qu'il 3. __possède__ (posséder) un énorme nez. Cyrano 4. __rouspète__ (rouspéter) et

5. __provoque__ (provoquer) ses adversaires en duel. Il

6. __gagne__ (gagner) toujours.

Cyrano 7. __aime__ (aimer) secrètement la belle Roxane, sa cousine. Malheureusement Roxane 8. __préfère__ (préférer) le beau Christian. Cyrano 9. __cède__ (céder) aux prières de Christian. Il 10. __accepte__ (accepter) de créer des poèmes que Christian 11. __envoie__ (envoyer) à Roxane.

Cyrano 12. _emmène_ (emmener) Christian sur le champ de bataille mais promet à Roxane de 13. _protéger_ (protéger) son amoureux. Il

14. _essaie_ (essayer) de faire cela mais Christian

15. _décède_ (décéder) sur le champ de bataille.

Désespérée, Roxane s' 16. _enferme_ (enfermer) dans un couvent. À la fin du film, Cyrano 17. _révèle_ (révéler) son amour à Roxane avant de

18. _décéder_ (décéder) dans ses bras. C'est triste et romantique, n'est-ce pas?

EXERCICE 1·6

À vous d'écrire! *Your turn to write!* *Translate the following paragraph into French.*

Mr. and Mrs. Duport have a big family. They are raising five children. Unfortunately, they own a small home. So the children share two bedrooms. The Duports take the children to school every day. The big ones protect the little ones.

While the children spend the day at school, Mrs. Duport works at her office and Mr. Duport cleans the house and cooks.

The Duport family hopes to possess a big house someday! But for the moment, nobody's complaining!

M. et Mme. Duport ont une grande famille. Ils élèvent cinq enfants. Malheureusement, ils possèdent une petite maison. Alors, les enfants partagent deux chambres à coucher. Les Duports emmènt leurs enfants à l'école chaque jour. Les grands protègent les petits. Pendant les enfants passent la journée à l'école, Mme. Duport travaille à son bureau et M. Duport nettoie la maison et cuisine. La famille Duport espère de posséder une grande maison un jour! Mais pour le moment, personne ne proteste.

EXERCICE 1·7

Qui est-ce? *Who is this?* *After reading this paragraph, answer the questions that follow in complete sentences.*

Elle **répond** au nom d'Audrey en hommage à la célèbre actrice Audrey Hepburn. L'adolescente Audrey **grandit** dans une famille ordinaire. Elle **a** un père chirurgien-dentiste et une mère enseignante. Elle **a** aussi un frère et deux sœurs, mais Audrey **est** l'aînée des quatre enfants. Quand elle **finit** ses études de lycée, Audrey ne **va** à l'université qu'une année et puis elle **fait** quelques films pour la télévision. Elle **joue** son premier grand rôle au cinéma à l'âge de vingt-deux ans et elle **gagne** le César (Oscar) du premier espoir féminin en l'an 2000. Depuis cette année-là, la jeune actrice ne **cesse** pas de **jouer** des rôles cinématographiques importants qui la **rendent** célèbre dans le monde entier.

Qui est-ce? C'est Audrey Tautou, célèbre pour ses rôles dans les films *Le fabuleux destin d'Amélie Poulain, Coco avant Chanel* et *Da Vinci Code.*

1. Comment s'appelle la personne décrite dans ce passage?

   Elle répond au nom d'Audrey.

2. Dans quelle sorte de famille grandit-elle?

   Elle grandit dans une famille ordinaire.

3. Quelle est la profession de son père?

   Dentiste

4. Est-ce qu'elle est enfant unique?

   non, elle a un frère et deux soeurs.

5. Qu'est-ce qu'elle fait après un an d'université?

   Elle fait quelques films pour télévision.

6. Qu'est-ce qu'elle gagne en l'an 2000?

   Elle gagne le César (Oscar) du premier espoir féminin en l'an 2000

7. Quel est l'équivalent américain d'un César?

   Un Oscar.

8. Quels films la rendent célèbre?

   Elle joue des rôles cinématographiques importants.

Articles and genders

Review of articles and genders

Review the following rules of thumb to help you determine the gender of a noun, but remember there are exceptions to the rules, and whenever possible it will be safer verifying the gender of a noun in a book or dictionary. Review the following chart in which nouns are classified by gender according to their endings:

MASCULINE NOUN ENDINGS	FEMININE NOUN ENDINGS
-eau	-e
-on	-son
-oir	-tion
-eur	-euse
-ou	-ette
-é	-té
-er	-ère
-in/ain	-ine

Now look at the following examples and note the patterns:

MASCULINE NOUNS		FEMININE NOUNS	
le bateau	*boat*	l'affiche	*poster*
le bureau	*office/office desk*	la chaise	*chair*
le jumeau	*twin boy*	la jumelle	*twin girl*
le jambon	*ham*	la maison	*house*
le raton	*little rat*	la saison	*season*
le ton	*tone*	la raison	*reason*
le soir	*evening*	la composition	*composition*
le rasoir	*razor*	la nation	*nation*
le manoir	*manor*	la résolution	*resolution*
le professeur	*teacher (male)*	la vendeuse	*saleslady*
le coiffeur	*hairdresser (male)*	la coiffeuse	*hairdresser (female)*
le menteur	*liar (male)*	la menteuse	*liar (female)*
le bijou	*jewel*	la chambrette	*little room*
le chou	*cabbage*	la coquette	*flirt (female)*
le clou	*nail*	la fillette	*little girl*

MASCULINE NOUNS		FEMININE NOUNS	
le blé	*wheat*	la célébrité	*fame*
le thé	*tea*	la fierté	*pride*
le dé	*die (n.)*	la beauté	*beauty*
le boucher	*butcher (m.)*	la bouchère	*butcher (lady)*
l'épicier	*grocery clerk (m.)*	l'épicière	*grocery store clerk (f.)*
l'ouvrier	*worker (m.)*	l'ouvrière	*worker (f.)*
le copain	*friend (m.)*	la copine	*friend (f.)*
le voisin	*neighbor (m.)*	la voisine	*neighbor (f.)*
le pain	*bread*	la farine	*flour*

Using the appropriate article

Remember that articles almost always precede a noun, and they vary according to the gender and number of the noun they accompany. Look at the following summary chart for articles.

GENDER AND NUMBER	INDEFINITE ARTICLES	DEFINITE ARTICLES	DEMONSTRATIVE ARTICLES	PARTITIVE ARTICLES
Masculine singular	un	le/l'	ce/cet	du/de l'
Feminine singular	une	la/l'	cette	de la/de l'
Plural	des	les	ces	des

Remember to use indefinite articles in French when talking about countable things or people.

| J'ai **une** meilleure amie. | *I have **a** (one) best friend.* |
| Tu as **un** beau sweat. | *You have **a** beautiful sweatsuit.* |

The plural indefinite article must be used in French even though it may be implied in English.

| Nous avons **des** roses rouges. | *We have (**some**) red roses.* |
| Elle a **des** cheveux longs. | *She has (**some**) long hair.* |

The plural indefinite article **des** should not be used before an adjective. It is replaced by **de**.

| Il a **de** beaux yeux. | *He has beautiful eyes.* |

Remember to use definite articles in French when talking about things in general even when the definite article is omitted in English.

| **Le** blé pousse bien en Alsace. | *Wheat grows well in Alsace.* |
| L'argent ne fait pas **le** bonheur. | *Money does not guarantee happiness.* |

Use definite articles before days of the week or moments of time when meaning regularly on that day or at that moment of time.

Le samedi, je ne travaille pas.	*On Saturdays, I do not work.*
Le matin, j'ai toujours sommeil.	*In the mornings, I am always sleepy.*
L'été, il fait chaud.	*In the summer, it is hot.*

Make necessary adjustments to singular articles that precede a vowel sound.

DEFINITE ARTICLES:	**Le** and **la** become **l'** before a vowel sound.
MASCULINE SINGULAR:	**le** garçon (*the boy*), **l'**arbre (*the tree*), **l'**hôtel (*the hotel*)
FEMININE SINGULAR:	**la** fille (*the girl*), **l'**affiche (*the poster*), **l'**histoire (*the story*)
DEMONSTRATIVE ARTICLES:	The masculine article **ce** becomes **cet** before a vowel sound, e.g., **ce** métier (*this job*), **cet** emploi (*this job*).
PARTITIVE ARTICLES:	**Du** and **de la** become **de l'** before a vowel.
MASCULINE SINGULAR:	**du** gâteau (*some cake*), **de l'**or (*some gold*), **de l'**humus (*some humus*)
FEMININE SINGULAR:	**de la** limonade (*some lemonade*), **de l'**eau (*some water*), **de l'**hésitation (*some hesitation*)

Do not use indefinite and partitive articles in negative sentences. Simply use **de** before the noun. Look at the following examples:

AFFIRMATIVE SENTENCE		NEGATIVE SENTENCE	
J'ai **un** frère.	*I have a brother.*	Je n'ai pas **de** frère.	*I do not have a brother.*
Elle a **une** voiture.	*She has a car.*	Elle n'a pas **de** voiture.	*She does not have a car.*
Je prends **du** lait.	*I'm having milk.*	Je ne prends pas **de** lait.	*I'm not having (any) milk.*
J'ai **de la** patience.	*I have patience.*	Je n'ai pas **de** patience.	*I do not have (any) patience.*
Je veux **des** bonbons.	*I want candy.*	Je ne veux pas **de** bonbons.	*I do not want (any) candy.*

Review the following chart of possessive adjectives, as these function as articles:

GENDER AND NUMBER	MY	YOUR (FAMILIAR)	HIS/HER	OUR	YOUR (FORMAL)	THEIR
Masculine singular	mon	ton	son	notre	votre	leur
Feminine singular	ma	ta	sa	notre	votre	leur
Plural	mes	tes	ses	nos	vos	leurs

Je rejoue **mes** films préférés plusieurs fois.	*I replay my favorite movies several times.*
Tu portes **ton** nouveau jean et **ta** nouvelle chemise?	*Are you wearing your new jeans and your new shirt?*

Use the masculine singular possessive adjective **mon/ton/son** before a feminine singular noun that starts with a vowel sound.

MASCULINE NOUN	FEMININE NOUN STARTING WITH A VOWEL SOUND
mon ami (*my male friend*)	**mon** amie (*my female friend*)
ton père (*your father*)	**ton** affaire (*your affair*)
son chalet (*his/her chalet*)	**son** habitation (*his/her habitation*)

Contractions

Always contract the prepositions **à** (*at, in, to*) and **de** (*from, of*) with the definite articles **le** and **les**.

	le	les		le	les
à	au	aux	**de**	du	des

Tu vas **au** bureau ce matin?	*Are you going to the office this morning?*
Dis **aux** enfants qu'il faut faire les devoirs!	*Tell (to) the children that they must do the homework!*
Je pars de la maison à sept heures **du** matin et je rentre à six heures **du** soir.	*I leave the house at 7 A.M., and I come back at 6 P.M.*
Ce sont les cahiers **des** élèves.	*These are the students' notebooks.*

Omitting articles

There are instances when nouns are not preceded by articles.

- After the prepositions **en**, **comme**, **sans**, **entre** when expressing generalities

En hiver, nous faisons du ski.	*During the winter, we go skiing.*
Comme dessert, je voudrais de la glace.	*For dessert, I would like some ice cream.*
Sans loisirs, la vie est monotone.	*Without leisure-time activities, life is monotonous.*
Entre amis, on peut tout se dire.	*Among friends, we can say everything.*

- After the negative adverbs **ni... ni**

Je n'ai **ni** confiture **ni** beurre en ce moment.	*I have neither jam nor butter right at this moment.*

- After expressions of quantity such as **assez de** (*enough*), **beaucoup de** (*many*), **peu de** (*little of*), **un peu de** (*a little of*), **trop de** (*too much*); and **un litre de** (*a liter of*), **un kilo de** (*a kilo of*); or **une douzaine de** (*a dozen of*), **une bouteille de** (*a bottle of*), **une tasse de** (*a cup of*), and **un verre de** (*a glass of*)

Donnez-moi **un litre de lait**.	*Give me a liter of milk.*
Je voudrais **un peu de sucre**.	*I would like a little sugar.*

- After certain verbal expressions such as **avoir besoin de** (*to need*), **être couvert/rempli de** (*to be covered/filled with*)

Ces chiens **ont besoin de nourriture**.	*These dogs need food.*
Leurs bols sont **remplis d'eau**.	*Their bowls are filled with water.*

- Before unmodified occupations and professions, after the verbs **être** (*to be*) and **devenir** (*to become*)

Elle est gérante.	*She is a manager.*
Nous devenons étudiants.	*We are becoming students.*

Conversation du matin. *Morning conversation. Translate the following short dialogues into French. Use the familiar* **tu** *form for verbs and the appropriate articles before nouns whenever necessary.*

1. What do you want, lemonade or water? —A little water, please!

   Qu'est-ce que tu veux, de la limonade ou de l'eau? - Un peu d'eau s'il te plaît.

2. Do you have coffee in the morning? —Yes, I always have a cup of coffee.

   Est-ce que tu prends du café le matin? - Oui, je prends toujours une tasse de café.

3. Do you need some sugar in your coffee? —Yes, I need a lot of sugar.

   Est-ce que tu as besoin de sucre dans son café? Oui, j'ai besoin beaucoup de sucre.

4. Can you buy a bottle of wine for dinner? —Sure, a dinner without wine is not a real dinner.

   Peux-tu acheter une bouteille de vin pour le souper? Bien sûr un souper sans vin n'est pas un vrai souper.

5. Do not bring any flowers this time! —Why not? You love flowers.

   N'apporte pas de fleurs cette fois! - Pourquoi pas? Tu aimes les fleurs.

6. Yes, but I have lots of roses from the garden. —May I bring a dessert?

   Oui, mais j'ai beaucoup de roses du jardin. Est-ce que je peux apport

7. No, thanks. We have fruit for dessert. —Fruit is perfect in the summer, you're right!

   apporter un dessert?
   no, merci. Nous avons des fruits pour le dessert - les fruits sont parfaits en été, tu as raison.

8. See you tonight! —Or this afternoon!

   À ce soir! Ou cet après-midi!

Que veux-tu faire dans la vie, Marc? *What do you want to do in life, Mark? Write the following questions in French. Use the familiar* **tu** *form for your verbs and the appropriate articles before nouns whenever necessary. Use* **est-ce que** *in your questions.*

1. Are you a student?

   Est-ce que tu es étudiante?

2. What is your favorite subject this year?

   Quel est ton sujet préféré cette année?

3. What do you want to be in ten years?

Qu'est que tu veux faire dans dix années?

4. Do you want to be a teacher, a hotel manager, an astronaut, an actor?

Est-ce que tu veux être professeur, gérant d'hôtel, astronaut ou acteur?

5. What is important? Money, fame, pride?

Qu'est-ce qui interessant? L'argent, la célébrité ou la fierté

EXERCICE 2·3

Les voitures. *Cars. Complete each French sentence with the appropriate definite, indefinite, demonstrative, or possessive article so that it corresponds to the English sentence. Write X on the line provided if no article is necessary.*

Individual cars appear at the end of the 18th century in our societies.

1. _Les_ voitures individuelles paraissent à 2. _la_ fin du 18ème siècle dans

3. _nos_ sociétés.

(appear)

Electric cars have existed since the 1900s but lose their appeal when Henry Ford invents his gas-powered engine.

4. _Les_ voitures électriques existent depuis 5. _les_ années 1900 mais perdent de

6. _leur_ attrait quand Henry Ford invente 7. _son_ moteur à l'essence.

Our world counts around a billion cars today.

8. _Notre_ monde compte aujourd'hui près d'un milliard de 9. _X_ voitures.

One disadvantage of the proliferation of this type of car is our dependence on oil.

10. _Un_ inconvénient de la prolifération de 11. _ce_ type de voitures est

12. _notre_ dépendance du pétrole.

Another one is the damage to the environment.

Un autre en est les dégâts à 13. _l'_ environnement.

When are we going to drive cars that use neither gas nor electricity?

Quand allons-nous conduire 14. _des_ voitures qui n'utilisent ni 15. _X_ essence ni

16. _X_ électricité?

The definite article with parts of the body

In French, parts of the body are preceded by a definite article rather than a possessive adjective when it is obvious whose part of the body is referred to. Look at the following examples, and note that this is especially true in commands:

Tu fermes **les** yeux, tu t'endors et tu te sens mieux.	*You close **your** eyes, you fall asleep, and you feel better.*
Sors **le** doigt du nez, Cécile! Ne suce pas **le** pouce, Jeannot!	*Take your finger out of **your** nose, Cécile! Do not suck **your** thumb, Jeannot!*
Levez **la** main, les enfants! Vous deux, fermez **les** yeux!	*Raise **your** hands, children! You two, close **your** eyes.*

VOCABULAIRE UTILE. *Useful vocabulary.*

Examine this vocabulary list before doing the following exercises.

l'épaule (*f.*)	*shoulder*	le bras	*arm*
l'oreille (*f.*)	*ear*	le cou	*neck*
l'orteil (*m.*)	*toe*	le coude	*elbow*
la bouche	*mouth*	le doigt	*finger*
la cheville	*ankle*	le dos	*back*
la dent	*tooth*	le genou	*knee*
la figure	*face*	le nez	*nose*
la jambe	*leg*	le pied	*foot*
la joue	*cheek*	le poignet	*wrist*
la main	*hand*	le pouce	*thumb*
la nuque	*nape of neck*	le ventre	*belly*
la poitrine	*chest*	les cheveux	*hair*
la tête	*head*	les yeux	*eyes*

À l'entraînement! *Boot camp! You are at boot camp, and these are the orders you hear. Complete each command as directed.*

Rentrez 1. _Le ventre_ (*your belly*)! Redressez 2. _la poitrine_

(*your chest*)! Ne baissez pas 3. _les yeux_ (*your eyes*)! Mettez

4. _la main._ (*your hand*) sur 5. _la poitrine_ (*your chest*)!

Haussez 6. _le menton_ (*your chin*)! Fermez 7. _la bouche_ (*your*

mouth) et ne montrez pas 8. _les dents_ (*your teeth*)! Mettez

9. _les pieds_ (*your feet*) l'un à côté de l'autre! Rentrez

10. _les genoux_ (*your knees*)!

Dans la salle d'attente chez le docteur. *In the waiting room at the doctor's office. Translate what you hear various patients complain about. Use the idiom* **avoir mal à** *to express* to hurt. *The first sentence has been done for you.*

1. My head has been hurting for five days.

   J'ai mal à la tête depuis cinq jours.

2. My right leg hurts a lot. I can't walk.

   J'ai mal à la jambe droite. Je ne peux pas marcher

* 3. My toe hurts. I think it is broken.

   J'ai mal à l'orteil. Je crois qu'il est cassé.

* 4. My wrist hurts. I play tennis too often.

   J'ai mal au poignet. Je joue trop souvent au tennis

5. My belly hurts. I can't eat.

   J'ai mal au ventre. Je ne peux pas manger

6. My chest hurts. I must have bronchitis (**une bronchite**).

   J'ai mal à la poitrine. Je pense que j'ai une bronchite.

7. My nose hurts. I have a cold (**un rhume**).

   J'ai mal au nez. J'ai un rhume

8. I have a toothache. I need a dentist.

   J'ai mal aux dents. J'ai besoin d'un dentiste

9. I have a scratch (**une griffure**) on my face.

   J'ai une griffure à la figure

10. My elbow hurts.

    J'ai mal au coude

The present tense and idiomatic uses of the irregular verbs **aller**, **avoir**, **être**, and **faire**

·3·

The present tense conjugation of the irregular verbs **aller**, **avoir**, **être**, and **faire**

Remember that the present tense conjugation of some basic verbs is irregular and requires memorization of each verbal form. See the following conjugations:

aller (to go)	**avoir** (to have)	**être** (to be)	**faire** (to do/make)
je vais	j'ai	je suis	je fais
tu vas	tu as	tu es	tu fais
il/elle/on va	il/elle/on a	il/elle/on est	il/elle/on fait
nous allons	nous avons	nous sommes	nous faisons
vous allez	vous avez	vous êtes	vous faites
ils/elles vont	ils/elles ont	ils/elles sont	ils/elles font

Je **vais** à l'université deux fois par semaine.	*I go to the university twice a week.*
Mes amis **vont** au Canada une fois par an.	*My friends go to Canada once a year.*
On **a** de la chance quand on gagne la loterie.	*One is lucky when one wins the lottery.*
Vous **avez** beaucoup de courage.	*You have a lot of courage.*
Tu **es** un excellent ami.	*You are an excellent friend.*
Tes sœurs **sont** à croquer.	*Your sisters are adorable (to eat).*
Je **fais** des fautes en français.	*I make mistakes in French.*
Monsieur, vous **faites** une erreur.	*Sir, you are making a mistake.*

Idiomatic uses of aller

The verb **aller** is used in idiomatic expressions that do not translate literally from French to English. Here is a list of **aller** expressions that you may be able to use in this chapter.

aller à la pêche	*to go fishing*
aller au fond des choses	*to get to the bottom of things*
aller avec quelque chose	*to go with something/to match/to fit*
aller bien/mal	*to feel well/bad*
aller bon train	*to go at a good speed/rhythm*

18

aller chercher (quelqu'un ou quelque chose)	to go get (someone or something)
aller de l'avant	to move forward
aller droit au but	to go straight to the goal/get straight to the point

Nous **allons bien** aujourd'hui.	We are fine today.
Va chercher le courier!	Go get the mail!
Ce foulard **va bien avec** ton chemisier.	This scarf goes well with your shirt.
Vous **allez bon train**. Continuez!	You are going at a good speed. Continue!
Je **vais droit au but**: il me faut de l'argent.	I'm getting straight to the point: I need money.

Note the following idiomatic phrases:

Ça va de soi.	It is self-evident.
Ça va sans dire.	It goes without saying.
Ça va!	I'm fine!/It works!
Ça va comme ça?	Is that OK?/Does it work?

Tu vas en France cet été? —**Ça va sans dire.**	Are you going to France this summer? —That goes without saying.
Salut, Jeanne! **Ça va?** —**Ça va bien**, merci.	Hi, Jeanne! How are you? —I'm fine, thank you.
Comment **va** le travail? —**Il va bien**, merci.	How is work? —It is fine, thank you.

Bonjour. Comment ça va? *Hello, how are you? Translate Denise and Johnny's conversation.*

1. DENISE: Hi, Johnny! How are you?

   Salut Johnny! Ça va?

2. JOHNNY: Fine, thanks. How about you?

   Ça va bien, merci. Et toi?

3. DENISE: Fine. Goes without saying: I'm on vacation.

   Bien. Ça va sans dire: Je suis en vacances

4. JOHNNY: Let's go fishing this afternoon!

   Allons à la pêche cet après-midi!

5. DENISE: This afternoon I'm going to get my new dress.

   Cet après-midi, je vais chercher ma nouvelle robe.

6. JOHNNY: The pretty dress that goes with my tuxedo (**le smoking**)?

La jolie robe qui va avec mon smoking?

7. DENISE: Yes, for Saturday. I'm keeping a good pace, right?

Oui, pour samedi. Je vais bon train, n'est-ce pas?

8. JOHNNY: That's (self-) evident.

Ça va de soi.

Idiomatic uses of avoir

The verb **avoir** is used in many idiomatic expressions that do not translate literally from French to English. Here is a list of **avoir** expressions that you may be able to use in this chapter:

avoir besoin de	*to need*
avoir bonne/mauvaise conscience	*to have a clear/guilty conscience*
avoir chaud/froid	*to be hot/cold*
avoir confiance en	*to trust*
avoir de la chance/de la malchance	*to be lucky/unlucky*
avoir envie de	*to feel like/to want*
avoir hâte (de)	*to be in a hurry (to)*
avoir honte (de)	*to be ashamed (of)*
avoir l'air (heureux/heureuse...)	*to look (happy . . .)*
avoir l'habitude de	*to be used to*
avoir l'impression de	*to get the impression/to have the feeling that*
avoir l'intention de	*to intend to*
avoir lieu	*to take place*
avoir peur de	*to be afraid to*
avoir pleine conscience de	*to be fully aware of*
avoir raison/tort	*to be right/wrong*
avoir sommeil	*to be sleepy*
avoir... ans	*to be . . . old*

Il fait zéro degré Celsius. **J'ai froid.**	*It is zero degrees Celsius. I am cold.*
Nina **a envie d**'aller au cinéma.	*Nina feels like going to the movies.*
J'ai l'impression de connaître ce monsieur.	*I have the feeling I know this gentleman.*
Tu **as hâte d**'arriver, n'est-ce pas?	*You are in a hurry to arrive, aren't you?*
Nous **avons confiance en** nos parents.	*We trust our parents.*
Vous **avez si hâte** que ça de partir?	*Are you so anxious to leave?*
Tes amis **ont l'air** heureux.	*Your friends look happy.*

Quelle expression choisir? *What expression should we choose?* *Choose the appropriate expression and write it on the line provided. Be sure to include the correct form of the verb* **avoir**.

hurry	age	feel like	sleepy	impression
hâte	ans	envie	sommeil	l'impression
right	intention	ashamed	luck	need
raison	l'intention	honte	de la chance	besoin

1. J'*ai l'impression* que tu as chaud. Attends! J'ouvre la fenêtre.

2. Vous *avez raison*. Audrey Tautou est une excellente actrice.

3. Marc gagne toujours à la loterie. Il *a de la chance*!

4. Le film commence dans deux minutes. J'*ai hâte* d'arriver.

5. Après le dîner, ma grand-mère *a sommeil*.

6. Mon grand-père *a* soixante *ans*.

7. Jeannot *a honte* quand il va à l'école sans ses devoirs.

8. Les étudiants *ont besoin* de beaucoup de livres.

9. Yvonne *a envie* de rester à la maison le soir.

10. Nous *avons l'intention* de voyager cet été.

Trouvons les synonymes. *Let's find synonyms.* *Rewrite the italicized part of the sentence using the appropriate* **avoir** *idiom from the ones listed in the previous exercise.*

1. *Nous comptons* rester chez nous ce weekend. *nous avons l'intention de rester chez nous*

2. *Tu crois* être malade? *J'ai l'imprenion d'être malade*

3. *Tu voudrais dormir?* *Tu as sommeil*

4. *Vous voulez* une bonne pizza ce soir? *Vous avez envie de manger une pizza*

5. Il n'a pas fait son travail. *Il a mauvaise conscience.* *Il a honte.*

6. Je suis en retard. *Je suis pressé* d'arriver. *J'ai hâte d'arriver*

7. *D'habitude nous mangeons* ensemble. *Nous avons l'habitude de manger ensemble*

8. *Ils n'ont pas de chance.* Ils perdent à la roulette. *Ils ont de la malchance.*

9. Marie *semble* fatiguée aujourd'hui. *Marie a l'air fatiguée*

10. Ce prof est qualifié. *Je crois* qu'on va apprendre. *J'ai l'imprenion.*

Examine this list of vocabulary before doing the next exercise.

alors	*so, then*	penser	*to think*
le bruit	*noise*	silencieux	*silent, quiet*
le chiot	*puppy*	trembler	*to shiver, tremble*
le réconfort	*comfort*		

EXERCICE
3·4

À vous d'écrire! *Your turn to write! Translate the following paragraph into French using the* **vous** *form for you.*

Lolo and Lili are puppies, and they are brother and sister. They are afraid of loud noises. When they hear a noise, they start to tremble. The Duport children are fully aware of that. They are used to avoiding noises. Unfortunately, their friends do not always feel like being silent. So they shout, and the puppies need comfort. They trust the Duport family. You think that they are lucky to have a nice family? You are right!

Lolo et Lili sont chiots, et ils sont frère et soeur. Ils ont peur des bruits forts. Quand ils entendent un bruit, ils commencent à trembler. Les enfants Duport sont pleinement conscients de ça. Ils ont l'habitude d'éviter les bruits. Malheureusement, leurs amis n'ont pas toujours envie d'être silencieux. Alors, ils crient et les chiots ont besoin de réconfort. Ils ont confiance en la famille Duport. Vous pensez qu'ils ont de la chance d'avoir une famille sympa? Vous avez raison.

Idiomatic uses of être

The verb **être** is used idiomatically in expressions that do not translate literally from French to English.

♦ **C'est** + **à** + stress pronoun + **de** + infinitive verb. This structure is used to express that it is someone's turn to do something.

C'est à moi de nettoyer la cuisine.	*It's my turn to clean the kitchen.*
C'est à lui de vider les ordures.	*It's his turn to empty the garbage.*
C'est à elles de préparer le dîner.	*It's their turn to prepare dinner.*

- ◆ **C'est/Il est/Elle est** + **à** + person or stress pronoun. This structure is used to express possession.

C'est à maman.	*It belongs to Mom.*
Le journal, **il est à** papa.	*The newpaper belongs to Dad.*
Elle est à moi, cette serviette.	*This towel belongs to me.*

- ◆ The form **est** can be just part of a phrase, such as the following:

C'est ça!	*That's it!*
Ça y est!	*Done!*
C'est tout.	*That's all.*
Ça m'est égal.	*It's all the same to me/I don't care.*
Tu as raison! **C'est ça.**	*You are right! That's it!*
J'ai fini. **Ça y est!**	*I finished. Done!*
Je n'ai pas envie de manger. **C'est tout.**	*I do not feel like eating. That's all.*
Il pleut? **Ça m'est égal.** Je sors.	*It's raining? I don't care. I'm going out.*
C'est bien fait pour toi!	*It serves you right!*

- ◆ The verb **être** is also used in the following expressions:

être à court de	*to be short of (something)*
être d'accord	*to agree*
être de retour	*to be back*
être en train de	*to be in the process/middle of*
être en vacances	*to be on vacation*
être sur le point de	*to be about*

Ce film est ennuyeux. **Je suis d'accord** avec toi.	*This movie is boring. I agree with you.*
Thierry est de retour de son voyage en Italie.	*Thierry is back from his trip to Italy.*
Il est sur le point d'annuler la conférence.	*He is about to cancel the conference.*
Ils sont en train de téléphoner.	*They are in the middle of a call.*
À la fin du mois, **je suis à court d'**argent.	*At the end of the month, I am short on money.*

- ◆ **Nous sommes** is used with days of the week to indicate what day it is.

Nous sommes lundi aujourd'hui.	*It is Monday today.*

Uses of c'est/ce sont and il(s)/elle(s) sont

C'est is followed by an adjective in the masculine form when expressing a general idea.

Jean arrive souvent en retard. **C'est vrai.**	*Jean often comes late. It's true.*
Tu penses qu'il pleut déjà? **C'est possible!**	*You think it is already raining? It's possible!*

C'est/ce sont are followed by noun phrases that describe people or things.

C'est/ce sont + article + noun phrase
(includes article and may include adjective)

C'est le nouveau professeur de chimie.	*He is the new chemistry teacher.*
C'est un printemps bizarre.	*It is a weird spring.*
Ce sont des familles célèbres.	*They are famous families.*
Ce sont nos affaires.	*It is our business.*

Il/elle est and **Ils/elles sont** are followed by adjectives or unmodified occupations.

Il/elle est/Ils/elles sont + adjective

Noëlle? **Elle est** très gentille.
Les albums de photos? **Ils sont** beaux.

Noëlle? *She is very nice.*
The photo albums? *They are beautiful.*

Il/elle est/Ils/elles sont + unmodified occupation
(no article or adjective included)

Jean et Thomas? **Ils sont** peintres.
Madeleine? Elle est esthéticienne.

Jean and Thomas? *They are painters.*
Madeleine? She is a cosmetician.

EXERCICE
3·5

Complétez! *Complete! Choose the appropriate expression from the list. Then complete each sentence. Be sure to include a subject such as* **je, c', il(s),** *or* **elle(s)** *and the correct form of the verb* **être.** *The first one is done for you.*

samedi	à court	x actrice	à moi	heureuse
sur le point	tout	à toi	professeur	égal

1. J'ai d'excellents résultats. _Je suis heureuse._

2. Audrey Tautou? ____elle est____ une excellente ____actrice____.

3. M. Rétaud? ____il est____ de chimie.

4. Tu me donnes un seul petit sandwich. ____c'est tout____? Mais j'ai faim.

5. Nina, ____c'est à toi____ de débarrasser la table!

6. Attention! Ne touche pas cet iPad! ____Il est à moi____.

7. Mais non! Je ne vais aux cours. ____c'est samedi____ aujourd'hui.

8. Tu as besoin d'argent? Désolé! Je ____suis à court____ d'argent aussi.

9. Tu n'es pas content parce que je n'ai pas d'argent à te donner? ____Ce m'est égal____!

10. Nous ____sommes sur le point____ de finir nos préparatifs de voyage. Encore une minute et ça y est!

EXERCICE
3·6

Le dilemne d'Irène. *Irène's dilemma. Write the omitted part of the sentence using the appropriate* **être** *structure. Use the instructions in parentheses.*

1. ____C'est____ dimanche. (*It is*)

2. ____c'est à moi____ de préparer le déjeuner? (*It's my turn*)

3. Comment préparer mes omelettes? _Je suis à court_ d'œufs. (*I'm short of*)

4. Ma sœur Irène _est sur le point_ de sortir. (*is about*)

5. Je lui demande d'acheter une douzaine d'œufs. _Elle est d'accord_. (*She agrees*)

6. _Elle est gentille_, ma sœur! (*She is nice*)

7. Ah! _Ça y est_! (*Done*) _Irène est de retour_! (*Irène is back*)

8. _C'est formidable_ d'avoir une famille comme ça! (*It's great*)

Idiomatic uses of faire

The verb **faire** is used in many idiomatic expressions that do not translate literally from French to English. Here is a list of **faire** expressions that you may be able to use in this chapter:

Physical activities

faire du sport	*to do sports*
faire de la musculation/de la gymnastique	*to lift weights/to do gymnastics*
faire de la natation/de la plongée	*to swim/dive*
faire du football/du volleyball	*to play soccer/volleyball*
faire de la marche/des randonnées	*to go for walks/hikes*
faire des promenades (à vélo, en moto…)	*to go for (bicycle, motorcycle . . .) rides*

On **fait beaucoup de football** en Europe. — *They play a lot of soccer in Europe.*

Nous **faisons de la plongée** quand nous allons en Corse. — *We dive when we go to Corsica.*

Les touristes **font des promenades à cheval** en Camargue. — *Tourists go for horse rides in Camargue.*

Domestic activities

faire des achats/des courses	*to go shopping/run errands*
faire la vaisselle/le linge	*to do the dishes/the laundry*
faire le lit/le ménage	*to make the bed/do the household chores*

Papa **fait des achats** en ville pendant que maman fait les courses au marché. — *Dad is shopping in town while Mom runs errands at the market.*

Nous **faisons la vaisselle** tous les jours et **le linge** le samedi. — *We do the dishes every day and the laundry on Saturdays.*

Leisure time activities

faire des voyages	*to take trips*
faire de la photo/de la peinture	*to do photography/painting*
faire du texto	*to text*
faire la queue	*to wait in line*
faire un blog	*to blog*

Les Léonard **font de la photo** comme hobby.	*The Léonards do photography as a hobby.*
Moi, je **fais du texto** à longueur de journée.	*I text all day long.*

Weather

faire beau/mauvais	*to be nice/bad*
faire chaud/froid	*to be hot/cold*
faire du soleil/du brouillard	*to be sunny/foggy*

Il fait du soleil sur la Côte Méditerranée.	*It is sunny on the Mediterranean coast.*
Il fait toujours **du brouillard** tôt le matin.	*It is always foggy early in the morning.*

States of being

faire peur à	*to scare (someone)*
faire envie à	*to make (someone) feel like/to tempt someone*
faire semblant de	*to do as if/to pretend*
faire de son mieux	*to do one's best*

Les dentistes **font peur aux** enfants.	*Dentists scare children.*
Tu **fais semblant d'**être amoureux ou tu l'es vraiment?	*Do you pretend to be in love, or are you really (in love)?*

Educational activities

faire des études	*to study/to be a student*
faire son droit/sa médecine	*to study law/medicine*
faire son baccalauréat (bac)/sa thèse	*to take the baccalaureate exam/to do a thesis*

C'est en terminale que les étudiants **font leur bac**.	*It is in their senior year that students take their baccalaureate exam.*
Martin **fait sa médecine**. C'est long et difficile.	*Martin studies medicine. It's long and difficult.*

Phrases

Ça fait combien?	*How much is it?*
Ça fait douze euros.	*It costs 12 euros.*
Qu'est-ce que ça fait?	*What does it matter?*
Ça ne fait rien.	*It does not matter./No problem.*
Ça fait mal.	*It (that) hurts.*
Ça fait combien, ce collier?	*How much is this necklace?*
Il est cher mais **ça ne fait rien**. Je l'achète.	*It is expensive, but it does not matter. I'm buying it.*

The structure **faire** + *infinitive verb* is used to indicate that someone is having someone else do a job or task.

Nous faisons construire une maison.	*We are having a house built.*
Je fais nettoyer mes vêtements chers.	*I'm having my expensive clothes cleaned.*
Laurie **se fait couper les cheveux**.	*Laurie is having her hair cut.*

On sort ou on fait le ménage? *Are we going out or cleaning the house?* *Find the appropriate completion of each sentence among the choices, and write the corresponding letter on the line provided.*

1. __H__ Il fait beau aujourd'hui, alors... *It is beautiful today, so...*

2. __E__ Mais il faut faire... avant de sortir. *...nt, I must do... before leaving*

3. __G__ Bon, moi,... et alors on sort. *Good, me... and so we leave*

4. __F__ Mais, on a aussi le linge... *But, you also have the laundry...*

5. __B__ Ça ne fait rien! ... *that never works...*

6. __D__ D'accord. On peut aussi... *Agreed. You can also...*

7. __C__ Oui, mais ça... *yes, but that...*

8. __A__ Je ne sais pas mais ça me fait... *I don't know but that makes me...*

a. envie. *to tempt*

b. Je peux le laver demain. *I can wash it tomorrow*

c. fait combien? *make how many?*

d. faire laver le linge à la blanchisserie. *to clean the laundry with bleach*

e. le ménage *housework*

f. à faire. *to do*

g. je fais le lit, *to do the bed.*

h. allons faire une promenade! *go do a walk*

Mireille et Mathieu ont une discussion. *Mireille and Mathieu have a discussion.* *Write Mathieu's replies to Mireille. Follow the instructions in parentheses.*

1. MIREILLE: Dis, Mathieu, c'est à toi de faire les courses pour la semaine. *Say, Mathieu, it is for you to do the errands for the week.*

   MATHIEU: _mais, j'ai envie de faire un tour en vélo._

   (But I feel like going for a bike ride. The weather is nice.)

2. MIREILLE: Je suis très occupée aujourd'hui. Tu sais que ce n'est pas facile de faire son droit. *I am very busy today. You know that it isn't easy to do law.*

   MATHIEU: _Ce beau temps me fait envie. C'est tout_

   (This beautiful weather is simply tempting. That's all.)

3. MIREILLE: Moi aussi, mais je fais mon travail. *me too, but I must do my work.*

   MATHIEU: _D'accord. Je fais les courses. Tu fais ton droit._

   (Agreed. I run the errands. You study your law.)

4. MIREILLE: Et qui fait le ménage et le linge ce weekend? *And who does the cleaning and laundry this weekend?*

   MATHIEU: _Ça fait combien à faire nettoyer la maison?_

   (How much is it to have the house cleaned?)

5. MIREILLE: C'est trop cher pour notre budget, mon petit Mathieu.

It's too much for our budget, my little Mathieu.

MATHIEU: _Ça fait rien. Je doit faire mon sport._

(*It doesn't matter. I have to do my exercise.*)

6. MIREILLE: Ça y est! Le mois prochain, on est ruiné à cause de toi.

Done! Next month, we are ruined because of you.

MATHIEU: _Bon. Je fais mon mieux aujourd'hui_

(*Fine. I'll do my best today.*)

EXERCICE 3·9

C'est une grande artiste! *She is a big artist. Write each verb in parentheses in the appropriate present tense form.*

Céline Dion 1. _____est_____ (être) une chanteuse canadienne. Céline

2. _____habite_____ (habiter) d'abord à Montréal. Sa mère

3. _____est_____ (être) violoniste, et son père accordéoniste. À l'âge de cinq ans,

elle 4. _____chante_____ (chanter) pour la première fois devant un public pour le

mariage de son frère.

En 1980, quand Céline Dion 5. _____a_____ (avoir) douze ans, sa mère

6. _____envoie_____ (envoyer) une cassette musicale à René Angélil, figure du monde

musical au Québec. Le monsieur 7. _____adore_____ (adore) la voix de Céline; cela

8. _____va_____ (aller) de soi.

En 1984, elle 9. _____va_____ (aller) de l'avant et

10. _____représente_____ (représenter) la jeunesse de son pays pour la venue du pape.

Céline Dion est aujourd'hui une grande artiste internationale. Sa chanson *My Heart Will*

Go On 11. _____fait_____ (faire) partie d'un album qui est un de ses plus grands

succès.

Adjectives and comparisons

Use and agreement of adjectives

There are several types of adjectives in the French language. Some serve as articles for nouns and noun phrases, while others are descriptive and serve to give you attributes and characteristics of nouns.

Possessive and demonstrative adjectives (see Chapter 3) function as articles and accompany a noun or noun phrase. Like any adjective in the French language, these adjectives agree in gender (masculine, feminine) and in number (singular, plural) with the noun they accompany.

mon père	*my father*	**ma** mère	*my mother*	**mes** amis favoris	*my favorite friends*
ce plateau	*this tray*	**cette** tasse	*this cup*	**ces** bouteilles	*these bottles*

The indefinite adjective tout

The indefinite adjective **tout** can serve as the article of a noun and is part of many phrases.

- In the singular forms, **tout/toute** usually means *whole* in English. Look at the following examples:

Tu manges **tout** le gâteau?	*Are you eating the whole cake?*
Tu veux **toute** la salade?	*Do you want the whole salad?*

    Now note the variety of translations of **tout/toute** in the following phrases:

Toute la journée, je lis.	*All day long, I read.*
Tout le monde veut être heureux.	*Everybody wants to be happy.*
Pendant **tout l'hiver**, ils skient.	*Throughout the winter, they ski.*
Tout acte criminel doit être puni.	*Any criminal act must be punished.*
J'ai **toute raison** de croire qu'il est honnête.	*I have every reason to believe he is honest.*
C'est de **toute importance**.	*This is of high importance.*

- In the plural forms, **tout/toute** usually means *all* in English. Look at the following examples:

Tous nos copains sont drôles.	*All our friends are funny.*
Toutes nos affaires sont là.	*All our things are here.*

Now, note the variety of translations of **tous/toutes** in the following phrases:

Allons-y, **tous les trois**!	*Let's go, all three of us!*
Je vais au gym **tous les deux jours**.	*I go to the gym every other day.*
Tu vas au cours **tous les jours**?	*Do you go to class every day?*
Il roule **à toute vitesse**.	*He drives at full speed.*
C'est **toute une histoire**, ça!	*That's quite a story!*

EXERCICE
4·1

Pierre et Luc trouvent des billets de concert à bon prix. *Pierre and Luc find well-priced concert tickets. Write the correct form of the adjective **tout** in the space provided.*

1. _tous_ les billets pour ce concert sont en baisse.

2. Allons-y, _tous_ les deux! D'accord?

3. _tout_ le monde va vouloir acheter des places à ce prix!

4. Achetons nos billets à _toute_ vitesse!

5. _toute_ la semaine, je vais penser à ce concert.

6. _tous_ nos copains vont être jaloux de nous.

7. On invite _toute_ la bande?

8. Et c'est toi qui vas payer pour _tous_ les copains!

The adjective **quel**

The interrogative adjective **quel** can serve as the article of a noun and agrees in gender and number with the noun it accompanies.

Quel couteau veux-tu?	*Which knife do you want?*
Quelle couleur préfère-t-il?	*What color does he prefer?*
Quels jours vient-elle?	*On which days does she come?*
Quelles photos sont à moi?	*Which photos are mine?*
Quelle heure est-il?	*What time is it?*

The adjective **quel**—in all its forms—can also be used in exclamations.

Quel film!	*What a movie!*
Quelle journée!	*What a day!*
Quels parents généreux!	*What generous parents!*
Quelles histoires!	*What stories!*

Now note the variety of translations of the various forms of **quel** in the following phrases:

Quel temps fait-il?	*How is the weather?*
Quel dommage!	*Too bad!/What a pity!*
Tu achètes **n'importe quelles** serviettes.	*You buy any napkins whatsoever.*
Quelle que soit la conclusion, je dois savoir.	*Whatever the conclusion may be, I have to know.*

Quel film pouvons-nous aller voir? *What movie can we go see? Complete each sentence appropriately with a phrase from the list. One of the options may be used more than once.*

x quelle   x n'importe quel   quel que soit   x quel   x quel dommage

1. ____Quel____ film tu veux voir? La comédie ou le film d'aventure?

2. A ____Quelle____ heure est-ce qu'il commence, le film d'aventure?

3. A quinze ou à dix-huit heures! Trop tôt pour moi! ___Quel dommage___ !

4. Non, je ne veux pas voir ___n'importe quel___ film!

5. Écoute! ___Quel que soit___ le type de film, je ne peux pas aller au ciné avant vingt heures.

6. Ah oui! Le film autobiographique! ____Quelle____ histoire incroyable!

Descriptive adjectives

Descriptive adjectives are used to describe things or people; they provide attributes or characteristics for nouns. Look at the following list of adjectives, which will be useful in upcoming exercises. Note that adjectives may be colors such as **blanc** (*white*), nationalities such as **américain** (*American*), and numerical such as **premier** (*first*). Adjectives may also be used to convey physical, psychological, moral, and emotional attributes such as **fort** (*strong*) or **franc** (*frank*).

actif	*active*	franc	*frank*
aimable	*amiable*	français	*French*
américain	*American*	gentil	*nice*
annuel	*annual*	grand	*tall*
assis	*seated*	gris	*gray*
attentif	*attentive*	gros	*fat/big*
bas	*low*	haut	*high*
blanc	*white*	heureux	*happy*
bleu	*blue*	honnête	*honest*
bon	*good*	impoli	*rude*
canadien	*Canadian*	inactif	*inactive*
chanceux	*lucky*	indiscret	*indiscrete*
cher	*expensive/dear*	inquiet	*worried*
complet	*complete*	jaune	*yellow*
concret	*concrete*	jeune	*young*
court	*short*	léger	*light*
cruel	*cruel*	lourd	*heavy*
dernier	*last*	malheureux	*unhappy*
différent	*different*	malhonnête	*dishonest*
discret	*discrete*	mauvais	*bad*
fâché	*angry*	muet	*mute*
faible	*feeble/weak*	noir	*black*
faux	*false*	pareil	*similar/same*
fier	*proud*	paresseux	*lazy*
fort	*strong*	petit	*small*

peureux	*easily frightened*	rouge	*red*
placide	*placid*	sec	*dry*
plaintif	*plaintive*	secret	*secret*
poli	*polite*	sot	*dumb/silly*
premier	*first*	sportif	*athletic*
réussi	*well done*	sympathique	*friendly*
riche	*rich*	vert	*green*
rose	*pink*	violet	*purple/violet*

Position of descriptive adjectives

In contrast to English adjective-noun phrases, most French adjectives follow rather than precede the noun.

un exemple **concret**	*a concrete example*
un enfant **gentil**	*a nice child*
une histoire **drôle**	*a funny story*
une femme **heureuse**	*a happy woman*
une fleur **jaune**	*a yellow flower*
un écrivain **américain**	*an American writer*

Commonly used adjectives such as **autre** (*other*) and **même** (*same*) precede the noun in French just as in English.

une **autre** fois	*another time*	**d'autres** raisons	*other reasons*
la **même** chose	*the same thing*	les **mêmes** jours	*the same days*

Many of the adjectives that precede the noun can be remembered as pertaining to **B**eauty, **A**ge, **G**ood (and bad), and **S**ize. Look at the following BAGS chart:

BEAUTY	AGE	GOOD/BAD	SIZE
beau	jeune	bon	grand/gros
joli	vieux	mauvais	long
	nouveau		petit

Quel **joli rosier**!	*What a pretty rose bush!*
Regarde ce **beau chat**!	*Look at that beautiful cat!*
C'est un **jeune prof**.	*It's a young teacher.*
Quel **vieux manoir**!	*What an old manor!*
Voilà mon **nouveau vélo**.	*There is my new bike.*
Quel **bon gâteau**!	*What a good cake!*
Donne-moi ce **gros livre**!	*Give me this big book!*
Le **petit garçon** est mignon.	*The little boy is cute.*

Some adjectives are used before or after the noun. Beware that their meaning usually changes according to their position. Look at the following sets of sentences, and compare the meanings of the adjectives in each set:

C'est mon **seul ami**.	*This is my only friend.*
Un **chien seul** est triste.	*A lonely dog is sad.*
Mon **ancien prof** est encore au lycée.	*My former teacher is still at the high school.*
Ce **site ancien** attire les touristes.	*This ancient site attracts tourists.*
Cet acteur a un **certain regard** mystérieux.	*This actor has a certain mysterious look.*
C'est une **victoire certaine** pour notre équipe.	*It is a sure victory for our team.*

Nous étudions les **grands hommes** de l'histoire.   *We are studying important historical men.*
Cet **homme grand** là-bas, c'est mon père.   *That tall man over there is my father.*

Prends ta **propre serviette**!   *Take your own towel!*
Prends une **serviette propre**!   *Take a clean towel!*

Je lis la **dernière page** du **dernier chapitre**.   *I'm reading the last page of the last chapter.*

Le mois dernier, il a fait chaud.   *Last month, it was hot.*

La prochaine fois, je vais rester chez moi.   *Next time, I'm going to stay home.*
L'an prochain, nous allons voyager.   *Next year, we are going to travel.*

EXERCICE 4·3

Quelle réponse est logique? *Which answer is logical?* *Write the letter of the best completion of each sentence on the line provided.*

1. ___J___ Ne prends pas ma voiture!   a. On peut le manger?
2. ___G___ Nous sommes déjà le 4 juillet.   b. Il est mignon et poli.
3. ___H___ Marius a gagné la loterie.   c. Ils gardent mes secrets.
4. ___I___ Aujourd'hui tu vas au cours.   d. Ils ont plus de charme.
5. ___F___ Cette année, pas de vacances!   e. Il n'a pas plus de trente ans.
6. ___E___ Quel jeune professeur!   f. Mais l'an prochain, je veux aller au Canada.
7. ___B___ Quel petit garçon adorable!   g. Le mois prochain, nous partons à la mer.
8. ___C___ J'ai des copains discrets.   h. C'est un homme chanceux.
9. ___D___ Je préfère les vieux hôtels.   i. C'est le premier ce semestre, n'est-ce pas?
10. ___A___ Quel gâteau réussi!   j. C'est la dernière fois que je te le dis!

EXERCICE 4·4

C'est à vous d'écrire! *It is your turn to write!* *Write the following phrases in French. Beware of the position of the adjective in the phrase.*

1. my only son

   mon seul fils

2. a lonely man

   un homme seul

3. his own father

   son propre père

4. a certain charm

   un certain charme

5. a definite day

   un jour certain

6. a clean sweater

   un pull propre

7. a bad dinner

   un mauvais dîner

8. an angry gentleman

   un monsieur fâché

9. a heavy book

   un livre lourd

10. her former boyfriend

    son ancien copain

Feminine agreement of descriptive adjectives

French adjectives agree in number and gender with the nouns they describe. There are several patterns of masculine/feminine forms for adjectives as well as several patterns of singular/plural forms. In addition, there are irregular feminine and plural adjective forms.

Look at the following chart showing some masculine to feminine adjective patterns. These adjectives were previously listed. You may refer to the list for the meanings.

NO CHANGE e → e	x → se/sse	s/t/d/é/i/u + e	f → ve	l → lle
aimable	heureux/heureuse	petit/petite	actif/active	annuel/annuelle
jeune	peureux/peureuse	grand/grande	attentif/attentive	cruel/cruelle
riche	chanceux/chanceuse	fâché/fâchée	plaintif/plaintive	gentil/gentille
rouge	faux/fausse	réussi/réussie	sportif/sportive	pareil/pareille

Look at the following chart showing some additional masculine to feminine patterns for adjectives:

CONSONANT → DOUBLE CONSONANT + e	er → ère	et → ète	c → che
bas/basse	cher/chère	complet/complète	blanc → blanche
bon/bonne	dernier/dernière	concret/concrète	franc → franche
gros/grosse	fier/fière	discret/discrète	sec → sèche
muet/muette	léger/légère	inquiet/inquiète	
sot/sotte	premier/première	secret/secrète	

Remember to check a dictionary for new adjectives to verify that their feminine form is not irregular. Here are some examples of adjectives that have irregular feminine forms:

beau/belle	*handsome/beautiful*	mou/molle	*soft*
doux/douce	*gentle*	nouveau/nouvelle	*new*
fou/folle	*crazy*	public/publique	*public*
frais/fraîche	*fresh*	vieux/vieille	*old*
long/longue	*long*		

Quelle **belle** vue!	*What a beautiful view!*
La brise est **douce**.	*The breeze is gentle.*
Elle est un peu **folle**, cette actrice.	*This actress is a little crazy.*
J'adore la salade **fraîche** du jardin.	*I love fresh salad from the garden.*
C'est une **longue** histoire.	*It's a long story.*
Cette balle **molle** est bonne pour les petits.	*This soft ball is good for the little ones.*

Beau, nouveau, vieux

Remember that **beau**, **nouveau**, and **vieux** have two masculine singular forms depending on whether the noun that follows starts with a consonant or vowel sound. However, they have only one feminine singular form.

Masculine singular

vieil homme	*old man*	nouvel an	*New Year's*	bel arbre	*beautiful tree*
vieux château	*old castle*	nouveau pull	*new sweater*	beau bijou	*beautiful jewel*

Feminine singular

vieille toilette	*old attire*	nouvelle photo	*new photo*	belle étoile	*beautiful star*

EXERCICE 4·5

Les jumeaux Luc et Lucie. *The twins Luc and Lucie. These identical twins have everything in common. Apply to Lucie the adjective that describes Luc.*

1. Luc est beau. Lucie est ___belle___.

2. Il est petit. Elle est ___petite___.

3. Il est peureux. Elle est ___peureuse___.

4. Il est souvent inquiet. Elle est souvent ___inquiète___.

5. Il n'est pas gros. Elle n'est pas ___grosse___.

6. Il peut être un peu fou. Elle peut être un peu ___folle___.

7. Il n'est pas sot. Elle n'est pas ___sotte___.

8. Il est américain. Elle est ___américaine___.

9. Il est plutôt actif. Elle est plutôt ___active___.

10. Il n'est pas du tout cruel. Elle n'est pas du tout ___cruelle___.

EXERCICE 4·6

Décrivez! *Describe!* *Using the nouns in the word bank, write the following phrases in French.*

✗ la salade ✗ la personne ✗ la laine ✗ la robe ✗ la mère
✗ la garde-robe ✗ la prière ✗ la brioche ✗ la démonstration ✗ la voix

1. a fresh salad — la salade fraîche
2. a crazy person — la personne folle
3. a soft wool — la laine douce
4. an expensive dress — la robe chère
5. a proud mother — la mère fière
6. a complete wardrobe — la garde-robe complète
7. a silent prayer — la prière silencieuse
8. a dry brioche — la brioche sèche
9. a public display — la démonstration publique
10. a low voice — la voix basse.

Plural agreement of descriptive adjectives

Most French adjectives add an -s in their plural forms, in the masculine as well as their feminine forms. However, no -s can be added if the adjective already ends in -s or -x. Look at the following chart:

MASCULINE SINGULAR	MASCULINE PLURAL	FEMININE SINGULAR	FEMININE PLURAL
bleu	bleus	bleue	bleues
petit	petits	petite	petites
assis	assis	assise	assises
jaune	jaunes	jaune	jaunes
heureux	heureux	heureuse	heureuses
actif	actifs	active	actives
doux	doux	douce	douces
fou	fous	folle	folles
blanc	blancs	blanche	blanches

Il a les yeux **bleus**.	*He has blue eyes.*
Nous avons des roses **jaunes**.	*We have yellow roses.*
Les enfants **actifs** sont **sains**.	*Active children are healthy.*
Nous sommes **assis** devant vous.	*We are seated in front of you.*
Les nappes **blanches** sont belles.	*The white tablecloths are beautiful.*

Now look at the following chart, and note that the adjectives **beau**, **nouveau**, and **vieux** have two masculine singular forms but only one masculine plural form:

MASCULINE SINGULAR	MASCULINE PLURAL	FEMININE SINGULAR	FEMININE PLURAL
beau/bel	**beaux**	belle	belles
nouveau/nouvel	**nouveaux**	nouvelle	nouvelles
vieux/vieil	**vieux**	vieille	vieilles

Ces **beaux** tableaux sont chers.	*These beautiful paintings are expensive.*
Ces **nouveaux** hôtels sont magnifiques.	*These new hotels are magnificent.*
Ces **vieux** arbres doivent être coupés.	*These old trees must be cut.*

EXERCICE 4·7

Désirable ou indésirable? *Desirable or undesirable?* *Place a check mark next to only what you find desirable.*

1. __X__ de vieilles chaussures

2. __X__ des employés malhonnêtes

3. __✓__ de gros diamants

4. __✓__ de nouvelles Corvettes

5. __X__ des amies folles

6. __✓__ de beaux enfants

7. __✓__ de bonnes notes aux examens

8. __X__ de mauvais parents

EXERCICE 4·8

J'en veux beaucoup. *I want many of them.* *Finish the sentence* **Je veux beaucoup de** *(I want many) with all of the following phrases. Remember you do not use an article after* **beaucoup de.**

Je veux beaucoup de...

1. red roses — *roses rouges*.

2. new books — *nouveaux livres*.

3. active children — *enfants actifs*.

4. gentle dogs — *chiens doux*.

5. good dinners — *bons dînes*.

6. beautiful clothes — *beaux vêtements*.

7. old cars — *vielles voitures*.

8. expensive jewels — *bijoux chers*.

9. fresh apples   _Pommes fraîches_.

10. long vacations   _Longues vacances_.

11. happy friends   _Amis heureux_.

12. honest workers   _Ouvriers honnête_.

Adverbial use of descriptive adjectives

Some descriptive adjectives can be used as adverbs to modify the meaning of the verb. Note how the adjective **droit** (*straight*) is an adjective describing the noun **ligne** (*line*) in the first example that follows, but is an adverb modifying the meaning of the verb **aller** in the second example that follows:

C'est une **ligne droite**.	*It is a straight line.*
Tournez à gauche et **allez droit** jusqu'au coin!	*Turn left and go straight to the corner!*
aller droit	*to go straight*
couper court	*to cut short*
croire ferme	*to firmly believe*
dire tout haut	*to say out loud*
il fait mauvais	*the weather is bad*
parler bas/haut	*to speak in a low/loud voice*
parler fort	*to speak loudly*
payer cher	*to pay a lot*
tenir bon	*to hold your position/to hold out*
tout bronzé(e)	*all tanned*
Il est un peu sourd. Il faut **parler fort**.	*He is a little deaf. You must speak loudly.*
J'ai payé cher pour ce mobilier.	*I paid a lot for this furniture.*
Dans un marathon, il faut **tenir bon** jusqu'à la fin.	*In a marathon, you have to hold out until the end.*

EXERCICE

4·9

Quelle expression est appropriée? *What expression is appropriate?* Write the letter of the appropriate supplement to what is being stated.

1. __C__   _stop zigzagging_   Arrête de zigzaguer!   x a. _I cannot pay a lot_   Je ne veux pas payer cher.

2. __A__   _I found a small house_   Je cherche une petite maison.   x b. _Express yourself outloud_   Exprime-toi tout haut!

3. __E__   _The baby sleeps_   Le bébé dort.   x c. _Go straight_   Va droit!

4. __F__   _Watch the little girl in the red dress_   Regarde la petite fille en robe rouge.   x d. _It's all clean_   Il est tout propre!

5. __B__   _You can be frank_   Tu peux être franc.   x e. _Speak quieter_   Parlez bas!

6. __D__   _Why are you washing the sweater_   Pourquoi tu veux laver ce pull?   x f. _She is very pretty_   Elle est toute jolie.

VOCABULAIRE UTILE. *Useful vocabulary.*

Examine the following vocabulary list before doing the next exercise.

l'époque (*f.*)	*era*	entourer	*to surround*	audacieux	*audacious*
le bicentenaire	*bicentennial*	envisager	*to imagine*	incroyable	*incredible*
le Parisien	*Parisian*	partager	*to share*	innombrable	*numerous*
le pied	*foot*	réaliser	*to realize*	majestueux	*majestic*
le siècle	*century*			neuf	*new*

EXERCICE 4·10

La tour Eiffel. *The Eiffel Tower. Fill in each blank in the following paragraphs with the most appropriate adjective from the list provided. Remember to pay attention to the gender and number as well as the meaning of the adjective.*

technical ✗ techniques	*bold* ✗ audacieuse	*big* ✗ grande	*19th* ✗ dix-neuvième	*whole* ✗ entier
✗ innombrables *innumerable*	✗ populaire *popular*	✗ haute *high*	✗ français *French*	✗ universelle *universal*

L'ambition de réaliser une tour 1. _____haute_____ de plus de mille pieds

est une idée 2. _____audacieuse_____ mais 3. _____populaire_____ dans le monde

4. _____entier_____ au 5. _____dix-neuvième_____ siècle. Mais il y a d'

6. _____innombrables_____ problèmes 7. _____techniques_____. En France, vers

1878, le gouvernement envisage l'organisation d'une 8. _____grande_____ Exposition

9. _____universelle_____ pour l'année 1889, le bicentenaire de la révolution

10. _____française_____.

Public ✗ publique	*majestic* ✗ majestueuse	*new* ✗ neuves	*surprise* ✗ surpris	*remarkable* ✗ remarquables
Wonder ✗ émerveillés	✗ métallique *metallic*	✗ hostiles *hostile*	✗ chère *expensive*	✗ originales *original*
✗ incroyable (*use twice*) *incredible*				

Gustave Eiffel propose une tour 11. _____métallique_____. Cette idée est jugée

un peu 12. _____incroyable_____ et beaucoup trop 13. _____chère_____. Mais M.

Eiffel gagne le support de l'opinion 14. _____publique_____ et on décide de

construire la tour Eiffel au centre de la ville de Paris. M. Eiffel est entouré d'hommes

15. _____remarquables_____ qui partagent ses idées 16. _____neuves_____.

Malheureusement il y a aussi de 17. _____grands_____ hommes de l'époque comme

Alexandre Dumas qui sont 18. _____émerveillés_____ à l'idée de la tour Eiffel. Cependant,

les Parisiens, 19. _____surpris_____ et 20. _____émerveillés_____, vont voir la

21. _____majestueuse_____ élévation de la tour, au rythme 22. _____incroyable_____

de douze mètres par mois.

·5· The present tense of irregular verbs ending in -oir, -re, and -ir

Verbs ending in -oir

Although many verbs have irregular patterns of conjugation in the present tense, grouping them in families of verbs makes it easier to remember their conjugations. Pay attention to the following -oir verbs.

The first three forms of irregular forms are usually very similar.

> je **doi**s
> tu **doi**s
> il/elle/on **doi**t

For its **nous** and **vous** forms, the stems of the verbs **devoir**, **savoir**, and **recevoir** are derived from their infinitive forms.

> devoir → **dev** → **nous dev**ons, **vous dev**ez
> savoir → **sav** → **nous sav**ons, **vous sav**ez
> recevoir → **recev** → **nous recev**ons, **vous recev**ez

The verb **voir** has a pattern of conjugation similar to **devoir**, **savoir**, and **recevoir** in the singular forms, but its stem remains constant except for the **y**, which takes the place of **i** in the **nous** and **vous** forms.

	devoir (to have to)	**voir** (to see)	**savoir** (to know)	**recevoir** (to receive)
je	dois	vois	sais	reçois
tu	dois	vois	sais	reçois
il/elle/on	doit	voit	sait	reçoit
nous	**dev**ons	**voy**ons	**sav**ons	**recev**ons
vous	**dev**ez	**voy**ez	**sav**ez	**recev**ez
ils/elles	doivent	voient	**sav**ent	reçoivent

Je dois nettoyer ma chambre aujourd'hui.	*I must clean my room today.*
Ils voient tout de leur fenêtre.	*They see everything from their room.*
Tu vois bien avec ces lunettes?	*Do you see well with those glasses?*
Nous **recevons** des compliments pour un travail bien fait.	*We receive compliments for a job well done.*

The verb **savoir** means *to know for a fact* or *to know how to*.

Vous savez bien qu'il est français.	*You know (that) he is French.*
Je sais jouer du piano.	*I know how to play the piano.*

The verbs **pouvoir**, **vouloir**, and **valoir** have similar patterns of conjugation. Note that as for the previous **-oir** verbs, their **nous** and **vous** forms have a stem derived from their infinitive forms.

	pouvoir (to be able to)	**vouloir** (to want to)	**valoir** (to be worth)
je	peux	veux	vaux
tu	peux	veux	vaux
il/elle/on	peut	veut	vaut
nous	**pouv**ons	**voul**ons	**val**ons
vous	**pouv**ez	**voul**ez	**val**ez
ils/elles	**peuv**ent	**veul**ent	**val**ent

Ma copine **peut** vraiment bien nager.
My girlfriend can swim really well.
Vous **pouvez** voir que c'est une championne.
You can see that she is a champion.
Mes amis **veulent** aller à l'université de Paris.
My friends want to go to the University of Paris.

Tu ne **veux** pas rester encore un moment?
Don't you want to stay another moment?

Note the following **vouloir** expressions:

en vouloir à quelqu'un — *to hold a grudge against/to be mad at*
vouloir bien — *to be willing*
vouloir du bien/du mal à quelqu'un — *to have good/bad intentions toward someone*

vouloir dire — *to mean*
sans le vouloir — *unintentionally*

J'en veux à mon copain. Il ne veut pas venir à la boum avec moi.
I am angry at my friend. He does not want to come to the party with me.
Dîne avec moi, Justin! —**Je veux bien!**
Have dinner with me, Justin! —Sure, glad to!

Les parents ne **veulent** que **du bien** pour leurs enfants.
Parents want nothing but good things for their children.
Que veux-tu dire? Je ne comprends pas.
What do you mean? I do not understand.

J'ai fermé la porte **sans le vouloir**.
I closed the door unintentionally.

The verb **falloir** (*to have to/must*) only exists in the third-person singular because it is an impersonal verb.

Il faut faire la vaisselle.
We/you/one must do the dishes.
Il faut savoir le français.
We/you/one must know French.
Il faut du courage pour persévérer.
We/you/one need(s) courage to persevere.
Il faut de la chance pour réussir.
We/you/one need(s) luck to succeed.

Also note the translation of **Il ne faut pas** in the following example:

Il ne faut pas perdre courage.
We/you/one must not lose courage.

The verb **valoir** (*to be worth*) is often used in the third-person singular or plural when estimating costs and as part of the expression **il vaut mieux** (*it is better*).

Ce tableau **vaut** une fortune.
This painting is worth a fortune.
Ces bijoux ne **valent** pas grand-chose.
These jewels are not worth much.
Il vaut mieux attendre encore un peu.
It is better to wait a little longer.

EXERCICE 5·1

D'accord ou pas d'accord? *Agree or disagree?* *Place a check mark next to only the statements you agree with.*

1. _____ Il ne faut pas aider ses amis.
   You should not help your friends

2. _____ Il faut en vouloir aux professeurs stricts.
   You should want a strict professor

3. __✓__ Il faut vouloir du bien à ses amis et à sa famille.
   You should want good things for your friends + family

4. __✓__ Les étudiants peuvent travailler et gagner de l'argent.
   Students can work and make money

5. _____ Les parents savent toujours tout.
   Parents know everything

6. __✓__ Beaucoup de gens voient très bien sans lunettes.
   Many people see well w/o glasses

7. __✓__ On peut voir la Tour Eiffel à Paris.
   We can see the Eiffel Tower in Paris

8. __✓__ Vouloir, c'est pouvoir.
   To want is power

9. __✓__ Un tableau de Monet vaut énormément d'argent.
   A monet painting is worth an enormous amount of money

10. _____ Il vaut mieux ne pas manger du tout le soir.
    It's worth more not to eat anything in the evening

EXERCICE 5·2

Que savez-vous faire et que devez-vous faire? *What do you know how to do, and what must you do?* *Écrivez en français.*

1. In the evening, I have to study.

   Le soirée, je dois étudier

2. My parents know that I am a serious student.

   Mes parents savent que je suis un étudiant sérieux

3. My brother John knows how to speak French.

   Mon frère John sait parler français

4. In my French class, we must do written exercises after each class.

   Dans mon cours de français, nous devons faire des devoirs écrits après chaque clase.

5. We must not use electronic translators to do the work.

   Nous ne devons pas utiliser de traducteurs électroniques pour faire les devoirs

6. My brother has to help me sometimes.

   Mon frère doit m'aider quelquefois.

7. Sometimes I ask: "What do you mean?" because he knows more than me.

Quelquefois je demand, "que voulez-vous dire" parce qu'il sait plus que moi

8. Unintentionally, he makes (**rendre**) my work more difficult.

Par hasard, il rend mes devoirs plus difficile.

Verbs ending in -re

There are many families of verbs and patterns of conjugation among -**re** verbs.

Verbs like connaître, mettre, and prendre

- The verbs **connaître** (*to know a place or a person*) and **reconnaître** (*to recognize*) belong to the same family. Once you know how to conjugate **connaître**, just add the prefix -**re** to each verbal form to conjugate the verb **reconnaître**.

- The verbs **mettre** (*to put/put on*), **permettre** (*to permit/allow*), **promettre** (*to promise*), and **remettre** (*to postpone/delay*) belong to the same family. Once you know how to conjugate **mettre**, just add the appropriate prefix to each verbal form to conjugate the other verbs in this family.

- The verbs **prendre** (*to take*), **apprendre** (*to learn*), **comprendre** (*to understand*), and **surprendre** (*to surprise*) belong to the same family. Once you know how to conjugate **prendre**, just add the appropriate prefix to each verbal form to conjugate the other verbs in this family.

	connaître	**mettre**	**prendre**
je	connais	mets	prends
tu	connais	mets	prends
il/elle/on	connaît	met	prend
nous	**connaiss**ons	**mett**ons	**pren**ons
vous	**connaiss**ez	**mett**ez	**pren**ez
ils/elles	**connaiss**ent	**mett**ent	**prenn**ent

Vous connaissez mon ami David?	*Do you know my friend David?*
Je connais la ville de Strasbourg.	*I know the city of Strasbourg.*
Nous reconnaissons ce café.	*We recognize this café.*
Je **mets** mon manteau.	*I put on my coat.*
Les professeurs ne nous **permettent** pas d'écouter nos mobiles.	*The teachers do not allow us to listen to our portables.*
Tu me **promets** de venir?	*Do you promise me to come?*
Il faut **remettre** la fête à dimanche prochain.	*We have to postpone the party to next Sunday.*
Mes copains **prennent** le bus.	*My friends take the bus.*
J'**apprends** facilement le français.	*I am learning French easily.*
Tu ne me **surprends** jamais.	*You never surprise me.*

Verbs like lire, dire, and écrire

These verbs have similar patterns of conjugation and other verbs that belong to their respective family.

	lire (to read)	**dire** (to say/tell)	**écrire** (to write)
je/j'	lis	dis	écris
tu	lis	dis	écris
il/elle/on	lit	dit	écrit
nous	**lis**ons	**dis**ons	**écriv**ons
vous	**lis**ez	**dites**	**écriv**ez
ils/elles	**lis**ent	**dis**ent	**écriv**ent

By attaching a given prefix to one of the previous verbs, you obtain a new verb.

lire → relire
to read → to read again

dire → redire
to tell → to tell again
dire → prédire
to tell → to predict
dire → médire
to tell → to talk badly about/slander

écrire → récrire
to write → to write over
écrire → décrire
to write → to describe
écrire → prescrire
to write → to prescribe

Je **relis** ce livre pour la troisième fois.	*I am reading this book over for the third time.*
Ne me **redis** pas toujours la même chose.	*Don't always repeat the same thing to me.*
Les voyants **prédisent** le futur.	*Clairvoyants predict the future.*
Nous ne **médisons** pas car nous sommes honnêtes.	*We do not slander, because we are honest.*
Je **récris** ma dissertation.	*I'm writing my essay over.*
Le médecin me **prescrit** un médicament.	*The doctor prescribes me a medication.*

EXERCICE
5·3

La biographie de Nostradamus. *The biography of Nostradamus. Write the verbs in parentheses in the correct present tense forms.*

1. _connaissez_ -vous (connaître) Nostradamus? C'

2. _est_ (être) un médecin et astrologue de la Renaissance. En 1538, à cause de la peste (*the plague*), il 3. _perd_ (perdre) sa femme et ses deux enfants. Alors il 4. _parcourt_ (parcourir) toute la France et il

5. _secourt_ (secourir) de nombreuses victimes de la peste. Dans ses textes, Nostradamus 6. _décrit_ (décrire) certaines de ses interventions médicales. Il

7. _écrit_ (écrire) aussi des almanachs astrologiques. Ces almanachs

8. _connaissent_ (connaître) un grand succès. On 9. _dit_

(dire) qu'en 1524, Nostradamus 10. ____prédit____ (prédire) l'avenir du jeune roi (king) Henri de Navarre. En 1566, il 11. ____annonce____ (annoncer) que sa mort est proche et 12. ____écrit____ (écrire) son testament. Peu après, il 13. ____décède____ (décéder). En 1791, les révolutionnaires 14. ____pillent____ (piller) son tombeau (tomb). Ils 15. ____espèrent____ (espérer) trouver un trésor mais, au lieu de cela, ils 16. ____découvrent____ (découvrir) seulement la date où son tombeau est profané.

De nos jours, beaucoup de gens 17. ____lisent____ (lire) et 18. ____relisent____ (relire) les manuscrits de Nostradamus. On 19. ____reconnaît____ (reconnaître) l'importance historique de ce personnage intriguant. Ses prédictions 20. ____permettent____ (permettre) des discussions intéressantes.

The verbs boire and croire

These two verbs drop their infinitive ending -**re** and add the following endings -**s**, -**s**, and -**t** for their singular forms. Note that their endings in the plural forms are -**ons**, -**ez**, and -**ent**.

	boire (to drink)	**croire** (to believe)
je	bois	crois
tu	bois	crois
il/elle/on	boit	croit
nous	**buv**ons	**croy**ons
vous	**buv**ez	**croy**ez
ils/elles	**boiv**ent	**croi**ent

On **boit** beaucoup d'eau minérale à la maison. *We drink a lot of mineral water at home.*
Vous **buvez** du jus d'orange. C'est bon. *You drink orange juice. That's good.*
Tu **crois** qu'il faut partir? *Do you think/believe we must leave?*
Vous **croyez** qu'elle ment? *Do you believe she is lying?*

The verbs craindre, éteindre, and peindre

These verbs drop -**dre** from their infinitive endings for their singular forms and add the following endings -**s**, -**s**, and -**t** for their singular forms. To obtain their plural forms, just change the **d** consonant from the stem to **gn** and add -**ons**, -**ez**, and -**ent**.

	craindre (to fear)	**éteindre** (to turn off)	**peindre** (to paint)
je	crains	éteins	peins
tu	crains	éteins	peins
il/elle/on	craint	éteint	peint
nous	**craign**ons	**éteign**ons	**peign**ons
vous	**craign**ez	**éteign**ez	**peign**ez
ils/elles	**craign**ent	**éteign**ent	**peign**ent

Pourquoi est-ce que tu **crains** tellement les araignées?	*Why do you fear spiders so much?*
Éteignons la lumière! On verra mieux l'écran.	*Let's turn off the light! We'll see the screen better.*
Il **peint** si bien! Que c'est beau!	*He paints so well. How beautiful this is!*

The verb plaire (to please)

Like other irregular -**re** verbs, this verb drops its -**re** infinitive ending and adds -**s**, -**s**, and -**t** in its singular forms. Once you know its plural stem **plais**-, just add -**ons**, -**ez**, and -**ent** to obtain its plural forms.

je plais	nous plaisons
tu plais	vous plaisez
il/elle/on plaît	ils/elles plaisent

Although this verb can be conjugated in all its forms, note that the third-person singular and plural are the most frequently used because this verb is often used to express likes and dislikes.

Also remember to place what is liked at the beginning of the sentence and use it as a subject of the verb **plaire**.

Cette voiture de sport me **plaît** beaucoup.	*I like this sports car a lot.*
Ces chaussures ne me **plaisent** pas du tout.	*I do not like these shoes at all.*

Note the special meaning of the verb **plaire** in the following sentences:

Tu me **plais**, Jean-Luc.	*I'm attracted to you, Jean-Luc.*
Mon frère admire Myriam. Elle lui **plaît**.	*My brother admires Myriam. He is attracted to her.*

EXERCICE
5·4

Que penses-tu de Marc? *What do you think of Marc?* *Write the following sentences addressed to Jeanine in French. Use the verb* **plaire** *to translate the verb to like, and use* intonation *for asking questions.*

1. I like this beautiful painting. Do you like it too, Jeanine?

Ce tableau me plaît. Il te plaît aussi, Janine?

2. How about these paintings? Do you like them?

Et ces tableau? Ils te plaisent?

3. Look who is there. Do you like Marc, Jeanine?

Regarde qui est là. Marc te plaît, Janine?

4. He is handsome. Everybody is attracted to him.

Il est beau. Il plaît à tout le monde.

5. Do you know that he paints really well?

Sais-tu qu'il peint très bien?

6. Believe me! He is excellent.

Crois-moi! Il est excellent.

7. Don't be afraid to speak to him! He is nice!

N'aie pas peur de lui parler. Il est gentil.

8. Oh! They are turning off the lights. It must be time to leave.

Oh! Ils éteignent les lumières. Il doit être l'heure de partir.

Verbs ending in -ir

There are several patterns of conjugations and families of verbs among **-ir** verbs. Let's examine verbs that have similar patterns as well as their extended families.

Verbs like **venir** and **tenir**

The verbs **devenir** (*to become*), **prévenir** (*to warn*), **provenir** (*to come from*), **revenir** (*to come back*), **survenir** (*to occur/to arise*), and **parvenir à** (*to manage to*) belong to the **venir** (*to come*) family. Similarly, the verbs **retenir** (*to retain*) and **soutenir** (*to support*) belong to the **tenir** (*to hold*) family.

	venir	**tenir**
je	viens	tiens
tu	viens	tiens
il/elle/on	vient	tient
nous	**ven**ons	**ten**ons
vous	**ven**ez	**ten**ez
ils/elles	**vienn**ent	**tienn**ent

Vous **venez** au concert ce soir?	*Are you coming to the concert tonight?*
Ce garçon **devient** de plus en plus beau avec l'âge.	*This boy becomes more and more handsome with age.*
Nous **revenons** de vacances le 8 juin.	*We are coming back from vacation on June 8.*
Chaque fois qu'un délai **survient**, nous **parvenons** à rentrer quand même.	*Each time a delay occurs, we manage to come home anyway.*
Retenez ce client, s'il vous plaît!	*Keep this client, please.*
Cet argent **provient** de mon travail de l'été passé.	*This money comes from my work last summer.*
Les lois **soutiennent** le système de justice.	*Laws support the system of justice.*
Préviens-moi s'il y a beaucoup de bouchons sur la route!	*Warn me if there are many jams on the road!*

The verb **tenir** is often used idiomatically as in the expressions that follow:

ne pas tenir en place	*to be restless*
tenir à + *infinitive*	*to absolutely want to/insist on*
tenir à l'œil	*to keep an eye on*
tenir une promesse	*to keep a promise*
tenir (la route)	*to hold (the road)*

Elle **tient à** devenir astronaute.   *She wants to be an astronaut.*

Je **tiens** mon chiot **à l'œil** car il **ne peut**   *I keep an eye on my puppy because he is restless.*
pas tenir en place.

Cette nouvelle voiture **tient** bien la route.   *This new car holds the road well.*

Il faut **tenir** ses promesses, n'est-ce pas?   *We must keep our promises, right?*

Note the following idiomatic expressions, which include an imperative form of the verb **tenir**:

Tiens! Regarde!   *Look at this!*

Tenez! C'est à vous.   *Take it! It's yours.*

EXERCICE

5·5

La grammaire française. *French grammar. Complete each sentence with the correct form of the verb in parentheses.*

1. Cette leçon ___devient___ de plus en plus compliquée. (devenir)

2. Je ___retiens___ beaucoup de bonnes idées quand même. (retenir) *hold back*

3. Et toi, tu ___parviens___ à comprendre tout cela? (parvenir) *achieve*

4. D'où ___viennent___ toutes ces règles de grammaire? (venir)

5. Est-ce que ces mots ___proviennent___ du latin? (provenir)

6. Je ___tiens___ à maîtriser la grammaire française. (tenir)

7. Quand une difficulté ___survient___, je consulte ce livre de grammaire. (survenir)

8. Dans mon cours de français, mon prof ___tient___ à l'œil tous les étudiants. (tenir)

9. Nous ___tenons___ tous à bien apprendre la langue. (tenir)

10. La plupart du temps, nous ___parvenons___ à bien nous exprimer. (parvenir)

11. ___Tiens___, regarde! Voilà notre prof! (tenir, *imperative familiar*)

12. ___tenez___, Madame Desjardins! Je vous rends mon devoir! (tenir, *imperative formal*)

Verbs like courir and sortir

The verbs **dormir** (*to sleep*) and **servir** (*to serve*) as well as **sortir** (*to go out*), **partir** (*to leave*), and **mentir** (*to lie*) follow the same pattern of conjugation in the present tense. However, note that while **dormir** loses its **m**, **servir** loses its **v**, and **partir**, **sortir**, and **mentir** lose their **t** in the stem of their singular forms, the verb **courir** (*to run*) does not lose the consonant **r** from its stem in the singular forms.

	courir	dormir	servir
je	cours	dors	sers
tu	cours	dors	sers
il/elle/on	court	dort	sert
nous	**cour**ons	**dorm**ons	**serv**ons
vous	**cour**ez	**dorm**ez	**serv**ez
ils/elles	**cour**ent	**dorm**ent	**serv**ent

Ne **cours** pas si vite! Tu vas tomber.   *Don't run so fast! You're going to fall.*
Les enfants **dorment** encore?   *Are the children still sleeping?*
Servons la quiche!   *Let's serve the quiche!*

	sortir	partir	mentir
je	sors	pars	mens
tu	sors	pars	mens
il/elle/on	sort	part	ment
nous	**sort**ons	**part**ons	**ment**ons
vous	**sort**ez	**part**ez	**ment**ez
ils/elles	**sort**ent	**part**ent	**ment**ent

Sortez, les enfants! Il fait beau.   *Go out, children! The weather is nice.*
Quand est-ce qu'ils **partent** en vacances?   *When do they leave on vacation?*
Il ne faut pas mentir. Quand on **ment**,   *One must not lie. When people lie, they*
on est malhonnête.   *are dishonest.*

Note that the verb **sortir** (*to go out/to take out*) can be transitive or intransitive. An intransitive verb does not admit an object, whereas a transitive verb admits an object. In the following sentence, the verb is followed by the adverbial phrase **tous les samedis**. The verb is not followed by an object.

Jérôme **sort** tous les samedis.   *Jérôme goes out every Saturday.*

In the following sentences, the verb is followed by the direct object **la voiture/les billets**:

Je **sors** la voiture du garage.   *I'm taking the car out of the garage.*
Les passagers **sortent** leurs billets.   *The passengers take out their tickets.*

Note the usage of the intransitive verb **courir** (*to run*) and the transitive verbs **parcourir** (*to run/cover a distance*) and **secourir** (*to come to someone's help/aid*). In the following sentence, the verb is followed by a prepositional phrase **pour attraper**. The verb is not followed by an object and is intransitive.

Rémy **court** pour attraper le bus.   *Rémy runs to catch the bus.*

In the following sentence, the verb is followed by a direct object: **trente kilomètres**. The verb is transitive.

Rémy **parcourt** trente kilomètres à   *Rémy runs a distance of thirty kilometers today.*
pied aujourd'hui.

In the following sentence, the verb is followed by a direct object: **la victime**. The verb is transitive.

Le secouriste de garde **secourt** la victime de l'accident.	*The paramedic on call comes to the aid of the accident victim.*

Note the usage of the intransitive verb **dormir** (*to sleep*) and that of the transitive verb **endormir** (*to put to sleep*). In the following sentence, the verb is followed by a prepositional phrase **jusqu'à huit heures**. The verb **dormir** is an intransitive verb, which does not admit a direct object.

Gigi **dort** jusqu'à huit heures.	*Gigi sleeps until eight o'clock.*

In the following sentence, the verb is followed by a direct object: **le bébé**. The verb **endormir** is a transitive verb, which admits a direct object.

Gigi **endort** le bébé en lui chantant une berceuse.	*Gigi puts the baby to sleep by singing him a lullaby.*

Note this special intransitive use of the verb **servir**:

À quoi **sert** ce truc?	*What is this thing for?*
Il **sert à** peler les tomates.	*It is used to peel tomatoes.*

EXERCICE
5·6

Mon weekend. *My weekend. Complete each sentence with the correct form of the appropriate verb in parentheses.*

1. En général, je ___dors___ jusqu'à neuf heures le samedi. (dormir/endormir)

2. Je fais du jogging. Je ___parcours___ deux ou trois kilomètres. (courir/parcourir)

3. C'est vrai! Je ne ___mens___ pas. Je suis sportive, tu sais. (mentir/servir)

4. À quoi ça ___sert___ de courir? Mais c'est excellent pour la forme! (sortir/servir)

5. Si je vois une victime, je la ___secours___ si je peux. (sortir/secourir)

6. Après mon jogging, mes amis et moi ___sortons___ déjeuner. (mentir/sortir)

7. Je ___pars___ généralement de la maison vers 11 heures. (endormir/partir)

8. Dans ma voiture, j'écoute la musique rock car les autres musiques m' ___endorment___. (dormir/endormir)

9. Au café, ma serveuse favorite nous ___sert___. (servir/secourir)

10. Ginette ne ___ment___ jamais. Elle nous prévient quand quelque chose n'est pas bon. (servir/mentir)

L'histoire de l'escargot et de la tortue. *The story of the snail and the turtle.* *Complete each sentence with the correct form of the appropriate verb in parentheses.*

Un jour, l'escargot 1. ___demande___ (demander) à sa camarade la tortue

de le laisser voyager sur son dos. Il 2. ___dit___ (dire) qu'il

3. ___est___ (être) malade aujourd'hui et que la tortue

4. ___doit___ (devoir) le secourir et l'emmener chez son oncle le médecin.

La très gentille tortue 5. ___est___ (être) d'accord et se

6. ___met___ (mettre) en route avec l'escargot sur son dos. Elle

7. ___tient___ (tenir) bien la route mais elle 8. ___parcourt___

(parcourir) seulement un mètre en une heure et l'escargot ne 9. ___tient___

(tenir) plus en place. L'escargot 10. ___craint___ (craindre) de mourir en cours de

route. Il 11. ___dit___ (dire) à la tortue qu'il 12. ___connaît___

(connaître) un raccourci (*shortcut*) mais il faut traverser la rivière. La tortue

13. ___prend___ (prendre) le raccourci; elle 14. ___nage___ (nager)

très bien et 15. ___arrive___ (arriver) de l'autre côté de la rivière en deux minutes.

Mais où 16. ___est___ (être) son ami l'escargot? Elle le

17. ___voit___ (voir) au milieu de la rivière et 18. ___revient___

(revenir) le secourir. À ce moment l'oncle de l'escargot 19. ___voit___ (voir) la

tortue et l'escargot sortir de la rivière et il 20. ___court___ (courir) vers eux

(*toward them*). L'escargot 21. ___dit___ (dire) que l'eau de la rivière

22. ___doit___ (devoir) être magique parce qu'il 23. ___va___

(aller) beaucoup mieux. Son oncle lui 24. ___dit___ (dire) qu'il

25. ___fait___ (faire) très chaud et qu'il faut beaucoup

26. ___boire___ (boire) par ce temps. La tortue, elle

27. ___assure___ (assurer) à son ami l'escargot qu'il 28. ___vaut___

(valoir) mieux ne pas 29. ___rentrer___ (rentrer) à la maison ce soir. C'

30. ___est___ (être) trop loin. L'escargot 31. ___promet___

(promettre) à la tortue qu'elle 32. ___peut___ (pouvoir) passer la nuit chez son oncle.

C'est une histoire à dormir debout, n'est-ce pas? *This is an unbelievable story, isn't it?*

Prepositions, prepositional phrases, and verbal structures after prepositions

·6·

Prepositions and prepositional phrases introducing nouns or pronouns

Prepositions and prepositional phrases (groups of words serving as a preposition) serve to introduce noun phrases or pronouns. They give details pertaining to the manner in which something is done, the location where something happens, a time element, or a detail such as with whom or because of what.

Look at the following list of simple prepositions (one word) and prepositional phrases (a group of words).

à	*at/in/to*	à cause de	*because of*
après	*after*	à côté de	*next to*
avant	*before*	à droite de	*to the right of*
avec	*with*	à gauche de	*to the left of*
chez	*at/to someone's home or office*	au centre de	*at the center of*
contre	*against*	au dessus de	*above*
dans	*in*	au lieu de	*instead of*
de	*from/of*	au milieu de	*in the middle of*
depuis	*for/since*	au sujet de	*about/on the subject of*
derrière	*behind*	de la part de	*on behalf of*
devant	*in front of*	de peur de	*for fear of*
en	*in/on/upon*	en dehors de	*outside of*
entre	*between*	en dessous de	*underneath*
envers	*toward*	en face de	*across from*
malgré	*in spite of*	en plus de	*in addition to*
pendant	*during*	grâce à	*thanks to*
pour	*for*	jusqu'à	*until/up to*
sans	*without*	le long de	*alongside of*
sauf	*except for*	loin de	*far from*
selon	*according to*	près de	*near*
sous	*under*	quant à	*regarding/as for*
sur	*on/on top of*	vis-à-vis de	*vis-a-vis*
vers	*toward*		

In the following examples, the preposition introduces a noun:

Après les cours, ils vont au café. — *After classes, they go to the café.*
Entre le restaurant et le théâtre, il y a des magasins. — *Between the restaurant and the theater, there are stores.*
Je ne bois pas de café **sans** sucre. — *I do not drink coffee without sugar.*
On dîne **vers** 19 heures. — *We have dinner around 7 P.M.*

Remember to make appropriate contractions when the prepositional phrase is followed by **le** or **les**.

à + le → au   de + le → du
à + les → aux   de + les → des

On ferme les routes **à cause des** tempêtes. — *They close the roads because of storms.*
Les touristes restent **jusqu'au** mois d'août. — *The tourists stay till the month of August.*
Regarde la vache **au milieu du** chemin! — *Look at the cow in the middle of the path!*
Quant aux concerts, ils sont annulés. — *As for the concerts, they are cancelled.*

In the following sentences, note that prepositions are followed by stress pronouns (**moi, toi, lui, elle, nous, vous, eux, elles**).

Tout le monde est dehors **sauf moi**. — *Everyone is outside except for me.*
Selon toi, il va faire mauvais temps? — *According to you, the weather is going to be bad?*
Je fais tout **pour eux**. — *I do everything for them.*

EXERCICE 6·1

Le cours d'histoire de Jeanie. *Jeanie's history class.* *Write in French.*

1. We go to school around 8 A.M.

   nous allons à l'école vers 08h00.

2. We have class every day except for Sundays.

   Nous avons cours chaque jour sauf le dimanche.

3. My first class on Mondays is my favorite class thanks to the teacher.

   Mon première cours le lundi est mon cours favouri grâce au prof.

4. I sit between my good friends Frank and Jerry.

   J'assise entre mes bons amis, Frank et Jerry.

5. My history class today is about World War II.

   Mon cours d'histoire aujourd'hui est à propos de la dieuxième guerre mondiale

6. In spite of Frank who talks during class, I am very attentive.

   Malgré Frank, qui parle pendant le cours, je suis très attentive

7. Sometimes, because of him, the teacher stops talking in the middle of a sentence.

   Quelquefois, à cause de lui, le prof cesse de parler au milieu d'une phrase

8. In front of me, there is a map.

Devant moi, il y a une carte.

9. On the map, we can see all the countries.

Sur la carte, nous pouvons voir tous les pays

10. For me, this is a very interesting class.

Pour moi, c'est un cours très intéressant.

Geographical prepositions à, de, en

Several prepositions are used to express *in*, *to*, or *from* a geographical place. If the place is a city or town, use **à** to express *in* or *to* the city, and use **de** to express *from* or *of* the city.

Le prince Albert **habite à** Monaco.	*Prince Albert lives in Monaco.*
Nous allons **à Montréal** cet été.	*We are going to Montreal this summer.*
Mon copain vient **d'Ottawa**.	*My friend comes from Ottawa.*
Je ne sais pas qui est le maire **d'Ottawa**.	*I do not know who the mayor of Ottawa is.*

To determine which preposition to use for various geographical entities such as regions and countries, identify the gender and number of the name of the area. Use **en**, **au**, or **aux** to express *to* the place and use **du**, **de**, or **des** to express *from* the place as indicated in the following chart:

	MASCULINE SINGULAR PLACE	FEMININE SINGULAR PLACE	MASCULINE OR FEMININE PLURAL PLACE
in/to	au	en	aux
from	du	de	des

Josée habite **au Canada** parce que **le** Canada est son pays natal.	*Josée lives in Canada because Canada is her country of birth.*
Elle parle anglais et français puisqu'elle est **du** Canada.	*She speaks English and French since she is from Canada.*
Mais Josée va souvent **en Martinique** parce que **la** Martinique est une belle île.	*But Josée goes to Martinique often because Martinique is a beautiful island.*
Quand elle rentre **de** Martinique, elle est bronzée.	*When she comes back from Martinique, she is tanned.*
Quelquefois elle voyage aussi **aux États-Unis** parce que **les** États-Unis sont intéressants.	*Sometimes she travels to the United States because the United States is interesting.*
Quand elle revient **des États-Unis**, son anglais est meilleur.	*When she comes back from the United States, her English is better.*

Note that all continents have the feminine gender.

l'Amérique du nord/du sud (*f.*)	*North/South America*
l'Australie (*f.*)	*Australia*
l'Afrique (*f.*)	*Africa*
l'Europe (*f.*)	*Europe*
l'Asie (*f.*)	*Asia*

Le Vietnam est **en Asie**.	Vietnam is in Asia.
La Suisse est **en Europe**.	Switzerland is in Europe.
Le Burkina Faso est **en Afrique**.	Burkina Faso is in Africa.
La ville de Sydney est **en Australie**.	The city of Sydney is in Australia.
La ville de Québec est **en Amérique du nord**.	The city of Quebec is in North America.

Look at the following chart and note that *of* the feminine country is not the same as *from* the feminine country:

	MASCULINE SINGULAR PLACE	FEMININE SINGULAR PLACE	MASCULINE OR FEMININE PLURAL PLACE
of	du	**de la**	des
from	du	**de**	des

| Tunis est la capitale **de la** Tunisie. | Tunis is the capital city of Tunisia. |
| La recette de ce couscous vient **de** Tunisie. | The recipe of this couscous dish comes from Tunisia. |

VOCABULAIRE ET CULTURE. *Vocabulary and culture.*

LES PAYS FRANCOPHONES D'EUROPE ET LEURS CAPITALES	LES PAYS FRANCOPHONES D'AFRIQUE ET LEURS CAPITALES	LES RÉGIONS FRANCOPHONES D'AMÉRIQUE ET LEURS CAPITALES
la Belgique: Bruxelles *Belgium: Brussels*	l'Algérie (*f.*): Alger *Algeria: Alger*	Haïti: Port-au-Prince *Haïti: Port-au-Prince*
la France: Paris *France: Paris*	le Burundi: Bujumbura *Burundi: Bujumbura*	la Guyane (française): Cayenne *(French) Guiana: Cayenne*
la Suisse: Berne *Switzerland: Bern*	le Cameroun: Yaounde *Cameroun: Yaounde*	la Louisiane: la Nouvelle Orléans *Lousiana: New Orleans*
le Luxembourg: Luxembourg *Luxemburg: Luxemburg*	le Mali: Bamako *Mali: Bamako*	la Martinique: Fort-de-France *Martinique: Fort-de-France*
Monaco: Monaco *Monaco: Monaco*	le Sénégal: Dakar *Senegal: Dakar*	le Québec: Québec *Quebec: Québec City*

EXERCICE 6·2

Un voyage dans des régions francophones du monde. *A trip to French-speaking regions of the world. Write in French.*

1. I'm going to Luxembourg. The capital of Luxembourg is Luxembourg.

   Je vais au Luxembourg. La capitale du Luxembourg est Luxembourg

2. I'm going to Quebec. The capital of Quebec is Québec City.

   Je vais au Québec. La capitale du Québec est la ville de Québec.

3. I'm going to Burundi. The capital of Burundi is Bujumbura.

Je vais au Burundi. La capitale du Burundi est Bujumbura

4. I'm going to French Guiana. The capital of French Guiana is Cayenne.

Je vais en Guyane Française. La capitale de la Guyane Française est Cayenne.

5. I'm going to Belgium. The capital of Belgium is Brussels.

Je vais en Belgique. La capitale de la Belgique est Bruxelles

6. I'm going to Martinique. The capital of Martinique is Fort-de-France.

Je vais en Martinique. La capitale de la Martinique est Fort-de-France.

7. I'm going to Cameroun. The capital of Cameroun is Yaounde.

Je vais au Cameroun. La capitale du Cameroun est Yaounde

8. I'm going to France. The capital of France is Paris.

Je vais en France. La capitale de la France est Paris.

EXERCICE
6·3

D'où viennent-ils? _Where do they come from?_ _Based on the nationality of the following people, which you will easily recognize, complete each sentence by stating from which region or country they come. The first one has been done for you._

1. Monique est française. _Elle vient de France/Elle vient de Martinique._

2. Ivoline est camerounaise. Elle vient _du Cameroun_ .

3. Abou est sénégalais. Il vient _du Senegal_ .

4. Jean-François est belge. Il vient _de Belgique_ .

5. Régine est suisse. Elle vient _de Suisse_ .

6. Éric est burundais. Il vient _du Burundi_ .

7. Sylvie est québecoise. Elle vient _du Quebec_ .

8. Meg est louisianaise. Elle vient _de Louisiane_ .

9. Fatima est algérienne. Elle vient _d'Algerie_ .

10. Hassane est malien. Il vient _du Mali._ .

Prepositions and prepositional phrases followed by verbal structures

Some prepositions introduce specific verbal forms such as infinitives, past infinitives, and present participles. Look at the following chart:

PREPOSITION OR PREPOSITIONAL PHRASE	MEANING	FOLLOWED BY	
après	*after*	Past infinitive	**avoir** or **être** in the infinitive form + past participle
pour	*in order to*	Infinitive	Verb ending in
sans	*without*	or	**-er, -ir, -re, -oir** ending
avant de	*before*	Past infinitive	**avoir** or **être** in the infinitive form + past participle
au lieu de	*instead of*		
de peur de	*for fear that*		
de	*of/from*	Infinitive	Verb ending in
after adjectives or		or	**-er, -ir, -re, -oir** ending
verbs		Past infinitive	**avoir** or **être** in the infinitive form + past participle
en	*while/upon/by*	Present participle	**nous** form of present tense **-ons** + **-ant**

Après + past infinitive

When this preposition is followed by a verb, it is always followed by the past infinitive structure, which consists of the auxiliary verb **avoir** (*to have*) or **être** (*to be*) and a past participle. Remember that the past participle of regular verbs is obtained by dropping the infinitive ending of the verb and adding **é** for **-er** verbs, **i** for **-ir** verbs, and **u** for **-re** verbs. (For more on past infinitive structures, see Chapter 15.)

First look at the following chart of regular verbs using **avoir** as an auxiliary verb:

INFINITIVE	PAST PARTICIPLE	PAST INFINITIVE
apporter	apporté	après avoir apporté
to bring	*brought*	*after having brought*
choisir	choisi	après avoir choisi
to choose	*chosen*	*after having chosen*
perdre	perdu	après avoir perdu
to lose	*lost*	*after having lost*

Après avoir mangé, nous regardons les nouvelles.	*After eating, we watch the news.*
Après avoir travaillé toute la semaine, ils sont fatigués.	*After working all week, they are tired.*
Après avoir fini le diner, nous regardons les nouvelles.	*After having finished dinner, we watch the news.*
Après avoir répondu à un texto, j'ai fermé mon iPad.	*After having answered a text message, I closed my iPad.*

Some verbs have irregular past participles. The following is a list of common irregular past participles:

avoir	*to have*	eu	*had*
connaître	*to know*	connu	*known*
courir	*to run*	couru	*run*
croire	*to believe*	cru	*believed*
devoir	*to have to*	dû	*had to*
dire	*to say/tell*	dit	*said/told*
écrire	*to write*	écrit	*written*
être	*to be*	été	*been*
faire	*to do*	fait	*done*
lire	*to read*	lu	*read*
mettre	*to put (on)*	mis	*put (on)*
offrir	*to offer*	offert	*offered*
ouvrir	*to open*	ouvert	*opened*
plaire	*to please*	plu	*pleased*
pouvoir	*to be able to*	pu	*been able to*
prendre	*to take*	pris	*taken*
recevoir	*to receive*	reçu	*received*
savoir	*to know*	su	*known*
voir	*to see*	vu	*seen*
vouloir	*to want*	voulu	*wanted*

Après avoir dit la vérité, on se sent mieux.	*After having told the truth, one feels better.*
Après avoir été en vacances, nous sommes reposés.	*After having been on vacation, we are rested.*
Après avoir connu un ami pendant longtemps, on peut bien le décrire.	*After having known a friend for a long time, one can describe him well.*
Après avoir reçu un premier prix, il est content.	*After having received a first prize, he is happy.*
Après avoir fait une promenade, je rentre chez moi.	*After having taken a walk, I go home.*

Remember that families of verbs have similar past participles. Look at how the families of **prendre** and **mettre** verbs form their past participles.

prendre → pris	mettre → mis
to take → taken	*put (on) → put (on)*
apprendre → appris	remettre → remis
to learn → learned	*to put back (on) → put back (on)*
comprendre → compris	permettre → permis
to understand → understood	*to allow → allowed*
surprendre → surpris	promettre → promis
to surprise → surprised	*to promise → promised*

Après avoir pris le mauvais train, je dois retourner.	*After having taken the wrong train, I have to go back.*
Après avoir appris le vocabulaire, je l'utilise.	*After having learned the vocabulary, I use it.*
Après avoir promis un beau cadeau, je dois acheter quelque chose de bien.	*After having promised a beautiful gift, I have to buy something good.*
Après avoir remis sa cravate, il est prêt à partir.	*After having put his tie back on, he is ready to leave.*

Now look at the following list of verbs using **être** as an auxiliary verb. Remember that these verbs are mostly verbs of coming and going but also include the verbs **rester** (*to stay*), **naître** (*to be born*), and **mourir** (*to die*).

aller	*to go*
arriver	*to arrive*
partir/repartir	*to leave/to leave again*
sortir/resortir	*to go out/to go back out*
retourner	*to return/to go back*
entrer/rentrer	*to enter/to go back*
venir/devenir/revenir	*to come/to become/to come back*
rester	*to stay*
monter/remonter	*to go up/to go back up*
descendre/redescendre	*to go down/to go back down*
tomber/retomber	*to fall/to fall again*
passer/repasser	*to pass by/to pass by again*
naître/renaître	*to be born/to be reborn*
mourir	*to die*

Note that among **être** verbs, the following have irregular past participles:

venir/devenir/revenir → venu/devenu/revenu
naître → né
mourir → mort

Après être descendu, il va au garage.	*After having come down, he goes to the garage.*
Après être revenu de France, il parle vraiment bien français.	*After having come back from France, he speaks French really well.*

Remember to make the past participle and the subject agree when forming the past infinitive of an **être** verb. Add **-e** for the feminine singular agreement, add **-s** for the masculine plural agreement, and add **-es** for the feminine plural agreement with the subject.

Après être rentrée à la maison, elle promène son chien.	*After getting home, she walks her dog.*
Après être montés en haut de la Tour Eiffel, ils ont une vue magnifique.	*After going up the Eiffel Tower, they have a magnificent view.*
Après être tombées plusieurs fois, elles ont peur.	*After having fallen several times, they are afraid.*

EXERCICE 6·4

Les héritières des parfumeries Fragonard. *The heirs of the Fragonard perfume factories.* *Complete each sentence with the past participle of the verb in parentheses.*

1. Après avoir _____*ouvert*_____ (ouvrir) une usine à Grasse en 1926, Eugène Fuchs l'a nommée Fragonard en l'honneur du peintre Jean-Honoré Fragonard.

2. Après avoir _____*acheté*_____ (acheter) un magasin à Grasse où il vend directement ses produits, Eugène commence bientôt à vendre ses parfums à des parfumeurs dans le monde entier.

3. Après avoir _____créé_____ (créer) des parfums célèbres, la maison Fragonard développe un petit empire et ouvre deux musées à Paris.

4. Après avoir _____travaillé_____ (travailler) pour leur père à l'usine de parfum Fragonard, Agnès et Françoise Costa, petites-filles d'Eugène Fuchs, prennent en main l'entreprise Fragonard.

5. Après avoir d'abord _____continué_____ (continuer) la tradition des parfums Fragonard, les deux sœurs sont maintenant dans les vêtements, les bijoux et toutes sortes de choses bien en dehors de la parfumerie traditionnelle.

EXERCICE
6·5

L'histoire de Jean et d'Élise. *Jean and Élise's story.* *Complete each sentence with the past infinitive form of the verb in parentheses.*

1. Après _____être allé_____ au lycée pendant quatre ans, Jean finit ses études secondaires. (aller)

2. Après _____avoir fini_____ ses études secondaires, Jean passe le baccalauréat. (finir)

3. Après _____avoir réussi_____ au baccalauréat, Jean commence des études de médecine à la faculté. (réussir)

4. Après _____être allée_____ au lycée pendant quatre ans, Élise veut aller en Afrique. (aller)

5. Après _____avoir fait_____ du bénévolat pour le Corps de la Paix, Élise rentre en France. (faire)

6. Après _____avoir fini_____ ses études de médecine, Jean devient médecin. (finir)

7. Après _____être rentrée_____ d'Afrique, Élise travaille comme infirmière pour Jean. (rentrer)

8. Après _____être tombé_____ amoureux d'Élise, Jean épouse Élise. (tomber)

9. Après _____avoir épousé_____ Élise, Jean décide qu'il est temps d'avoir des enfants. (épouser)

10. Après _____avoir pris_____ la décision d'avoir des enfants, Jean comprend qu'Élise ne veut pas d'enfants. (prendre)

11. Après _____avoir compris_____ qu'Élise ne veut pas encore d'enfants, Jean est très déçu. (comprendre)

12. Après _____avoir été_____ déçu, Jean décide qu'il vaut mieux attendre un peu. (être)

13. Après _____avoir attendu_____ un peu, Élise a changé d'avis. Ils ont maintenant trois enfants. (attendre)

Prepositional phrase + infinitive or past infinitive

A prepositional phrase is followed by an infinitive verb when the action of that verb takes place simultaneously with the action of the main verb in the sentence. In addition, the subject of the main verb must be the same as the subject of the infinitive verb.

Avant de sortir, tu finis tes devoirs!	*Before going out, you finish your homework!*
Au lieu de jouer aux jeux vidéo, il doit travailler.	*Instead of playing video games, he must work.*
Pour avoir un bon salaire, il faut un bon emploi.	*To have a good salary, one needs a good job.*
Il part **sans dire** au revoir?	*He is leaving without saying good-bye?*
À force d'essayer, il va réussir.	*By trying, he is going to succeed.*

A prepositional phrase is followed by a verb in the past infinitive when the action of that verb takes place before the action of the main verb in the sentence. In addition, the subject of the main verb must be the same as the subject of the infinitive verb.

Elle révise son essai **de peur d'avoir omis** quelque chose.	*She reviews her essay fearing she omitted something.*
Il n'est pas bon d'aller travailler **sans avoir mangé**.	*It is not good to go to work without having eaten.*

EXERCICE 6·6

Ce petit coquin! *This little rascal! Complete each sentence as directed using the appropriate prepositional phrase followed by an infinitive verb.*

1. Toto veut toujours jouer _au lieu de faire ses devoirs_.
   (*instead of doing his homework*)

2. Il court dans les corridors de l'école _au lieu de marcher_.
   (*instead of walking*)

3. Il travaille rapidement _pour sortir jouer_.
   (*in order to go out and play*)

4. Il sort _sans demander pour permission_.
   (*without asking permission*)

5. Un jour, il va être puni _pour avoir désobéi_.
   (*for having disobeyed*)

Regretter de + infinitive verb or past infinitive

The verb **regretter** (*to regret*) can be followed by the preposition **de** and an infinitive verb. The two actions must take place simultaneously. In addition, the subject of the main verb must be the same as the subject of the infinitive verb.

J'accepte **de faire** ce projet.	*I accept to do this project.*
Nous **regrettons de ne pas avoir** de patience.	*We are sorry we do not have any patience.*

The verb **regretter de** can be followed by a verb in the past infinitive. The action of the verb in the past infinitive must precede the action of the main verb. In addition, the subject of the main verb must be the same as the subject of the infinitive verb.

Je **regrette de vous avoir dérangé**.   *I regret I disturbed you.*

See Chapter 7 for more verbs like **regretter**.

EXERCICE
6·7

Quel dommage! *What a pity!* *Write in French. Beware that some sentences require an infinitive structure, while others require a past infinitive structure.*

1. I regret I do not have this book.

   Je regrette de ne pas avoir ce livre.

2. He regrets he is not able to come to the party.

   Il regrette de ne pas pouvoir venir à cette fête

3. She regrets that she is busy today.

   Elle regrette d'être changé aujourd'hui

4. We regret we have forgotten to bring the cake.

   nous regrettons d'avoir oublié d'apporter le gâteau

5. Our friends regret that they have not written.

   Nos amis regrettent de ne pas avoir écrit.

6. You (*familiar*) regret that you sold your car, don't you?

   Tu regrettes d'avoir vendu ta voiture, n'est-ce pas?

Adjectives + **de** + infinitive verb or past infinitive

Look at the following sets of sentences, and note that in the first sentence of each set, the verbal structure after the preposition **de** is the infinitive because the action takes place simultaneously with the action of the main verb. Note also that in the second sentence of each set, the verbal structure after the preposition **de** is the past infinitive because the action takes place before the action of the main verb. In all sentences, the subject of the main verb is the same as the subject of the infinitive or past infinitive verb.

Elle est contente **d'être** en bonne santé.	*She is happy to be in good health.*
Elle est contente **d'avoir rencontré** ses amis.	*She is happy to have met her friends.*
Ils sont désolés **de ne pas pouvoir** aller au cinéma.	*They are sorry they cannot go to the movies.*
Ils sont désolés **d'être arrivés** en retard.	*They are sorry they arrived late.*

Quel dommage! *What a pity! Write in French. Beware that some sentences require an infinitive structure, while others require a past infinitive structure.*

1. I am happy I have many friends.

   Je suis contente d'avoir beaucoup d'amis.

2. He is satisfied he is in good health.

   Il est content d'être en bonne santé

3. She is delighted to be living in France.

   Elle est ravie d'habiter en France

4. We are sad to be leaving soon.

   Nous sommes triste de partir bientôt

5. You (*m., pl.*) are jealous that you are not rich.

   Vous êtes jaloux de ne pas être riches.

6. They (*m.*) are angry that they have to work this weekend.

   Ils sont fâchés de devoir travailler ce weekend

7. I am sorry that I did not go for a walk before the rain.

   Je regrette de ne pas avoir fait de promenade avant la pluie

8. We are unhappy that we did not pass this exam.

   Nous sommes malheureux de ne pas avoir réussi à cet examen

9. He is sorry that he was late.

   Il est désolé d'avoir été en retard

10. They (*f.*) are mad they have no invitation.

    Elles sont fâchée de ne pas avoir d'invitation

Preposition en + present participle

This preposition **en** is followed by a present participle to express *while*, *upon*, or *by* when the main verb and the verb following the preposition have the same subject. To form the present participle of a verb, drop the -**ons** ending of the **nous** form of the present tense and add -**ant**.

En écoutant attentivement, j'ai entendu l'oiseau.	*By listening attentively, I heard the bird.*
En lisant beaucoup de livres de science-fiction, tu as développé ton imagination.	*Upon reading many science fiction books, you developed your imagination.*
Il est tombé **en courant**.	*He fell while running.*

See Chapter 7 for more on present participles.

C'est comme cela. *That's how it is.* *Write the letter of the most appropriate completion of each sentence on the line provided.*

1. __F__ *one is reasonable* On est raisonnable   ✗ a. *in lying* en mentant.

2. __D__ *one shows its appreciation to its friends* On montre qu'on apprécie ses amis   ✗ b. *in perservering in his efforts* en persévérant dans ses efforts.

3. __E__ *one keeps his friends* On garde ses amis   ✗ c. *in disobeying* en désobéissant.

4. __G__ *one is discreet* On est discret   ✗ d. *in thanking them* en les remerciant.

5. __C__ *one deceives his parents* On déçoit ses parents   ✗ e. *in being trustworthy* en étant fidèle.

6. __H__ *one learns a lot* On apprend beaucoup   ✗ f. *in choosing good friends* en choisissant de bons amis.

7. __B__ *one is successful in everything* On réussit en tout   ✗ g. *in keeping their secrets* en gardant nos secrets.

8. __A__ *one loses trust in people* On perd la confiance des gens   ✗ h. *in doing research* en faisant des recherches.

Un projet de camping. *A camping project.* *Complete each sentence with the present participle, infinitive, or past infinitive, form of the verb in parentheses as appropriate.*

1. Nous achetons une tente pour ___faire___ du camping. (faire)

2. Nous ne pouvons pas partir sans ___organiser___ tout le matériel. (organiser)

3. À force de/d' ___escalader___ des montagnes, toi, tu es en pleine forme. (escalader)

4. En ___faisant___ beaucoup de sports en plein air, les sportifs restent en forme! (faire)

5. Après ___avoir suivi___ de régulières sessions d'athlétisme, moi aussi, je suis prêt. (suivre)

6. Je n'ai pas peur de ___participer___ à tes randonnées. (participer)

7. Je souhaite seulement ___avoir___ plus d'expérience. (avoir)

8. Mais, peu importe! Je suis ravi d'___accepter___ de t'accompagner. (accepter)

Imperative, infinitive, and present participle structures

Imperative structures

The imperative forms of a verb are used for instructions, suggestions, and commands. They are mostly used in oral communication. Written instructions are often expressed with infinitives in the French language.

Formation of imperative forms

Although the imperative is a mood, its conjugated forms are borrowed from the present tense indicative for regular **-er**, **-ir**, and **-re** verbs as well as for irregular verbs.

Remember to use the second-person singular (**tu**), and the first- and second-person plurals (**nous** and **vous**) of the present tense conjugation of a verb to create imperative forms.

Tu choisis. → **Choisis!**	*You are choosing. → Choose!*
Nous choisissons. → **Choisissons!**	*We are choosing. → Let's choose!*
Vous choisissez. → **Choisissez!**	*You are choosing. → Choose!*

Remember that in the case of **-er** verbs, you must drop the **-s** from the **tu** form to obtain the familiar command form. This is also true for the verb **aller**.

Tu décides. → **Décide!**	*You are deciding. → Decide!*
Nous décidons. → **Décidons!**	*We are deciding. → Let's decide!*
Vous décidez. → **Décidez!**	*You are deciding. → Decide!*
Tu vas. → **Va!**	*You are going. → Go!*
Nous allons. → **Allons!**	*We are going. → Let's go!*
Vous allez. → **Allez!**	*You are going. → Go!*

Note that the dropped **-s** in the familiar command of the verb **aller** is back if the command includes the pronoun **y**.

Va! *Go!*	*but*	**Vas**-y! *Go there!*
Nous pouvons prendre un seul chien; alors **choisis**, Jeannot!		*We can take only one dog; so choose, Jeannot!*
Prenons le plus gros!		*Let's take the fattest one!*
Monsieur, **donnez** ce chiot à mon fils, s'il vous plaît!		*Sir, give this puppy to my son, please!*
Prends ton chiot et **va** attendre dans la voiture, Jeannot!		*Take your puppy and go wait in the car, Jeannot!*
Vas-y! J'arrive.		*Go there! I'm coming.*

Only a few verbs have imperative forms that are not obtained from the present tense indicative. Memorize the imperative stems for the following verbs:

avoir (to have)		**être** (to be)		**savoir** (to know)	
aie	*have*	sois	*be*	sache	*know*
ayons	*let's have*	soyons	*let's be*	sachons	*let's know*
ayez	*have*	soyez	*be*	sachez	*know*

Sachez, madame, que nous ne vendons que la meilleure qualité!	*Know that we sell only the best quality, madame!*
Sois poli, mon enfant!	*Be polite, my child!*
Ayons patience!	*Let's be patient!*

Use of the various imperative forms

The various forms of the imperative mood help distinguish whom an instruction is addressed to.

- The second-person singular and plural imperative forms are used to give direct instructions, suggestions, and commands.

Obéis et **fais** tes devoirs, Marie!	*Obey and do your homework, Marie!*
Ne **reste** pas trop longtemps dehors, mon chou!	*Don't stay out too long, honey!*
Arrosez les plantes et **coupez** l'herbe aujourd'hui, monsieur Jason!	*Water the plants and cut the grass today, Mr. Jason!*
Rentrez tout de suite, les enfants! Il va pleuvoir.	*Come home right away, children! It's going to rain.*

- The first-person plural imperative is used to command and instruct one other person or several other persons, but it includes the speaker as well.

Allons à la piscine!	*Let's go to the pool!*
Restons calmes!	*Let's stay calm!*

- Note the second-person plural imperative form of the verb **vouloir** is used in formal settings to give polite instructions and also at the end of a formal letter as part of a closing. It is followed by an infinitive verb.

Veuillez entrer, mesdames.	*Please enter, ladies.*
Veuillez accepter, madame, mes sincères salutations.	*Please accept, madam, my sincere salutations.*

- Note that the verb **vouloir** is used in the interrogative structure to soften an instruction or a command.

Veux-tu fermer la porte, s'il te plaît, Philippe.	*Please close the door, Philippe.*

Suivez bien ces instructions! *Follow these instructions well! Madame Jonat is out of town and left a list of instructions for her son. Complete each instruction with the correct imperative form of the verb in parentheses.*

1. N' _____ pas de vider la poubelle tous les jours! (oublier)

2. _____ le journal chaque jour. (rentrer)

3. _____ à l'école et _____ à l'heure! (aller/partir)

4. _____ tes devoirs diligemment! (faire)

5. _____ gentil et patient avec le chien! (être)

6. Ne _____ pas trop la télévision. (regarder)

7. _____ bien les amis que tu invites à la maison! (choisir)

8. _____ des fruits et des légumes chaque soir! (manger)

9. Ne _____ pas les mêmes jeans tous les jours. (mettre)

10. _____ -moi de tes nouvelles régulièrement! (donner)

Notre forum des étoiles. *Our star forum. Write the correct imperative form of each verb in parentheses, keeping in mind that this message is addressed to many potential Internet users.*

1. _____ (ouvrir) et 2. _____ (élargir) vos horizons! 3. _____ (devenir) membres de notre forum sur les galaxies et les étoiles! 4. _____ (vouloir) remplir le formulaire d'inscription! 5. N'_____ (oublier) pas d'inclure votre adresse e-mail et 6. _____ (recevoir) notre bulletin hebdomadaire.

7. _____ (être) rassurés! Nous ne nous servons pas de vos coordonnées à but commercial. 8. _____ (savoir) que notre forum est au profit des passionnés de la science. 9. _____ (explorer) et 10. _____ (discuter) ensemble notre univers!

Use of infinitive forms of verbs

There is a great variety of uses of the infinitive form of a verb in French. For example, an infinitive verb can be used to give instructions in recipes. An infinitive verb can also serve as the subject of a verb, thus assuming the function of a noun. In addition, verbs that follow a preposition such as **à** (*to*), **avant de** (*before*), **de** (*of, from*), **pour** (*in order to*), or **sans** (*without*) are in the infinitive form.

Infinitives used to give directions of instructions to a general public

In instructions addressed to a general public, such as recipes, assembly guides, parking instructions, or security measures, the infinitive form of verbs is preferred rather than imperative forms.

Mettre une pincée de sel et **laisser** bouillir.	*Put in a pinch of salt and let boil.*
Identifier les pièces A et B et les **mettre** l'une à côté de l'autre.	*Identify parts A and B and put them next to each other.*
Garer la voiture dans le parking indiqué.	*Park the car in the assigned parking lot.*
Ne pas abandonner les bagages.	*Do not abandon baggage.*

VOCABULAIRE UTILE. *Useful vocabulary.*

Examine the following vocabulary list before doing the next exercise.

l'œuf (*m.*)	*egg*	ajouter	*add*
la farine	*flour*	chauffer	*warm up/heat*
la pâte	*dough*	cuire	*cook*
la pincée	*pinch*	graisser	*grease*
la poêle	*pan*	laisser	*let*
le beurre	*butter*	mélanger	*mix*
le fouet	*whip*	mesurer	*measure*
le lait	*milk*	préparer	*prepare*
le sel	*salt*	reposer	*rest*
le sucre	*sugar*	verser	*pour*

EXERCICE
7·3

Découvrez la recette des crêpes! *Discover the recipe for crêpes! Writing letters A through J on the lines provided, put the following crêpe-making steps into the correct order.*

1. _____ Ajouter le lait et les œufs et mélanger avec le fouet ou le mixer.

2. _____ Laisser reposer la pâte.

3. _____ Verser la farine dans un bol.

4. _____ Préparer tous les ingrédients.

5. _____ Verser un peu de pâte dans la poêle et faire cuire.

6. _____ Faire chauffer la poêle.

7. _____ Mesurer la farine.

8. _____ Mettre une pincée de sel et un peu de sucre vanille dans le bol de farine.

9. _____ Graisser une poêle avec du beurre.

10. _____ Faire dorer la crêpe des deux côtés.

Infinitives used as subjects

Activities are often stated in the form of an infinitive verb, which functions as the subject of the conjugated verb in the sentence.

Faire du sport est essential pour rester en forme.	*Doing sports is essential to stay in shape.*
Nager me permet de faire de l'exercice tout en relaxant.	*Swimming allows me to exercise while relaxing.*
Manger représente un des grands plaisirs de la vie.	*Eating represents one of the great pleasures in life.*

EXERCICE
7·4

Un peu de tout! *A little of everything!* *Write in French.*

1. Reading all day, that's my hobby.

   _____

2. Answering my questions is urgent.

   _____

3. Walking alone in the streets at night is dangerous.

   _____

4. To pass this exam is my only goal.

   _____

5. Buying new clothes is fun.

   _____

6. To help friends is natural.

   _____

Infinitives after a conjugated verb

Remember that when two verbs have the same subject, the first one is conjugated and the second one stays in the infinitive form.

The verbs **aimer** (*to like/love*), **adorer** (*to love*), **désirer** (*to desire*), **devoir** (*to have to/must*), **pouvoir** (*to be able to/can*), **vouloir** (*to want to*), **savoir** (*to know*), **sembler** (*to seem*), and **souhaiter** (*to wish*) are among the many verbs followed by an infinitive verb.

J'adore **jouer** au tennis.	*I love to play tennis.*
Les touristes veulent **acheter** des souvenirs.	*Tourists want to buy souvenirs.*
Elle semble **avoir** des difficultés.	*She seems to have difficulties.*
Je souhaite **devenir** célèbre.	*I want to become famous.*

Sometimes the infinitive verb is used to express a goal. In that case the preposition **pour** (*in order to*) is omitted and implied.

Nous allons au club (pour) **rencontrer** des amis.	*We are going to the club (in order) to meet friends.*
Le professeur vient (pour) **corriger** nos examens.	*The professor comes (in order) to correct our exams.*
Vous partez (pour) **faire** des courses?	*Are you leaving (in order) to go shopping?*

Note that the verbs **dire** (*to say/tell*), **penser** (*to think*), and **croire** (*to think/to believe*) can be followed by an infinitive verb in French even though they are not in English.

Elle dit **avoir** raison.	*She says she is right.*
Pensez-vous **vendre** votre maison?	*Do you think you'll sell your house?*
Il croit **être** riche.	*He believes to be rich.*

Note the following special expressions:

laisser tomber quelque chose	*to drop something*
faire croire quelque chose à quelqu'un	*to make someone believe something*
Attention! **Ne laisse pas tomber** le vase!	*Careful! Don't drop the vase!*
Je n'ai pas l'intention de **laisser tomber** ce projet.	*I do not intend to give up this project.*
Tu **fais croire** à tout le monde que tout est bien.	*You make everyone believe that all is well.*

Infinitives after the preposition **de**

Some verbs are followed by a required preposition and an infinitive verb. Here are lists of such verbs that you may use in this chapter:

- **Avoir** expression + **de** + infinitive

avoir envie de	*to feel like (to want/wish to)*
avoir honte de	*to be ashamed to*
avoir l'habitude de	*to be used to*
avoir l'impression de	*to have the feeling that*
avoir l'intention de	*to intend to*
avoir l'occasion de	*to have the opportunity to*
avoir la chance de	*to be so lucky as to*
Tu as envie de **sortir** boire un pot?	*Do you want to go out for a drink?*
J'ai l'impression d'**être** malade.	*I feel sick.*
En France, tu as souvent l'occasion de **prendre** le train.	*In France you often have the opportunity to take the train.*
Nous avons la chance d'**être** si heureux.	*We are lucky to be so happy.*

- **Être** expression + **de** + infinitive

être à même de	*to be up to/able to*
être en train de	*to be in the middle/process of*
être sur le point de	*to be about to*
Tu es à même de **finir** ce travail?	*Are you up to finishing this job?*
Oui, je suis en train de **terminer**.	*Yes, I am finishing.*
Le restaurant est sur le point de **fermer**.	*The restaurant is about to close.*

◆ Adjective + **de** + infinitive

capable de	*able to*
certain(e)/sûr(e) de	*sure that*
déçu(e) de	*disappointed to*
désolé(e) de	*sorry to*
enchanté(e) de	*delighted to*
heureux(-se) de	*happy to*
ravi(e) de	*delighted to*

Enchanté de **faire** votre connaissance, madame.	*Delighted to make your acquaintance, madam.*
Tu es sûre de **pouvoir** venir?	*Are you sure you can come?*
Je suis déçu de **ne pas voir** mon copain.	*I am disappointed not to see my friend.*

◆ Verb + **de** + infinitive

accepter de	*to accept to*
arrêter de	*to stop*
décider de	*to decide to*
essayer de	*to try to*
faire semblant de	*to pretend to*
oublier de	*to forget to*
refuser de	*to refuse to*
regretter de	*to regret to*

Arrête de **fumer**!	*Stop smoking!*
Essaie de **faire** de ton mieux!	*Try to do your best!*
N'oublie pas **d'apporter** du pain!	*Don't forget to bring bread!*
Ils regrettent de ne pas **parler** français.	*They are sorry they do not speak French.*

EXERCICE
7·5

Jeannot est paresseux! *Jeannot is lazy! Write in French.*

1. Jeannot, stop playing this game!

_____

2. Do not pretend to do homework!

_____

3. You always forget to write what (**ce que**) you have to do.

_____

4. You are capable of having good grades.

_____

5. You are about to finish your high school studies.

_____

6. Are you not ashamed to be lazy?

_____

7. Do you intend to live on the street?

_____

8. You are lucky to have this family!

_____

Infinitives after the preposition à

There are verbs that are necessarily followed by the preposition **à** and an infinitive verb. There are also special expressions that include **à** followed by an infinitive. Note some of these expressions in the following sentences:

J'ai quelque chose à te dire.	_I have something to tell you._
Tu as quelque chose à faire?	_Do you have something to do?_
Cet outil **sert à couper** les œufs en tranches.	_This instrument is used to slice eggs._
Cet article est **facile à comprendre.**	_This article is easy to understand._
Tu n'as **rien à ajouter**?	_Do you have nothing to add?_
Ces instructions sont **difficiles à suivre.**	_These instructions are difficult to follow._
Il reste à payer la facture.	_What remains to be done is to pay the bill._
Il y a peu/beaucoup à faire ici.	_There is little/much to do here._

- Verb + **à** + infinitive

aider quelqu'un à	_to help someone to_
apprendre à	_to learn to_
apprendre à quelqu'un à	_to teach someone to_
arriver à	_to manage to_
commencer à	_to begin to_
continuer à	_to continue to_
obliger quelqu'un à	_to force someone to_
renoncer à	_to give up (doing something)_
réussir à	_to succeed in/to manage_

Il **apprend à conduire.**	_He is learning to drive._
Mon père **apprend à** ma petite sœur à **nager.**	_My father teaches my little sister how to swim._
Ma mère **oblige** Jeannot **à ranger** sa chambre.	_My mother forces Jeannot to clean up his room._
Je **renonce à faire** du ski.	_I'm giving up skiing._
Tu **réussis à comprendre**?	_Do you manage to understand?_

- Verb + **à quelqu'un** + **de** + infinitive

conseiller à quelqu'un de	_to advise someone to_
défendre à quelqu'un de	_to forbid someone from_
demander à quelqu'un de	_to ask someone to_
dire à quelqu'un de	_to tell someone to_
permettre à quelqu'un de	_to allow someone to_
suggérer à quelqu'un de	_to suggest for someone to_

Les conseillers conseillent **aux élèves de remplir** leur formulaire.

Counselors advise students to fill out their forms.

Maman dit toujours **à mon père de ne pas trop travailler**.

Mom always tells my dad not to work too much.

On permet **aux adhérents de mettre** des commentaires sur le site.

They allow subscribers to put comments on the site.

EXERCICE 7·6

Le travail d'un conseiller pédagogique. *The work of a school counselor.*
Write the letter of the most appropriate completion of each sentence on the line provided.

1. _____ Je fais un travail qui...

2. _____ Chaque jour, je conseille à des jeunes...

3. _____ Très souvent, ils me disent...

4. _____ J'apprends aux lycéens à...

5. _____ Je ne leur suggère jamais de...

6. _____ Quelquefois, ils font semblant de...

7. _____ Mais je ne renonce jamais...

8. _____ Ils arrivent généralement à...

9. _____ Je suis toujours ravi...

10. _____ J'ai quelquefois l'occasion...

11. _____ J'ai envie de continuer...

12. _____ Je n'ai pas l'intention...

a. de garder leurs secrets.

b. de les voir partir calmes et rassurés.

c. ce travail pour le reste de ma vie.

d. me parler sincèrement.

e. renoncer à leurs rêves.

f. à les aider.

g. ne pas m'écouter.

h. trouver des solutions à leurs problèmes.

i. de venir me confier leurs difficultés.

j. de laisser tomber ce travail!

k. permet d'aider les jeunes lycéens.

l. d'avoir de l'influence sur leurs projets d'avenir.

EXERCICE 7·7

La biographie de Gérard Depardieu. *Gérard Depardieu's biography.* *Write in French.*

1. Gérard Depardieu grows up (**grandir**) with five brothers and sisters.

_____

2. The adolescent decides (**décider de**) to steal (**voler**) cars.

_____

3. It is hard to believe (**croire**), but it's true!

_____

4. He manages (**arriver à**) to stop (**cesser de**) doing (**faire**) this.

_____

5. He starts (**commencer à**) to take (**suivre**) comedy classes in Paris.

_____

6. American cinema offers (**offrir à/de**) Depardieu to play (**jouer**) in *Green Card*.

_____

7. Depardieu learns (**apprendre à**) very fast to earn (**gagner**) a lot of money.

_____

8. He becomes (**devenir**) famous and rich and seems (**sembler**) to love (**adorer**) both.

_____

Infinitives after impersonal expressions

Impersonal expressions containing a conjugated verb other than the verb **être** are sometimes followed directly by an infinitive verb.

Il faut	*It is necessary*
Il vaut mieux	*It is better*

Remember that impersonal expressions should not be translated literally from French into English. Infer the subject from contextual clues, and translate accordingly into English.

Il faut **écouter** ton professeur, Philippe!	***You** have to listen to your teacher, Philippe!*
Il faut **partir**. Sinon, nous allons être en retard.	***We** have to leave. Otherwise, we'll be late.*
Il vaut mieux **ne pas mentir**, ma petite chérie.	***You'd** better not lie, my little darling.*

Some impersonal expressions containing a conjugated verb other than the verb **être** are followed by the preposition **de** and an infinitive verb.

Il suffit de sourire pour charmer les gens.	*It suffices to smile to charm people.*
Il importe d'être honnête.	*It is important to be honest.*

Many impersonal expressions that include an adjective are followed by **de** and an infinitive verb.

Il est bon/mauvais de	*It is good/bad to*
Il est dangereux de	*It is dangerous to*
Il est facile/difficile de	*It is easy/difficult to*
Il est défendu/permis de	*It is forbidden/allowed to*
Il est intéressant/ennuyeux de	*It is interesting/boring to*
Il est juste/injuste de	*It is just/unjust to*
Il est utile/inutile de	*It is useful/useless to*
Il est amusant/ennuyeux de	*It is fun/boring to*

Il est **défendu de fumer**.	It is forbidden to smoke.
Il est **dangereux de courir** sur une chaussée mouillée.	It is dangerous to run on a wet pavement.
Il est **bon de croire** en soi.	It is good to believe in oneself.
Il est **inutile d'insister**.	It is useless to insist.

EXERCICE

7·8

Vrai ou faux? *True or false?* *Write* V (**vrai**) *or* F (**faux**) *on the line provided.*

1. _____ Il est facile d'escalader les Alpes.

2. _____ Il est bon de voler les voitures.

3. _____ Il est juste d'être malhonnête.

4. _____ Il est utile de parler français.

5. _____ Il est défendu de brûler un feu rouge.

6. _____ Il est ennuyeux d'être à une bonne comédie.

7. _____ Il est dangereux de marcher sur l'autoroute.

8. _____ Il vaut mieux avoir un diplôme universitaire.

9. _____ Il faut être français pour comprendre le français.

10. _____ Il vaut mieux écouter le professeur.

EXERCICE

7·9

Pour réussir dans la vie. *To succeed in life.* *Write the appropriate verb from the list for each blank.*

| facile | amusant | être | croire |
| faut | persévérer | dangereux | travailler |

Pour réussir dans la vie, il suffit de 1. _____ dur et de

2. _____ dans ses initiatives. Évidemment il n'est pas toujours

3. _____ de faire cela. Il n'est pas 4. _____ de faire

des efforts inutiles. Il 5. _____ savoir que certains ont plus de chance dans

la vie que d'autres. Malgré tout, il est bon de/d' 6. _____ courageux face au

destin et il est 7. _____ de se laisser démoraliser. Il est permis de

8. _____ en soi.

The present participle

The present participle of a verb is formed by using the stem obtained from the first-person plural of the present tense -**ons** → **ant**.

regarder (*to watch*)	→ nous regardons	→ regardant
finir (*to finish*)	→ nous finissons	→ finissant
perdre (*to lose*)	→ nous perdons	→ perdant
faire (*to make/do*)	→ nous faisons	→ faisant
pouvoir (*to be able to*)	→ nous pouvons	→ pouvant

The verbs **avoir** (*to have*), **être** (*to be*), and **savoir** (*to know*) have irregular present participle stems, which must be memorized.

avoir → **ayant**   être → **étant**   savoir → **sachant**

The preposition **en** (*while/by/upon doing*) generally precedes the present participle but is sometimes omitted and implied. Use this verbal form only to express *while/by/upon* doing something.

Je fais des exercices d'aérobic **en regardant** la télé.	*I do aerobics while watching TV.*
Je maigris **en mangeant** moins et **en faisant** du sport.	*I lose weight by eating less and exercising.*
Sachant la réponse, je suis à même de l'expliquer.	*Knowing the answer, I am able to explain it.*
Étant bon élève, je réussis mes examens.	*Being a good student, I pass my exams.*

EXERCICE 7·10

Banalités et dictons. *Generalities and sayings.* Write the letter of the appropriate completion of each sentence on the line provided.

1. _____ On s'instruit   a. on garde ses amis.

2. _____ L'appétit vient   b. on est sûr de gagner sa vie.

3. _____ En écoutant bien   c. en devenant célèbre.

4. _____ On est aimable   d. on devient bilingue.

5. _____ En gardant les secrets   e. en voyageant.

6. _____ En travaillant dur   f. en mangeant.

7. _____ On devient riche   g. on finit par comprendre.

8. _____ En apprenant une langue étrangère   h. en offrant son aide.

Tout en faisant cela! *While doing this!* *Write the following sentences in French.*

1. By practicing a lot learning a new language becomes easy.

_____

2. While listening to the news in French, I am beginning to understand more.

_____

3. Upon doing grammar exercises, I can write French more correctly.

_____

4. But I sometimes have difficulties while doing my homework.

_____

5. People (**On**) become more tolerant while understanding other cultures.

_____

Des dictons! *Sayings!* *Translate the following common sayings into English.*

1. Il est dangereux de laisser libre cours à ses passions.

_____

2. Il faut avoir assez de force pour suivre la raison.

_____

3. Il est rare de trouver des politiciens sincères.

_____

4. Il est difficile de définir l'amour.

_____

5. Il est bon de poser des questions.

_____

6. C'est en souffrant qu'on devient fort.

_____

Examine the following vocabulary list before doing the next exercise.

la confiance	*trust*	avouer	*to admit/confess*
le buisson	*bush*	malin	*cunning*
le champ	*field*	marcher	*to walk*
le maître	*master*	ravi	*delighted*
le roi	*king*	récolter	*to harvest*
le sac	*bag*	rendre service	*to do favors*

EXERCICE 7·13

L'histoire du chat botté (Charles Perrault). *The story of Puss in Boots. Complete each sentence with the appropriate word from the list provided. Capitalize when necessary.*

récolter	chercher	rencontrer	marcher	trouvé
enchanté	rendant	désolé	quant au	sans
dans	à (*use twice*)	au		

1. _____ cette histoire, un chat très intelligent aide son maître qui est

2. _____ d'être pauvre. Le chat demande 3. _____ son

maître de lui donner un sac pour 4. _____ des fruits et des légumes et

aussi des bottes pour 5. _____ dans les champs et les buissons. Prétendant

6. _____ de la nourriture, le chat part à l'aventure.

En 7. _____ certains services 8. _____ roi, le chat

gagne sa confiance. Le chat permet alors 9. _____ son maître de

10. _____ la fille du roi qui tombe amoureuse de lui.

11. _____ avouer qu'il est très pauvre, le maître épouse la fille du roi. Le roi

est charmé d'avoir 12. _____ un bon mari pour sa fille. Le maître est

13. _____ d'avoir épousé la fille du roi et d'avoir un chat si malin.

14. _____ chat, il est ravi d'avoir un maître riche et heureux.

Reflexive verbs

Reflexive verbs in the present tense

Remember that reflexive verbs can be categorized into regular verb groups or families of irregular verbs like other verbs. Look at the following list of regular -**er** verbs used reflexively. Beware of the stem-changing verbs.

s'approcher (de)	*to get near/ close (to)*	se fâcher	*to get angry/ mad*
s'arrêter	*to stop*	se fatiguer	*to get tired*
s'excuser	*to excuse oneself/ apologize*	se laver	*to wash oneself*
s'habiller	*to get dressed*	se lever (e → è)	*to get up*
s'inquiéter (é → è)	*to be worried*	se maquiller	*to put on makeup*
se baigner	*to take a bath/ to bathe*	se préparer	*to get ready*
se balader	*to take a walk*	se présenter	*to introduce oneself*
se brosser les dents	*to brush one's teeth*	se promener (e → è)	*to take a walk*
se calmer	*to calm down*	se rappeler (l → ll)	*to remember*
se coiffer	*to style one's hair*	se reposer	*to rest*
se coucher	*to go to bed*	se réveiller	*to wake up*
se demander	*to wonder*	se sécher (é → è)	*to dry oneself*

Je m'excuse de vous déranger.	*I apologize for disturbing you.*
On se fatigue après une longue journée de travail.	*One gets tired after a long day of work.*
Ses parents se fâchent quand il rentre tard.	*His parents get mad when he comes home late.*
Les enfants se lavent les mains quand ils rentrent.	*Children wash their hands when they come home.*
Alors **ils se reposent**.	*Then they rest.*

Now look at the following list of irregular verbs used reflexively:

s'assoir	*to sit down*	se mettre en colère	*to get angry*
s'en aller	*to go away*	se mettre en route	*to start off/to get going*
s'endormir	*to fall asleep*	se rendormir	*to go back to sleep*
s'inscrire	*to enroll*	se souvenir (de)	*to remember*
se mettre d'accord	*to come to an agreement*		

Je m'en vais.	*I'm going away.*
Tu t'endors vite.	*You fall asleep fast.*
Nous nous mettons d'accord.	*We come to an agreement.*
Vous vous mettez en route?	*Are you setting off?*
Elles se rendorment toujours.	*They always go back to sleep.*
Pierre se souvient très bien de son séjour au Sénégal.	*Pierre remembers his stay in Senegal very well.*

You have seen how to conjugate most of the preceding verbs in a previous chapter of this book. Now look at the present tense conjugations of the verb **s'assoir** (*to sit down*).

je m'assois	je m'assieds
tu t'assois	tu t'assieds
il/elle/on s'assoit	il/elle/on s'assied
nous nous assoyons	nous nous asseyons
vous vous assoyez	vous vous asseyez
ils/elles s'assoient	ils/elles s'asseyent

Regarde! **Je m'assieds** près de toi.	*Look! I'm sitting next to you.*
Nous nous asseyons généralement devant tout le monde.	*We usually sit in front of everybody.*

Note the following imperative forms of the verb **s'assoir**:

Assieds-toi!	*Sit down!*	Ne t'assieds pas!	*Do not sit down!*
Asseyons-nous!	*Let's sit down!*	Ne nous asseyons pas!	*Let's not sit down!*
Asseyez-vous!	*Sit down!*	Ne vous asseyez pas!	*Do not sit down!*
Assieds-toi à côté de moi!	*Sit down next to me!*		
Ne vous asseyez pas là! C'est sale!	*Don't sit there! It's dirty.*		

Note that the verbs **s'approcher de** (*to get near*), **se souvenir de** (*to remember*), and **s'en aller** (*to go away*) only exist in the reflexive form.

Je m'approche de la maison.	*I get near my house.*
On se souvient de moments mémorables.	*One remembers memorable moments.*
Tu t'en vas déjà?	*Are you already leaving?*

Transitive verbs

Transitive verbs (verbs admitting a direct object) can be used reflexively or nonreflexively. Verbs are reflexive only if the action of the verb is done by the subject to him- or herself. Compare the following sets of sentences. In the first sentence, the verb is not used reflexively (the action is not done by the subject to itself), but in the second sentence, the same verb is used reflexively (the action is done by the subject to itself).

Cette musique **endort** tout le monde.	*This music puts everybody to sleep.*
Le bébé **s'endort**.	*The baby is falling asleep.*
Le professeur **rappelle** aux élèves qu'il faut étudier.	*The teacher reminds the students that they must study.*
Le professeur **se rappelle** qu'il doit rendre les devoirs.	*The teacher remembers that he must return the homework.*
Ce grand bruit **inquiète** les passagers.	*This big noise worries the passengers.*
Le pilote ne **s'inquiète** pas.	*The pilot is not worried.*

EXERCICE
8·1

Aujourd'hui je vais chez le coiffeur! *Today I'm going to the hair stylist!* *Write the appropriate form of the verbs in parentheses in the present tense on the lines provided.*

1. Le matin, je _____ vers six heures et je _____

dix minutes plus tard. (se réveiller/se lever) 2. Je _____ et je

_____. (se doucher/se maquiller) 3. Ensuite je _____ et

je _____ à aller chez le coiffeur. (s'habiller/se préparer)

4. Il _____ Jérôme et il _____ comme Elvis Presley.

(s'appeler/se coiffer) 5. Il ne _____ jamais de la coiffure que je veux et il

_____ naturellement. (se souvenir/s'excuser) 6. Souvent je

_____ dans ma chaise et Jérôme me _____.

(s'endormir/réveiller) 7. Jérôme _____ et _____ mes

cheveux. (sécher/coiffer) 8. Quand c'est fini, je _____ bien et si je suis

contente, je paie Jérôme et je _____. (se regarder/s'en aller)

Expressing reciprocity with reflexive verbs

Note that the following reflexive verbs may be used to express reciprocity from one subject to another.

s'admirer	*to admire oneself/one another*
s'aider	*to help oneself/one another*
s'aimer	*to love/like oneself/one another*
s'écrire	*to write to one another*
s'embrasser	*to kiss each other*
s'envoyer des mails	*to send e-mails to one another*
se dire bonjour	*to say hello to one another*
se donner des cadeaux	*to give gifts to one another*
se fiancer	*to get engaged to each other*
se marier	*to get married to each other*
se regarder	*to look at oneself/at one another*
se rencontrer	*to meet one another*

se revoir	*to say good-bye to one another*
se séparer	*to separate from one another*
se serrer la main	*to shake hands with one another*

Compare the following sets of sentences and the meanings of the reflexive verbs in each set:

Marie **se regarde** dans le miroir.	*Marie looks at **herself** in the mirror.*
Marie et Pierre **se regardent** tendrement.	*Marie and Pierre look at **each other** tenderly.*
Marie **se sépare** de son fiancé.	*Marie leaves (**separates herself** from) her fiancé.*
Marie et Pierre **se séparent**.	*Marie and Pierre split up (they **leave each other**).*

Reflexive verbs include a reflexive pronoun. The pronoun is **se** in the infinitive form but varies according to the subject pronoun in the conjugated forms. Look at the following conjugation of **se souvenir** in the present tense indicative:

je me souviens	**nous nous** souvenons
tu te souviens	**vous vous** souvenez
il/elle/on se souvient	**ils/elles se** souviennent

EXERCICE
8·2

Quand faut-il le verbe réfléchi? *When do we need the reflexive verb? Write and compare the two sets of sentences. Use the verb reflexively only when appropriate.*

1 a. We are watching a good movie. b. We watch each other.

a. _____

b. _____

2 a. The little girl says good-bye. b. The little girls say good-bye to each other.

a. _____

b. _____

3 a. I am helping my cousin Maurice. b. Maurice and I are helping each other.

a. _____

b. _____

4 a. They do not separate children. b. The two brothers do not like to be away (separate) from each other.

a. _____

b. _____

5 a. He shakes the gentleman's hand. b. The gentlemen shake hands.

a. _____

b. _____

6 a. The secretary is enrolling students. b. The student is enrolling in a course.

a. _____

b. _____

7 a. I am meeting Marianne. b. Marianne and I are meeting today.

a. _____

b. _____

8 a. You (**tu**) admire this pretty lady. b. You (**tu**) admire yourself in the mirror.

a. _____

b. _____

Reflexive verbs in the imperative mood

Remember to use the appropriate reflexive pronoun before the conjugated verb when giving negative instructions and commands with reflexive verbs.

Ne **te** fâche pas!	*Do not get angry!*
Ne **vous** inquiétez pas!	*Do not worry!*
Ne **nous** affolons pas!	*Let's not panic!*

Also remember to use the appropriate reflexive pronoun after the conjugated verb in affirmative instructions and commands.

Brosse-**toi** les dents!	*Brush your teeth!*
Approchez-**vous** de mon bureau!	*Approach my desk!*
Allongeons-**nous** ici!	*Let's lay down here!*

EXERCICE
8·3

Logique ou pas logique? *Logical or not logical?* Write L *if the statement is logical;* write PL *if it is not logical.*

1. _____ Il fait chaud. Habille-toi plus chaudement!

2. _____ Ne nous approchons pas de l'incendie! C'est dangereux.

3. _____ Ne te dépêche pas d'aller au cours! Le prof est strict.

4. _____ Ne te lave pas avant d'aller te coucher!

5. _____ Ne vous approchez pas de moi! Je suis malade.

6. _____ Mariez-vous puisque vous vous aimez!

7. _____ Ne vous arrêtez pas ici! C'est là que vous habitez.

8. _____ Brosse-toi les dents avant de manger!

9. _____ Souvenez-vous des bons moments!

10. _____ Serrez-vous la main puisque vous êtes réconciliés!

Les instructions du professeur aux élèves. *The teacher's instructions to the students. Write the following instructions a teacher gives his students in French.*

1. Hurry up!

   _____

2. Sit down!

   _____

3. Do not talk to each other!

   _____

4. Get up!

   _____

5. Approach the board!

   _____

6. Do not worry!

   _____

7. Remember the answers!

   _____

8. Talk to each other!

   _____

9. Agree with each other!

   _____

Use of the definite article with parts of the body

When used in conjunction with a reflexive verb, parts of the body are preceded by a definite article rather than a possessive article in a French sentence. Look at the following sentences:

Tu te casses **la** jambe, tu te retrouves à l'hôpital et puis, tu te déplaces avec des béquilles.	*You break **your** leg, you find yourself in the hospital, and then you move around with crutches.*
Je me lave **les** cheveux. Après, je me les sèche et puis, je me les boucle.	*I wash **my** hair. After that, I dry it, and then I curl it.*
Je me lave **la** figure. Après, je me maquille et puis, je me mets du mascara.	*I wash **my** face. Afterward, I put on makeup, and then I put on mascara.*

Tu te rases **le** menton. Après, tu t'essuies la **figure** et puis, tu te peignes **les** cheveux.

*You are shaving **your** chin. Afterward, you wipe **your** face, and then you comb **your** hair.*

On se serre **la** main, on se tient **la** main, on se fait **la** bise sur **la** joue.

We shake hands, we hold hands, we kiss on the cheek.

Les petites habitudes. *Common habits.* *Write in French.*

1. In the morning, Marie gets up, washes her face, brushes her teeth, puts on makeup, and gets dressed.

   _____

   _____

2. Jean-Marc wakes up, goes back to sleep for a few minutes, wakes up again, combs his hair, shaves his face, washes himself, dries himself, and dresses.

   _____

   _____

3. When men meet, they shake hands and say hello.

   _____

   _____

4. When women meet, they kiss on the cheek, and they give (**faire**) each other compliments.

   _____

   _____

Future tenses

The near future tense of verbs

This tense should theoretically relate to events in the relatively near future. It is, however, used in many instances instead of the simple future tense for any future event.

Je **vais** vite **acheter** du lait.	*I'm quickly going to buy some milk.*
Dans deux ans, tu **vas être** majeur.	*In two years, you are going to be an adult.*

The near future tense requires the appropriate conjugated form of the verb **aller** followed by an infinitive verb.

Je **vais venir** te voir après l'école.	*I am going to see you after school.*
Tu **vas jouer** au foot.	*You are going to play soccer.*
On **va prendre** le bus pour rentrer.	*We are going to take the bus to go home.*
Nous **allons dîner** vers 18 heures.	*We are going to eat dinner around 6 P.M.*
Les copains, vous **allez être** étonnés.	*Friends, you are going to be astonished.*

Note that the two negative adverbs hug the helping verb **aller** in the near future.

Mes parents **ne vont pas être** là.	*My parents are not going to be there.*
Ma sœur **ne va plus être** là non plus.	*My sister is not going to be there any more either.*

Also note that when a reflexive verb is used in the near future or after a conjugated verb, the reflexive pronoun must match the subject pronoun.

Je vais **me** reposer maintenant.	*I'm going to rest now.*
Elsa va **se** fâcher avec toi.	*Elsa is going to get mad at you.*
Nous allons **nous** baigner.	*We're going to take a bath.*
Vous voulez **vous** marier?	*You want to get married?*

Ils vont sortir ce soir. *They are going to go out tonight.* *Write this dialogue in French.*

1. JULIETTE: Are you going to come to the party tonight?

_____

2. CHRISTOPHE: Yes, but I am going to finish my math homework first.

_____

3. JULIETTE: Good. I'm going to wait for you at my house.

_____

4. CHRISTOPHE: Fine. I'm going to pick you up around seven o'clock.

_____

5. JULIETTE: I'm going to wear my new dress tonight.

_____

6. CHRISTOPHE: I can't wait to go to the party. It's going to be fun.

_____

On va s'amuser comme des fous! *We are going to have fun like crazy!* *Translate the following conversation. Use intonation when posing questions.*

1. JULIETTE: Are you getting dressed, Christophe?

_____

2. CHRISTOPHE: Yes, but I want to look at myself in the mirror. Wait!

_____

3. JULIETTE: Oh! You are handsome. Look at yourself!

_____

4. CHRISTOPHE: I am looking at myself. Not bad!

_____

5. JULIETTE: Now, look at me!

_____

6. CHRISTOPHE: You are beautiful! Come closer!

_____

The simple future tense of verbs

This tense is used to discuss what will happen in the future. It is a simple tense requiring a stem and an ending. The stem is usually the entire infinitive verb (except for -**re** verbs or irregular verbs ending in -**re**, which lose -**e** from the ending of the infinitive). The endings are -**ai**, -**as**, -**a**, -**ons**, -**ez**, -**ont**.

Look at the future tense conjugations of the following regular verbs:

	chercher (to pick up)	**saisir** (to seize)	**confondre** (to confuse)
je	cher**cher**ai	saisirai	confondrai
tu	cher**cher**as	saisiras	confondras
il/elle/on	cherchera	saisira	confondra
nous	chercherons	saisirons	confondrons
vous	chercherez	saisirez	confondrez
ils/elles	chercheront	saisiront	confondront

Demain je **chercherai** ton tailleur à la blanchisserie.	*Tomorrow I will get your suit at the cleaner's.*
Je vais t'expliquer mon idée et tu **saisiras**.	*I'm going to explain my idea to you, and you will get it.*
Il est sûr que nous **confondrons** les jumeaux.	*It is certain that we will confuse the twin boys.*

Remember that the only difference in conjugating a reflexive verb in the future tense is the reflexive pronoun in front of the conjugated verb.

Nous nous dirons au revoir à l'aéroport.	*We will say good-bye to each other at the airport.*
Je me souviendrai de toi.	*I will remember you.*

Remember that most verbs that have a stem change in the present tense will also have that stem change in all the forms of the future tense.

acheter → j'ach**è**terai, tu ach**è**teras, il/elle/on ach**è**tera, nous ach**è**terons, vous ach**è**terez, ils/elles ach**è**teront

appeler → j'appe**ll**erai, tu appe**ll**eras, il/elle/on appe**ll**era, nous appe**ll**erons, vous appe**ll**erez, ils/elles appe**ll**eront

jeter → je je**tt**erai, tu je**tt**eras, il/elle/on je**tt**era, nous je**tt**erons, vous je**tt**erez, ils/elles je**tt**eront

payer → je pa**i**erai, tu pa**i**eras, il/elle/on pa**i**era, nous pa**i**erons, vous pa**i**erez, ils/elles pa**i**eront

However, verbs like **répéter** are exceptional because they do not carry that stem-change over into the future.

répéter → je rép**é**terai, tu rép**é**teras, il/elle/on rép**é**tera, nous rép**é**terons, vous rép**é**terez, ils/elles rép**é**teront

Many frequently used verbs have an irregular future stem. Look at the following list of such verbs:

aller	→ ir
avoir	→ aur
courir	→ courr
devoir	→ devr
envoyer/renvoyer	→ enverr/renverr
être	→ ser

faire/refaire	→ fer/refer
mourir	→ mourr
pouvoir	→ pourr
recevoir	→ recevr
savoir	→ saur
tenir/obtenir/retenir	→ tiendr/obtiendr/retiendr
venir/devenir/revenir/survenir	→ viendr/deviendr/reviendr/surviendr
voir/revoir	→ verr/reverr
vouloir	→ voudr

The following impersonal expressions have irregular future stems:

Il faut	*It is necessary*	→ Il faudra	*It will be necessary*
Il vaut mieux	*It is better*	→ Il vaudra mieux	*It will be better*
Il pleut	*It rains*	→ Il pleuvra	*It will rain*
Il gèle	*It freezes*	→ Il gèlera	*It will freeze*

You have previously seen that the verb **s'asseoir** (*to sit down*) has two present tense conjugations. It also has two future tense conjugations.

je m'assiérai	je m'assoirai
tu t'assiéras	tu t'assoiras
il/elle/on s'assiéra	il/elle/on s'assoira
nous nous assiérons	nous nous assoirons
vous vous assiérez	vous vous assoirez
ils/elles s'assiéront	ils/elles s'assoiront

EXERCICE
9·3

Le monde de demain. *Tomorrow's world. Complete all the questions by writing the verb in parentheses in the future tense.*

Parlons d'abord de mode vestimentaire! Quelle 1. _____ (être) la

mode dans dix ans? Est-ce qu'il y 2. _____ (avoir) des mini-jupes, des pattes

d'éléphant ou est-ce qu'on 3. _____ (créer) quelque chose de totalement

nouveau? Est-ce que les gens 4. _____ (vivre) jusqu'à deux cents ans?

Est-ce qu'ils 5. _____ (rester) en bonne santé toute leur vie? Est-ce que les

maladies comme le Sida et le cancer 6. _____ (être) éradiquées? Qu'est-ce

que nos enfants et nos petits-enfants 7. _____ (faire) pour gagner leur vie?

Est-ce qu'ils 8. _____ (se promener) dans l'espace? Comment est-ce qu'ils

9. _____ (communiquer) entre eux ? Est-ce qu'ils

10. _____ (pouvoir) voyager à travers le temps?

Créons un héros ou une héroïne! *Let's create a hero or a heroine! Using the following phrases and conjugating the verbs in the future tense will allow you to paint the portrait of a superhero. You can start each sentence with* **Il** *or* **Elle**.

1. _____ (être) invincible.

2. _____ (porter) des vêtements aérodynamiques.

3. _____ (se transporter) n'importe où.

4. _____ (se transformer) en n'importe quoi.

5. _____ (se battre) contre des monstres.

6. _____ (sauver) les innocents.

7. _____ (n'avoir) peur de rien.

8. _____ (ne pas pouvoir) mourir.

9. _____ (savoir) résister aux forces du mal.

10. _____ (obtenir) le respect de tout le monde.

Ce weekend! *This weekend! Complete each sentence with the verb provided in the simple future tense.*

1. Je _____ (se lever) tard samedi et je _____ (prendre) une longue douche.

2. Je _____ (faire) un petit jogging et je _____ (courir) tout autour du parc.

3. Je _____ (rentrer) à la maison et je _____ (se faire) une omelette.

4. Je _____ (se faire) beau/belle et je _____ (s'habiller) pour sortir en ville.

5. Je _____ (se mettre) en route pour un rendez-vous avec des amis et j'_____ (envoyer) des texto.

6. Je _____ (rejoindre) les copains au café du centre-ville et je _____ (bavarder).

7. J'_____ (aller) au ciné et je _____ (regarder) un bon film américain.

8. Je _____ (s'assoir) à une terrasse de café et je _____ (boire) une limonade.

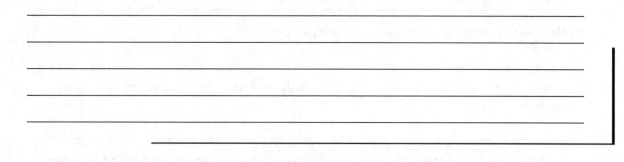

EXERCICE 9·6

Leurs projets de mariage. *Their wedding plans.* *Write the following paragraph in French using the verbs provided. They appear here in the order you need them.*

espérer	pleuvoir	paraître	arriver
avoir lieu	y avoir	se regarder	faire leurs vœux de mariage
s'embrasser	applaudir	se rendre	

Let's hope it will not rain next Sunday. Juliette will appear at the church with her bridesmaids (**les demoiselles d'honneur**), and then Roméo will arrive. The wedding will take place outside (**dehors**). There will be 50 guests. Juliette and Roméo will look at each other tenderly. Then they will say their wedding vows. They will kiss, and everyone will applaud. After the ceremony, all the guests will go to the garden.

_____

_____

_____

_____

_____

The future tense after **quand, lorsque, dès que, aussitôt que**

In contrast to English, the future tense is used in French after **quand** and **lorsque** (*when*) as well as after **dès que** and **aussitôt que** (*as soon as*) when the action of the verb that follows takes place in the future.

Téléphone-moi **quand tu arriveras** à Paris.

Call me when you arrive in Paris.

Envoie-moi un texto **dès que tu sauras** ta note d'examen.

Send me a text message as soon as you know your exam grade.

VOCABULAIRE UTILE. *Useful vocabulary.*

Examine the following vocabulary list before doing the next exercise.

après-demain	*the day after tomorrow*	à l'avenir	*in the future*
demain	*tomorrow*	à partir de...	*starting . . .*
demain après-midi	*tomorrow afternoon*	bientôt	*soon*
demain matin	*tomorrow morning*	dans dix jours	*in ten days*
demain soir	*tomorrow night*	ensuite	*then*
dimanche prochain	*next Sunday*	plus tard	*later*
l'année prochaine	*next year*	tout à l'heure	*in a while*
la semaine prochaine	*next week*	tout de suite	*right away*
le mois prochain	*next month*		

Une visite. *A visit.* *Write in French. Use the familiar form (**tu**).*

1. When you get off the plane, call me! I will come immediately. (**débarquer de l'avion, appeler, venir**)

   _____

2. As soon as you arrive, we will sit down to eat. (**arriver, s'asseoir, manger**)

   _____

3. Tomorrow we will get up early and visit the town. (**se lever, visiter**)

   _____

4. Next Sunday, you will meet my friends. (**rencontrer**)

   _____

5. Next week, we will have fun watching a big basketball game at the stadium. (**s'amuser, regarder**)

   _____

6. In 10 days, you will accompany my family to the Riviera. (**accompagner à la Côte d'Azur**)

   _____

7. I hope it will not rain when we stay in Nice. (**espérer, pleuvoir, rester**)

   _____

8. If it rains, we will not be able to sail. (**pleuvoir, pouvoir, faire de la voile**)

   _____

9. It will be better to go to the casino tomorrow night. (**valoir mieux, aller au casino**)

   _____

10. Next month, as soon as we finish our vacation, I will have to start school. (**finir, devoir, commencer**)

    _____

11. Starting tomorrow we will speak only in French to each other. (**se parler**)

    _____

12. Soon you will speak French very well. (**parler**)

    _____

Negative and interrogative structures

·10·

Negative expressions in simple tenses

Remember that in French two negative adverbs are necessary to make a verb negative. If a verb is conjugated in a simple tense such as the present or simple future tense (one verbal form consisting of a stem and an ending), the negative adverbs "hug" the single verbal form.

Review the following negative expressions:

Ne... pas	*not*
Ne... plus	*no more/no longer*
Ne... rien	*nothing/not anything*
Ne... jamais	*never/not ever*
Ne... personne	*nobody/not anybody*
Ne... que	*only/nothing but*
Ne... ni... ni	*neither . . . nor*
Ne... aucun(e) + nom	*none + noun*

Je **ne** veux **rien**, merci.	*I don't want anything, thank you.*
Nous **n'**allons **jamais** aux courses de chevaux.	*We never go to horse races.*
Elle **n'**a **ni** patience **ni** persévérance.	*She has neither patience nor perseverance.*
Je **n'**ai **aucune** idée.	*I have no idea (whatsoever).*
Demain, je **ne** ferai **rien**.	*Tomorrow I will do nothing.*

Some phrases do not include a verb. In that case **ne** is omitted.

Pas comme ca!	*Not like that!*
Jamais de la vie!	*Never in my/your life!*
Plus maintenant!	*Not now/anymore!*
Ni l'un **ni** l'autre!	*Neither one!*

It is possible in French to use two negative words together. Note that the adverb **pas** is never part of those phrases. The adverb **ne** is a part of the structure only when there is a verb in the sentence.

jamais personne	*never anybody/nobody ever*
jamais plus	*never again*
jamais rien	*never anything*
plus personne	*nobody left/nobody anymore*
plus que	*only . . . left/nothing left but*
plus rien	*nothing left/nothing anymore*

Qu'est ce que tu veux? —**Plus rien**, merci.
Est-ce qu'on peut fermer le
magasin? —Oui, il **n'**y a **plus personne**.
Il te reste de l'argent? —Non, je **n'**ai **plus qu'**un euro.

What do you want? —Nothing else, thanks.
*Can we close the store? —Yes, there is
nobody left.*
*Do you have any money left? —No, all I have
left is one euro.*

EXERCICE
10·1

Tout est négatif aujourd'hui! *All is negative today! Translate the negative answers
to the following questions.*

1. Tu vas souvent au gym?

Non, _____! (*never*)

2. Il y a beaucoup de monde à l'arrêt de bus tard le soir?

Non, _____! (*nobody*)

3. Vous voulez acheter quelque chose ici?

Non, _____! (*nothing*)

4. Qui vois-tu régulièrement au cours de statistiques?

_____! (*Never anybody*)

5. Tu voudrais encore un café ou un croissant?

_____! (*Neither one*)

6. Tu vois encore tes copains du lycée?

_____! (*Never again*)

EXERCICE
10·2

As-tu changé? *Have you changed? Write the letter of the most appropriate reply to
each statement or question on the line provided*

1. _____ Tu détestes les escargots.

2. _____ Tu rentres toujours encore vers 20h?

3. _____ Tu aimes toujours le vin rouge?

4. _____ Tu vas aux concerts de rock ou rap?

5. _____ Tu veux encore un café ou un croissant?

6. _____ Tu vois encore tes copains du lycée?

a. Plus jamais! Où sont-ils?

b. Non, merci, je n'ai plus faim.

c. Je ne vais ni à l'un ni à l'autre.

d. Non, je ne bois plus que le blanc.

e. Non, plus jamais. C'est trop tard.

f. C'est vrai. Je n'en mange jamais.

Negative expressions with infinitives

To make an infinitive verb negative, place the two negative adverbs before the infinitive.

Je suis désolée de **ne pas avoir** faim.	*I'm sorry that I'm not hungry.*
J'espère **ne pas revoir** cet homme.	*I hope I will not see this man again.*
Nous décidons **de ne plus fumer**.	*We decide not to smoke anymore.*
Ils prennent la résolution **de ne jamais faire** de drogues.	*They take the resolution to never do any drugs.*
J'adore **ne pas devoir** travailler.	*I love not having to work.*
Tu préfères **ne pas sortir** ce soir?	*Do you prefer to not go out tonight?*
Elle est d'accord pour **ne plus fumer**.	*She agrees not to smoke anymore.*
Ils considèrent **ne plus jamais** inviter cet impoli.	*They are thinking of never again inviting this rude man.*
J'ai envie de **ne rien faire** ce soir.	*I feel like doing nothing tonight.*

Consider the following exceptions, and note that **personne** and **que** appear after the infinitive verbs:

J'ai l'intention de **ne voir personne** demain.	*I intend to see nobody tomorrow.*
Nous décidons de **ne faire que** le minimum.	*We decide to only do the minimum.*

EXERCICE
10·3

Quelle vie ennuyeuse! *What a boring life!* Write in French.

1. Jeannot is capable of doing nothing on the weekend.

_____

2. He often decides to see no one and to do nothing.

_____

3. He prefers not to go to school anymore.

_____

4. He does not want to study anything anymore.

_____

5. He likes neither studying nor working.

_____

6. To have nothing to do all day seems boring!

_____

Negative expressions in compound tenses

In compound tenses such as the near future or the future perfect, which require an auxiliary verb, the negative adverbs **ne... pas** (*not*), **ne... pas encore** (*not yet*), **ne... plus** (*no more/longer*), **ne... jamais** (*never/not ever*), **ne... rien** (*nothing/not anything*) hug the auxiliary verb. Look at the following sentences, and note the place of **plus**, **pas**, **jamais**, and **rien** after the infinitive verb in the near future tense:

Nous **n'**allons **plus** rester longtemps.	*We are not going to stay much longer.*
Vous **n'**allez **pas** aimer ce film.	*You are not going to like this movie.*
Ils **ne** vont **plus jamais** revenir.	*They are never going to come again.*
Je **ne** vais **rien** changer.	*I am not going to change anything.*

In the following examples, note the place of **pas** and **pas encore** after the past participle in the future perfect tense:

Elle **n'**aura **pas** fini d'ici demain.	*She will not have finished by tomorrow.*
Ils **ne** seront **pas encore** arrivés à huit heures.	*They will not have arrived yet by eight o'clock.*

However, when using the negative phrases **ne... personne** (*nobody/no one*) and **ne... que** (*only*), place the adverb **ne** before the auxiliary verb, but place **personne** or **que** after the second verb, which is in the infinitive or in the past participle form. Look at the following sentences.

In the following examples, note the place of **personne** and **que** after the infinitive verb in the near future tense:

Elle **ne** va voir **personne** ce soir.	*She is going to see no one tonight.*
Tu **ne** vas recevoir **qu'**un cadeau de moi.	*You are going to receive only one gift from me.*

In the following examples, note the place of **personne** and **que** after the past participle in the near future perfect:

Nous **n'**aurons vu **personne**.	*We will have seen no one.*
Ils **n'**auront reçu **qu'**un ticket chacun.	*They will have received only one ticket each.*

Interrogative expressions in simple tenses

Questioning may require a yes or no answer or a specific piece of information. Regardless of which type of question you ask, several structures are always available to you.

Interrogative structures

Remember that French has several interrogative structures, and the inverted interrogative structure (verb-subject) is more formal.

Note that two interrogative structures do not require any change in word order, as you compare a statement with the corresponding question. Let's change the statement **Tu pars** (*you're leaving*) into the question *Are you leaving?*

STATEMENT	STATEMENT + INTONATION	STATEMENT + **EST-CE QUE**
Tu pars.	**Tu pars?**	**Est-ce que tu pars?**

Note that the third and more formal interrogative structure does require a change in word order, as you compare a statement with the corresponding question.

STATEMENT		QUESTION-INVERSION	
Tu pars.	*You are leaving.*	Pars-tu?	*Are you leaving?*
Il part.	*He is leaving.*	Part-il?	*Is he leaving?*

Remember not to use the inversion for the first-person singular of a verb except for a few standard phrases. Also remember that regular **-er** verbs and the verb **aller** require an inserted **-t-** in the third-person singular.

Mange-**t**-il?	*Does he eat?*
Chante-**t**-elle?	*Does she sing?*
Va-**t**-on au cinéma?	*Are we going to the movies?*

Remember that in inversions, the two negative adverbs hug the verb-subject phrase.

Ne mange-t-il **pas**?	*Does he not eat?*
Ne chante-t-elle **jamais**?	*Does she never sing?/Doesn't she ever sing?*
Ne va-t-on **plus** au cinéma?	*Are we no longer going to the movies?*

Note that the inversion structure exists in sentences where the subject is a noun. However, the subject-noun must remain at the beginning of the sentence.

STATEMENT	INVERSION-QUESTION
Marie parle bien français.	Marie parle-t-elle bien français?
Marie speaks French well.	*Does Marie speak French well?*
Ses parents voyagent souvent.	Ses parents voyagent-ils souvent?
Her parents travel often.	*Do her parents travel often?*

Interrogative words

Interrogative words are necessary because you want to know specific information such as *how* (**comment**), *who* (**qui**), *what* (**qu'est-ce que** or **qu'est-ce qui**), *where* (**où**), and *when* (**quand**).

Qui (Who)

Note that **qui** as subject of the verb is immediately followed by the verb. **Qui**, as subject of the verb, may also be followed by **est-ce qui** and the verb.

Qui + *verb*	Qui est-ce qui + *verb*
Qui vient régulièrement dîner?	**Qui est-ce qui vient** régulièrement dîner?
Who comes and dines regularly?	*Who comes and dines regularly?*

Note that **qui**, object of the verb, can be followed by **est-ce que** + statement. In a more familiar style, it can also be followed directly by the statement.

Qui (+ est-ce que) + *statement*	Qui + *inversion*
Qui est-ce que tu invites?/Qui tu invites?	**Qui invites-tu?**
Whom do you invite?	*Whom do you invite?*

Note how **qui** is used after stress pronouns or people's names to assign, confirm, and emphasize various roles.

C'est moi qui organise la soirée.
C'est toi qui envoies les invitations.
C'est Nicole qui apporte la musique.
Ce sont Jacques et Jeanine qui font les décorations.

Que (What)

Note that **que** is the direct object of the verb and is followed by **est-ce que** + statement or by an inversion.

Qu' + est-ce que + *statement*	Que + *inversion*
Qu'est-ce que tu voudrais?	**Que voudrais-tu?**
What would you like?	*What would you like?*

Note that **comment** (*how*), **où** (*where*), **pourquoi** (*why*), and **quand** (*when*) can be followed by **est-ce que** + statement, or in a more familiar style, directly by the statement. Each one of these question words can also, in a more formal style, be followed by an inversion.

Comment (+ est-ce que) + *statement*	Comment + *inversion*
Comment (est-ce que) vous venez?	**Comment venez-vous?**
How are you coming?	*How are you coming?*
Où (+ est-ce que) + *statement*	
Où (est-ce que) vous allez?	**Où allez-vous?**
Where are you going?	*Where are you going?*
Pourquoi (+ est-ce que) + *statement*	Pourquoi + *inversion*
Pourquoi (est-ce que) vous faites ça?	**Pourquoi faites-vous ça?**
Why are you doing this?	*Why are you doing this?*
Quand (+ est-ce que) + *statement*	Quand + *inversion*
Quand (est-ce que) vous arrivez?	**Quand arrivez-vous?**
When are you arriving?	*When are you arriving?*

Frequently used questions

Remember the following basic questions, which are often asked using the inversion structure:

Combien de temps est-ce qu'il faut?	*How much time is needed?*
Quelle heure est-il?	*What time is it?*
Quel temps fait-il?	*What is the weather like?*
Comment vas-tu?/Comment allez-vous?	*How are you?*

Also remember to use **depuis** and the present tense when you want to know for how long something has been going on.

Depuis quand (est-ce que) **tu fais** du yoga?	*For how long have you been doing yoga?*
Depuis quand Raymond a-t-il cet iPod?	*For how long has Raymond had this iPod?*
Depuis combien de temps (est-ce qu') **il pleut?**	*For how long has it been raining?*

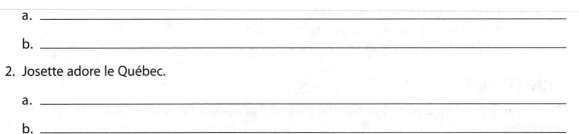

EXERCICE
10·4

Un petit tour en montagne? *A little trip to the mountains?* *Change each statement into a question using the* **est-ce que** *method on the first line and the* inversion *method on the second line.*

1. Tu pars en voyage cet été.

   a. _____

   b. _____

2. Josette adore le Québec.

   a. _____

   b. _____

3. Nous pouvons passer le weekend dans votre chalet de montagne.

   a. _____

   b. _____

4. Vous avez deux chiens là-bas.

   a. _____

   b. _____

5. Ils sont méchants.

   a. _____

   b. _____

6. Vos chiens sont des chiens de garde.

   a. _____

   b. _____

EXERCICE
10·5

Il faut quelques détails sur le tour en montagne. *We need a few details about the trip to the mountains. Using the familiar register for you (**tu**) and we (**on**), ask the following questions. Use **est-ce que** whenever possible. Do not use inversions.*

1. Are you organizing the tour?

   _____

2. Whom are you inviting?

   _____

3. Who is driving?

   _____

4. Do we all bring food (**à manger**)?

   _____

5. When are we leaving and at what time?

   _____

6. Where are we staying for the night?

   _____

7. What are we going to do on Sunday?

   _____

8. Why are we not leaving today?

_____

9. How do you know that the roads are good?

_____

10. How much time do we need to arrive?

_____

Prepositions and interrogative adverbs

To elicit specific information, prepositions and interrogative adverbs such as **qui** (*whom*) or **quoi** (*what*) can be used.

Avec **qui** partages-tu ta tente?	*With whom do you share your tent?*
Grâce à **qui** est-ce que tu trouves le moyen de payer?	*Thanks to whom do you have the means to pay?*
En face de **quoi** est-ce que vous installez votre tente?	*Across from what do you install your tent?*
Dans **quoi** est-ce que tu ranges ton sac de couchage?	*In what do you put away your sleeping bag?*

To elicit specific information, prepositions and noun phrases including the interrogative adjective **quel** (*which*) can be used. Remember that the adjective **quel** agrees in gender and number with the noun it describes.

Dans quel car tu arrives?	*In which bus do you arrive?*
De quels outils on a besoin?	*Which tools do we need?*
Sous quelle tente tu restes?	*Under which tent are you staying?*
Aux environs de quelles villes vous restez?	*In the vicinity of which cities are you staying?*

Review prepositions and prepositional phrases in Chapter 6.

EXERCICE
10·6

Parle-moi de tes vacances. *Tell me about your vacation.* *Write in French, using the familiar register and* **est-ce que** *whenever possible. Do not use inversions.*

1. Where are you going on vacation?

_____

2. With whom are you going?

_____

3. Next to whom are you sitting on the plane?

_____

4. In what hotel are you staying?

_____

5. Is your hotel near or far from the beach?

_____

6. On what beach is the hotel?

_____

7. Across from what other hotels is it?

_____

8. What do you need?

_____

9. For what meals are you paying in advance?

_____

10. Why are you not staying longer?

_____

VOCABULAIRE UTILE. *Useful vocabulary.*

Examine the following vocabulary before doing the next exercise.

disponible	*available*	lutter	*to fight*
médaillé	*decorated with a medal*	remporter	*to win*

EXERCICE
10·7

Carrière sportive de Tony Estanguet. *Tony Estanguet's sports career.* *Read the following paragraph, and match the questions and answers that follow.*

Tony, Aldric et Patrice Estanguet pratiquent le canoë et le kayak grâce à leur père. Patrice est médaillé de bronze en kayak aux Jeux olympiques d'été d'Atlanta en 1996. En l'an 2000, les deux frères Patrice et Tony doivent lutter pour s'offrir le deuxième billet disponible derrière Emmanuel Brugvin qualifié en tant que champion du monde. C'est finalement Tony qui obtient le billet.

Il représente son pays et remporte la médaille d'or aux Jeux olympiques d'été de 2000 à Sydney. En 2003, il remporte la coupe du monde. Début 2004, il se sélectionne facilement pour les Jeux olympiques d'été de 2004 à Athènes. Là, il remporte la médaille d'or face à Michal Martikan.

1. _____ Qui pratique le kayak?

2. _____ Grâce à qui les garçons Estanguet pratiquent-ils le kayak?

3. _____ Qui est médaillé de bronze aux Jeux olympiques en 1996?

a. Emmanuel Brugvin

b. Il faut lutter.

c. une médaille d'or

4. _____ Derrière qui les deux frères Tony et Patrice sont-ils pour les qualifications de champion du monde en 2000?

d. les trois frères Estanguet

5. _____ Qu'est-ce que Tony espère aussi remporter en 2000?

e. Patrice

6. _____ Quand et où est-ce que Tony gagne une médaille d'or?

f. Michal Martikan

7. _____ Face à qui Tony remporte-t-il la médaille d'or à Athènes en 2004?

g. en 2000 à Sydney

8. _____ Que faut-il faire pour avoir le succès de Tony Estanguet?

h. leur père

Interrogative structures in compound tenses

Interrogative structures are only impacted by the compound tense when the structure is an inversion. Let's first change the statement **Tu vas partir** (*You are going to leave*) into the question *Are you going to leave?* using intonation and **est-ce que** methods.

STATEMENT	STATEMENT + INTONATION	STATEMENT + **EST-CE QUE**
Tu vas partir.	**Tu vas partir?**	**Est-ce que tu vas partir?**

Now let's change the statement to a question using the inversion method. Note that the inversion is between the subject and the auxiliary verb.

STATEMENT		QUESTION-INVERSION	
Tu vas partir.	*You are going to leave.*	**Vas-tu** partir?	*Are you going to leave?*

Remember not to use the inversion for the first-person singular (**je**) of a verb. Also remember that the verb **aller** requires an inserted **-t-** in the third-person singular.

Va-**t**-il sortir?	*Is he going to go out?*
Va-**t**-elle venir?	*Is she going to come?*
Va-**t**-on faire ce projet?	*Are we going to do this project?*

Note that the sentence structure required for inversions in compound tenses such as the near future is the same in sentences where a conjugated verb is followed by an infinitive verb.

Pierre ne **sait-il** pas parler français?	*Does Pierre not know how to speak French?*
Tes amis n'**aiment-ils** pas le foot?	*Don't your friends like soccer?*
Ne **veux-tu** pas faire la cuisine?	*Don't you want to cook?*

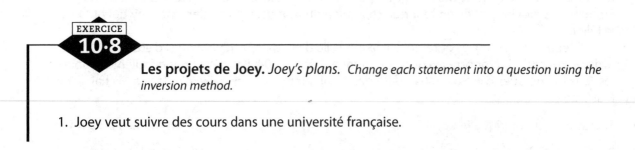

EXERCICE
10·8

Les projets de Joey. *Joey's plans. Change each statement into a question using the inversion method.*

1. Joey veut suivre des cours dans une université française.

_____

2. Ses parents vont payer les frais de scolarité.

_____

3. Son professeur de français va écrire une lettre de recommandation pour Joey.

_____

4. Joey va envoyer son dossier à l'université sans délai.

_____

5. Le comité d'admission doit étudier son dossier.

_____

6. Joey va recevoir une réponse au mois de mai.

_____

**EXERCICE
10·9**

Les Jeux olympiques de 2016. *The 2016 Olympic Games. Read the paragraph, and write questions about its content as instructed. Use the inversion method for each except for number 2.*

Les Jeux olympiques vont avoir lieu au Brésil, à Rio de Janeiro, en 2016. Le président du comité international va être Jacques Rogge. C'est lui qui doit organiser les préparatifs des Jeux.

Pour moderniser la ville de Rio et faciliter le transport, il va falloir exproprier des centaines de familles dans la banlieue ouest de la ville. La ville de Rio doit trouver une solution à ce problème.

1. Where and when are the Olympic Games going to take place?

_____

2. Who is the president of the international committee going to be?

_____

3. What must he organize?

_____

4. Why is it going to be necessary to expropriate hundreds of families?

_____

5. What must they do in the city of Rio?

_____

Imparfait and passé composé

Formation of **imparfait** tense

Remember that the **imparfait** is a simple tense; the conjugated verb consists of a stem and an ending. The stem is obtained by dropping the -**ons** ending of the **nous** form of the present tense of the verb. This is true for both regular and irregular verbs.

regarder	rougir	descendre	faire
(*to watch*)	(*to blush*)	(*to go down*)	(*to make/do*)
regardons →	rougissons →	descendons →	faisons →
regard	**rougiss**	**descend**	**fais**

The endings of the conjugated forms of the verb are as follows: -**ais**, -**ais**, -**ait**, -**ions**, -**iez**, -**aient**.

je fais**ais**	*I did/was doing*	nous fais**ions**	*we did/were doing*
tu fais**ais**	*you did/were doing*	vous fais**iez**	*you did/were doing*
il/elle/on fais**ait**	*he/she/one did/ was doing*	ils/elles fais**aient**	*they did/were doing*

The only verb for which the stem for the **imparfait** is not obtained in that fashion is the verb **être** (*to be*). The **imparfait** stem for **être** is **ét-**.

j'**ét**ais	*I was*	nous **ét**ions	*we were*
tu **ét**ais	*you were*	vous **ét**iez	*you were*
il/elle/on **ét**ait	*he/she/one was*	ils/elles **ét**aient	*they were*

Quand **j'allais** au gymnase chaque matin, **j'étais** en excellente forme.	*When I was going to the gym every morning, I was in great shape.*
Quand elle **allait** au cours régulièrement, elle **avait** de très bonnes notes.	*When she was going to class regularly, she had very good grades.*
Le matin nous **voyions** le soleil se lever.	*In the morning, we would see the sun rise.*
Le facteur **venait** à trois heures précises.	*The mailman would come at three o'clock sharp.*
Nous **connaissions** tous les voisins.	*We knew all the neighbors.*
Nous nous **arrêtions** et nous **disions** bonjour.	*We would stop and say hello.*

For **-ger** ending verbs, remember to insert an **e** after **g** in all conjugated forms of the **imparfait** except in the **nous** and **vous** forms in order to conserve the soft *g* sound.

manger (*to eat*)	**corriger** (*to correct*)	**plonger** (*to dive*)	**neiger** (*to snow*)
je mangeais	je corrigeais	je plongeais	il neigeait
tu mangeais	tu corrigeais	tu plongeais	
il/elle/on mangeait	il/elle corrigeait	il/elle/on plongeait	
nous mangions	nous corrigions	nous plongions	
vous mangiez	vous corrigiez	vous plongiez	
ils/elles mangeaient	ils/elles corrigeaient	ils/elles plongeaient	

Ils **mangeaient** comme des ogres.	*They were eating like ogres.*
Quand nous faisions des erreurs, les profs nous **corrigeaient**.	*When we made mistakes, the teachers corrected us.*
Nous **plongions** l'un après l'autre.	*We dove one after another.*
Il **neigeait** toujours quand nous allions en montagne.	*It always snowed when we went to the mountains.*

For **-cer** ending verbs, remember to insert a cedilla under the letter **c** in all conjugated forms of the **imparfait** except in the **nous** and **vous** forms in order to conserve the *s* sound in the stem.

annoncer (*to announce*)	**avancer** (*to advance*)	**commencer** (*to start*)	**lancer** (*to throw*)
j'annonçais	j'avançais	je commençais	je lançais
tu annonçais	tu avançais	tu commençais	tu lançais
il/elle/on annonçait	il/elle/on avançait	il/elle/on commençait	il/elle/on lançait
nous annoncions	nous avancions	nous commencions	nous lancions
vous annonciez	vous avanciez	vous commenciez	vous lanciez
ils/elles annonçaient	ils/elles avançaient	ils/elles commençaient	ils/elles lançaient

On **annonçait** l'arrivée du train.	*They were announcing the arrival of the train.*
Il **lançait** la balle aussi loin que possible.	*He was throwing the ball as far as possible.*
Ta montre **avançait**.	*Your watch was fast.*
Ils **commençaient** le repas.	*They were starting the meal.*

For **-ier** ending verbs, remember that the **nous** and **vous** forms of the **imparfait** will have an **i** in the stem and another **i** in the ending.

copier (*to copy*)	**étudier** (*to study*)	**oublier** (*to forget*)	**remercier** (*to thank*)
je copiais	j'étudiais	j'oubliais	je remerciais
tu copiais	tu étudiais	tu oubliais	tu remerciais
il/elle/on copiait	il/elle/on étudiait	il/elle/on oubliait	il/elle/on remerciait
nous copiions	nous étudiions	nous oubliions	nous remerciions
vous copiiez	vous étudiiez	vous oubliiez	vous remerciiez
ils/elles copiaient	ils étudiaient	ils/elles oubliaient	ils/elles remerciaient

Vous **copiiez** l'adresse.	*You were copying the address.*
Vous **oubliiez** toujours le numéro de ma maison.	*You always forgot the number of my house.*
Nous **étudiions** les cultures antillaises.	*We were studying Caribbean cultures.*
Nous **remerciions** la serveuse chaque fois qu'elle nous servait.	*We would thank the waitress each time she served us.*

Examine the following vocabulary, which appears in the upcoming exercise.

Il était une fois	*once upon a time*	le meuble	*furniture*
l'argent (*m.*)	*silver/money*	le miroir	*mirror*
l'or (*m.*)	*gold*	le sol	*floor*
la cadette	*youngest*	défendre	*to forbid*
la chasse	*hunting*	envier	*to envy*
la pêche	*fishing*	épouser	*to marry*
la tapisserie	*tapestry*	mort (e)	*dead*
le bonheur	*happiness*	prier	*to ask/beg*
le carrosse	*carriage*	s'amuser	*to have fun*
le corps	*body*	s'empêcher	*to help oneself*

EXERCICE 11·1

Barbe bleue (un conte de Charles Perrault). *Bluebeard (a Charles Perrault tale). Write all the verbs in parentheses in the appropriate **imparfait** form to create a version of this classic tale.*

Il 1. _____ (être) une fois un homme qui

2. _____ (avoir) de belles maisons, des montagnes d'or et d'argent, des

meubles richement décorés, et des carrosses luxueux. Cet homme 3. _____

(être) unique parce qu'il 4. _____ (avoir) une barbe bleue. Ses voisins

5. _____ (avoir) deux très belles filles. Il 6. _____

(vouloir) épouser une de ces filles. Chez Barbe bleue, il n'y 7. _____ (avoir)

que promenades, chasse, pêche, danses et festins. On ne 8. _____ (dormir)

pas, on 9. _____ (passer) toute la nuit à s'amuser.

Bientôt la cadette des deux belles filles 10. _____ (être) mariée à

Barbe bleue. Après un mois, Barbe bleue 11. _____ (prier) sa jeune épouse

de continuer de s'amuser pendant son absence. Elle 12. _____ (devoir)

inviter sa famille et ses amies. Elle 13. _____ (avoir) libre accès à toutes ses

possessions mais il lui 14. _____ (défendre) d'aller dans un seul petit

bureau.

Les amies de la jeune épouse 15. _____ (être) impatientes de

voir toutes les richesses de la maison. Elles 16. _____ (examiner)

toutes les belles choses de la maison: les tapisseries et les immenses miroirs où elles se

17. _____ (voir) et s' 18. _____ (admirer). Elles ne

19. _____ (pouvoir) pas s'empêcher d'envier le bonheur de leur amie.

   Mais la jeune épouse 20. _____ (être) terriblement curieuse de savoir

ce qu'il y 21. _____ (avoir) dans le petit bureau de son époux. Arrivée à la

porte du bureau, la tentation 22. _____ (être) si forte qu'elle ne

23. _____ (pouvoir) pas y résister. Une fois la porte ouverte, quelle horreur!

Il y 24. _____ (avoir) sur le sol des corps de femmes mortes. Qu'est-ce qu'il

25. _____ (falloir) faire? D'où 26. _____ (venir) ces

corps de femme?

(à suivre—*to be continued*)

Uses of the **imparfait**

A French verb in the **imparfait** tense can be translated into English with the progressive past tense (something was happening) as in the following example:

Tout le matin, les enfants **roulaient** à bicyclette.	*All morning long, the children were riding their bikes.*

A French verb in the **imparfait** tense can be translated into English with *would* or *used to* (something would or used to happen) as in the following example:

Quand elle était petite, Dara **jouait** à la poupée.	*When she was little, Dara would play with a doll.*
	or
	When she was little, Dara used to play with a doll.

A French verb in the **imparfait** tense can also be translated with the simple past when accompanied by adverbial phrases of time such as **toute la journée** (*all day long*) or **chaque matin** (*each morning*), which convey that the action was ongoing or that the action took place on a regular basis.

Il **partait** au travail à six heures chaque matin.	*He left for work at 6 A.M. each morning.*
Il **travaillait** toute la journée.	*He worked all day long.*

Similarly, the French verb in the **imparfait** can be translated into English by a simple past when there is any indication in the sentence that the action occurred for an unspecified number of times.

Il **rentrait** quand il en avait envie.	*He came home whenever he felt like it.*
Elle **étudiait** de temps en temps.	*She studied from time to time.*

The following expressions indicate that an action was habitual or regular and can therefore be cues that the past occurrence should be expressed in the **imparfait** tense.

le lundi, le mardi, le mercredi, le jeudi, le vendredi, le samedi, le dimanche
on Mondays, on Tuesdays, on Wednesdays, on Thursdays, on Fridays, on Saturdays, on Sundays

le matin, l'après-midi, le soir, la nuit
in the morning, in the afternoon, in the evening, at night

chaque année	*each year*	tous les ans	*every year*
chaque fois	*each time*	toutes les fois	*every time*
chaque jour	*each day*	tous les jours	*every day*
chaque mois	*each month*	tous les mois	*every month*
fréquemment	*frequently*	de temps en temps	*from time to time*
généralement	*generally*	d'habitude	*usually*
jamais	*never*	quand j'étais...	*when I was*
parfois/quelquefois	*sometimes*	quand il y avait...	*when there was*
rarement	*rarely*	quand il pleuvait	*whenever it rained*
souvent	*often*	quand il neigeait	*whenever it snowed*
toujours	*always*		

EXERCICE
11·2

Quand j'avais cinq ans. *When I was five years old.* *Write the following sentences in French.*

1. I often cried. (**pleurer**)

   _____

2. I always wanted my mommy. (**vouloir**)

   _____

3. I ate fruit every day. (**manger**)

   _____

4. I sometimes played with my brother. (**jouer**)

   _____

5. I rarely had homework. (**avoir**)

   _____

6. Whenever it snowed, my school was closed. (**neiger, être**)

   _____

7. I read from time to time. (**lire**)

   _____

8. I usually had friends at home in the afternoon. (**avoir**)

_____

9. Each time I had a new tooth (**la dent**), I received a dollar. (**avoir, recevoir**)

_____

10. I was never mean. (**être**)

_____

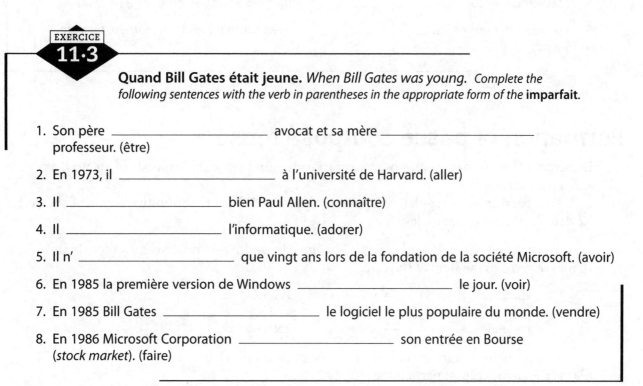

EXERCICE
11·3

Quand Bill Gates était jeune. _When Bill Gates was young._ _Complete the following sentences with the verb in parentheses in the appropriate form of the_ **imparfait.**

1. Son père _____ avocat et sa mère _____ professeur. (être)

2. En 1973, il _____ à l'université de Harvard. (aller)

3. Il _____ bien Paul Allen. (connaître)

4. Il _____ l'informatique. (adorer)

5. Il n' _____ que vingt ans lors de la fondation de la société Microsoft. (avoir)

6. En 1985 la première version de Windows _____ le jour. (voir)

7. En 1985 Bill Gates _____ le logiciel le plus populaire du monde. (vendre)

8. En 1986 Microsoft Corporation _____ son entrée en Bourse (_stock market_). (faire)

Imparfait after the adverb si

Note that the **imparfait** tense is used after the adverb **si** (_if_) to make suggestions. In this case, it does not express a past action.

Si on regardait un vieux film ce soir?	_How about watching an old movie tonight?_
Si on nettoyait le garage demain?	_How about cleaning the garage tomorrow?_
Si tu étudiais un peu plus, Jonas?	_How about studying a little more, Jonas?_
Si seulement tu faisais parfois ton lit!	_If only you made your bed sometimes!_

Si seulement... *If only . . . Complete the following sentences with the verb in parentheses in the appropriate form of the* **imparfait.**

1. Si seulement vous _____ moins impatients, mes amis! (être)

2. Si seulement nous _____ plus de temps, mes amis! (avoir)

3. Si seulement nos profs _____ moins de travail, mes amis! (donner)

4. Si seulement nous _____ partir en vacances, mes amis! (pouvoir)

5. Si seulement nous _____ à tous les examens, mes amis! (réussir)

6. Si seulement nous ne _____ pas travailler toute la journée, mes amis! (devoir)

Formation of passé composé tense

Remember that the **passé composé** tense is a compound tense that consists of an auxiliary verb and a past participle.

Past participles of regular verbs are easily derived from the infinitive forms of the verbs. Review the following examples:

The past participle of regular verbs is formed by adding -**é** for -**er** verbs, -**i** for -**ir** verbs, and -**u** for -**re** verbs to the stem of the verb.

chercher	→	cherch**é**
punir	→	pun**i**
prétendre	→	prétend**u**

Past participles of irregular verbs must be memorized. Here is a list of frequently used irregular verbs and their past participles:

aller	*to go*	**allé**	*gone*
avoir	*to have*	**eu**	*had*
connaître	*to know*	**connu**	*known*
devoir	*to have to*	**dû**	*had to*
dire	*to say/tell*	**dit**	*said/told*
dormir	*to sleep*	**dormi**	*slept*
écrire	*to write*	**écrit**	*written*
être	*to be*	**été**	*been*
faire	*to do*	**fait**	*done*
lire	*to read*	**lu**	*read*
offrir	*to offer*	**offert**	*offered*
ouvrir	*to open*	**ouvert**	*opened*
plaire	*to please*	**plu**	*pleased*
pleuvoir	*to rain*	**plu**	*rained*

pouvoir	*to be able to*	**pu**	*been able to*
recevoir	*to receive*	**reçu**	*received*
savoir	*to know*	**su**	*known*
voir	*to see*	**vu**	*seen*
vouloir	*to want*	**voulu**	*wanted*

All derivatives from **venir** have a past participle ending in **u**.

| venir: venu | devenir: devenu | revenir: revenu |
| *to come: came* | *to become: became* | *to come back: came back* |

All derivatives from **prendre** have similar past participles that include **pris**.

| prendre: pris | apprendre: appris | comprendre: compris | surprendre: surpris |
| *to take: taken* | *to learn: learned* | *to understand: understood* | *to surprise: surprised* |

All derivatives from **mettre** have similar past participles that include **mis**.

| mettre: mis | permettre: permis | promettre: promis | remettre: remis |
| *to put (on): put (on)* | *to allow: allowed* | *to promise: promised* | *to postpone/put back on: postponed/put back on* |

Formation of passé composé with auxiliary verb avoir

Remember that it is imperative to use the appropriate conjugated form of an auxiliary verb before the past participle to form the **passé composé** tense. The auxiliary verb is **avoir** (*to have*) for transitive verbs. In the following sentences, note that there are two English translations for each verb in the **passé composé**; although the first translation may be more common, the second translation exhibits the same verbal structure as the French **passé composé**.

J'**ai acheté** des billets de train en ligne.	*I bought/**have bought** train tickets online.*
Nous **avons pris** le train.	*We took/We **have taken** the train.*
Moi, j'**ai fini** de lire mon livre dans le train.	*I finished/**have finished** reading my book on the train.*
Toi, tu **as dormi** pendant une heure.	*You slept/**have slept** for an hour.*
Paul **a prétendu** dormir.	*Paul pretended/**has pretended** to sleep.*
Toi et Paul, vous **n'avez** rien **vu** du paysage.	*You and Paul saw/**have seen** none of the countryside.*
Mes parents **ont reçu** mon message.	*My parents received/**have received** my message.*
Il **a plu** hier soir.	*It rained/**has rained** yesterday.*

Now review the conjugation of the verb **prendre** in the **passé composé**. Note that the past participle of an **avoir** verb does not change in the conjugation. The exception to this rule will be explained in Chapter 15.

j'ai pris	*I took/have taken*
tu as pris	*you took/have taken*
il/elle/on a pris	*he/she/one has taken*
nous avons pris	*we took/have taken*
vous avez pris	*you took/have taken*
ils/elles ont pris	*they took/have taken*

Le rêve d'Evelyne. *Evelyne's dream.* Put the verbs in parentheses into the appropriate form of the **passé composé**.

Hier soir Evelyne 1. _____ (faire) un beau rêve. Dans son rêve elle

2. _____ (imaginer) qu'elle 3. _____ (réussir) à tous

ses examens de fin d'année. Ses professeurs 4. _____ (féliciter) Evelyne

pour ses bons résultats. Ses parents 5. _____ (offrir) une belle voiture de

sport à Evelyne comme récompense. Ses amis 6. _____ (prétendre) qu'ils

n'étaient pas du tout jaloux. Le beau Thomas 7. _____ (ouvrir) la portière

de la voiture pour Evelyne. Ce geste 8. _____ (plaire) à Evelyne. Alors elle

9. _____ (inviter) Thomas à l'accompagner dans sa belle voiture. Elle

10. _____ (dire) au revoir à tous ses copains. Mais ce n'était qu'un rêve! Zut!

Une invitation. *An invitation.* In the list provided, find the appropriate verb to fit each blank in the following paragraph, and put the verb into the correct form of the **passé composé**.

regarder	jouer	recevoir	devoir
répondre	prendre	faire	rendre
pleuvoir	manger	accepter	danser

Mes parents 1. _____ une invitation aujourd'hui pour rendre visite à

nos amis canadiens à Montréal. Tout de suite ils 2. _____ et naturellement ils

3. _____ affirmativement à l'invitation. L'année dernière nous

4. _____ visite à nos amis au mois de juillet. Nous

5. _____ un avion d'Air Canada. À Montréal, il y avait beaucoup à faire. Nous

6. _____ dans des restaurants chics. Maman et papa

7. _____ des achats dans les petites boutiques. Nous les jeunes, nous

8. _____ dans des boîtes de nuit. C'était chouette! Il faisait généralement

beau mais un jour il 9. _____ très fort et nous 10. _____

rester à la maison. Alors on 11. _____ des films et on

12. _____ au Monopoly.

Formation of **passé composé** with auxiliary verb **être**

The auxiliary verb **être** (*to be*) is used for intransitive verbs of movement. Review the list of such verbs, and note that they can often be remembered in pairs of opposites.

aller	*to go*	venir/revenir/ retourner/rentrer	*to come/come back/ return/go back*
arriver	*to arrive*	partir	*to leave*
descendre	*to go down*	monter	*to go up*
entrer	*to enter*	sortir	*to go out*
naître	*to be born*	mourir	*to die*
passer	*to pass by*	rester	*to stay*
tomber	*to fall*	devenir	*to become*

Among these verbs, the ones with irregular past participles are as follows:

(re)venir → (re)**venu**   naître → **né**   mourir → **mort**

It is imperative to use the appropriate conjugated form of the auxiliary verb **être** (*to be*) before the past participle of these verbs to form their **passé composé**. Review the conjugation of the verb **naître** (*to be born*) in the **passé composé**. You will observe that the second English translation of each verb does not reflect the French verbal structure; in English, we use only the auxiliary verb *have* in the past tense.

Je suis né/née.	*I was born/have been born.*
Tu es né/née.	*You were born/have been born.*
Il est né.	*He was born/has been born.*
Elle est née.	*She was born/has been born.*
On est né.	*We were born/have been born.*
Nous sommes nés/nées.	*We were born/have been born.*
Vous êtes né/née/nés/nées.	*You were born/have been born.*
Ils sont nés.	*They were born/have been born.*
Elles sont nées.	*They were born/have been born.*

Remember to make the past participle of the verb agree in gender and number with the subject of the verb.

- In the phrase **Il est né**, the past participle **né** remains in its original form because it reflects the masculine gender and singular number of the subject **il**.
- In the phrase **Elle est née**, the past participle **née** changes to the feminine form because it reflects the feminine gender and singular number of the subject **elle**.
- In the phrase **Ils sont nés**, the past participle **nés** reflects the masculine gender and plural number of the subject **ils**.
- In the phrase **Elles sont nées**, the past participle **nées** reflects the feminine gender and plural number of the subject **elles**.

Be especially aware of the many spelling possibilities of a past participle of a verb conjugated with **être** when the subject is **vous**. This subject pronoun **vous** could represent a male (**vous êtes né**), a female (**vous êtes née**), several males or a mixed group (**vous êtes nés**), and finally several females (**vous êtes nées**).

Bill Gates **est né** en 1955.	*Bill Gates was born in 1955.*
Sa femme Melinda **est née** en 1964.	*His wife, Melinda, was born in 1964.*
Venus et Serena Williams **sont nées** en 1980 et en 1981.	*Venus and Serena Williams were born in 1980 and 1981.*

En quelle année **êtes-vous né**, monsieur Dupont?	*In what year were you born, Mr. Dupont?*
En quelle année **êtes-vous nées**, mesdames?	*In what year were you born, ladies?*

The auxiliary verb **être** (*to be*) is also used for reflexive verbs in the **passé composé** tense. Review the conjugation of the reflexive verb **s'amuser** (*to have fun*) in the **passé composé**.

Je me suis amusé/amusée.	*I had fun/have had fun.*
Tu t'es amusé/amusée.	*You had fun/have had fun.*
Il s'est amusé.	*He had fun.*
Elle s'est amusée.	*She had fun.*
On s'est amusé.	*We had fun/have had fun.*
Nous nous sommes amusés/amusées.	*We had fun/have had fun.*
Vous êtes amusé/amusée/amusés/amusées.	*You had fun/have had fun.*
Ils se sont amusés.	*They had fun/have had fun.*
Elles se sont amusées.	*They had fun/have had fun.*

Note that the past participle agrees in gender and number with the reflexive pronoun (which has the same gender and number as the subject of the verb).

- In the sentence **Je me suis amusé**, the past participle **amusé** remains in its original form when the reflexive pronoun **me** represents a male. The pronoun **me** is the same person as **je**.
- In the sentence **Je me suis amusée**, the past participle **amusée** changes to its feminine form when the reflexive pronoun **me** represents a female. The pronoun **me** is the same person as **je**.

Now review the following sentences and note the spelling of the past participle for each verb. In the first sentence, the past participle **amusé** reflects the masculine gender of the pronoun **s'** (which represents Pierre). In the second sentence, the past participle **amusée** reflects the feminine gender of the pronoun **s'** (which represents Céline).

Pierre **s'est amusé** à la fête.	*Pierre had fun at the party.*
Céline **s'est amusée** aussi.	*Céline had fun, too.*

Now review the following sentences, and note the spelling of the past participle for each verb. In the first sentence, the past participle **amusés** reflects the masculine gender and the plural number of the pronoun **se** (which represents Pierre and Paul). In the second sentence, the past participle **amusées** reflects the feminine gender and the plural number of the pronoun **se** (which represents Céline and Marie-Louise).

Pierre et Paul **se** sont amusés au cirque.	*Pierre and Paul had fun at the circus.*
Céline et Marie-Louise **se** sont amusées à Disneyworld.	*Celine and Marie-Louise had fun at Disney World.*

EXERCICE

11·7

Comment s'est passé l'été de Nathalie? *How did Nathalie's summer go? In the following dialogue between Marc and Nathalie, write the verbs in parentheses in the **passé composé** taking care to make past participles agree with the subject.*

1. MARC: Dis, où est-ce que tu _____ au mois de juin? (aller)

2. NATHALIE: Je _____ en Corse. C'était bien. (aller)

3. MARC: Tu _____ combien de temps? (rester)

4. NATHALIE: Moi, je _____ trois semaines et ma tante aussi. (rester)

5. MARC: Et le reste de ta famille? Ils _____ ? (ne pas venir)

6. NATHALIE: Si, si. Mais papa et maman _____ à Paris après deux semaines. (rentrer)

7. MARC: Ah! Je vois! Mais tu _____ à Paris seulement en août, n'est-ce pas? (revenir)

8. NATHALIE: C'est vrai! Je _____ en Italie pour tout le mois de juillet. (aller)

9. MARC: Quelle voyageuse! Tu _____ amoureuse d'un Italien là-bas? (tomber)

10. NATHALIE: Oh la la! Je _____ en boîte tous les soirs. (sortir)

EXERCICE 11·8

Marc se plaint. *Marc is complaining.* *Write the verbs in parentheses in the* **passé composé** *taking care to make past participles agree with the reflexive pronoun.*

1. MARC: Tu sais, je _____ devant ta maison chaque jour. (s'arrêter)

2. NATHALIE: Quoi? Tu _____ sans moi, alors. (s'ennuyer)

3. MARC: Pour sûr! Je _____ cet été. (ne pas s'amuser)

4. NATHALIE: Oh! Je suis désolée! Nous _____ fréquemment en mai. (se voir)

5. MARC: Oui, justement! Mais tu _____ de partir en juin et pas de nouvelles de toi! (se dépêcher)

6. NATHALIE: Bon, bon. Ça va, Marc. Je _____ en Italie mais tu es toujours mon copain. (s'amuser)

Uses of the passé composé

The **passé composé** is used when referring to a past occurrence that took place at a precise moment of time such as **à ce moment** (*at that moment*), for a specified number of times such as **trois fois** (*three times*), or for a specific length of time such as **pendant quinze minutes** (*for fifteen minutes*).

A precise moment of time will often be indicated in a narrative by means of expressions such as the following:

avant-hier	*the day before yesterday*	lundi dernier	*last Monday*
hier	*yesterday*	la semaine dernière	*last week*
ce matin	*this morning*	le mois dernier	*last month*
hier matin	*yesterday morning*	l'an dernier/l'année dernière	*last year*
cet après-midi	*this afternoon*	l'automne dernier	*last fall*
hier après-midi	*yesterday afternoon*	l'hiver dernier	*last winter*
ce soir	*tonight*	l'été dernier	*last summer*
hier soir	*yesterday evening*	le printemps dernier	*last spring*

A precise moment of time can also be indicated in a narrative by means of expressions such as the following:

à ce moment	*at that moment*	enfin	*finally*
à huit heures	*at eight o'clock*	soudain	*suddenly*
alors/ensuite/puis	*then*	sur ce fait	*upon that fact*
après	*afterward*	tout à coup	*all of a sudden*
d'abord	*first of all*		

Papa **a pris** la voiture ce matin pour aller au travail.	*Dad took the car this morning to go to work.*
Maman **est allée** au marché deux fois aujourd'hui.	*Mom went to the market twice today.*
Hier après-midi, il y **a eu** un gros orage.	*Yesterday afternoon there was a big storm.*
Soudain l'orage s'**est interrompu**.	*Suddenly the storm stopped.*
Nous **sommes restés** à la maison pendant une heure seulement.	*We stayed at home for an hour only.*
Mais nous **n'avons pas pu** jouer au tennis.	*But we have not been able to play tennis.*

VOCABULAIRE UTILE. *Useful vocabulary.*

Review this list of vocabulary before doing the upcoming exercise.

l'épouse (*f.*)	*bride*	le sang	*blood*
la chambre	*bedroom*	malgré	*despite*
la tour	*tower*	menacer	*to threaten*
le cabinet	*little room/study*	remarquer	*to notice*

EXERCICE 11·9

Le conte de Barbe bleue. *Bluebeard's tale.* *Write the verbs in parentheses in the* **passé composé.** *Take care to use the appropriate auxiliary verb and past participle for each verb.*

Dans le bureau de Barbe bleue, la jeune épouse 1. _____ (avoir)

terriblement peur quand elle 2. _____ (voir) les corps des femmes mortes.

Alors elle 3. _____ (fermer) la porte du bureau et elle

4. _____ (remonter) à sa chambre. Mais elle 5. _____

(remarquer) qu'il y avait du sang sur la clef du bureau. Malgré ses efforts, elle 6.

_____ (ne pas pouvoir) nettoyer le sang de la clé. Ce soir-là, Barbe bleue

7. _____ (rentrer) de voyage. Il était d'abord content de revoir sa jeune

épouse mais il 8. _____ (voir) qu'elle semblait bien nerveuse. Barbe bleue

9. _____ (demander) à son épouse si tout allait bien et elle

10. _____ (répondre) avec hésitation que oui. Puis elle

11. _____ (confesser) qu'elle 12. _____ (perdre) une

clé. Barbe bleue 13. _____ (se fâcher) et 14. _____

(menacer) son épouse. Elle 15. _____ (demander) pardon, mais Barbe bleue

16. _____ (rester) froid face à sa pauvre épouse.

Il 17. _____ (dire) qu'elle devait mourir demain pour son crime. La pauvre

jeune femme 18. _____ (aller) voir sa sœur Anne. Elle

19. _____ (implorer) Anne de chercher ses frères pour l'aider. Et puis elle

20. _____ (monter) dans la plus haute tour pour voir approcher ses frères.

(à suivre—*to be continued*)

Using the **imparfait** and/or **passé composé** in a sentence

There are instances when it is very clear whether the **passé composé** or the **imparfait** is the appropriate tense to use in a sentence.

Passé composé or imparfait

In the next two sentences, the **passé composé** is clearly the tense to use because the past occurrences took place and were completed at a specific moment of time.

Elle **est née** le 9 janvier 1945.	*She was born on January 9, 1945.*
Elle **est morte** le 30 mars 1980.	*She died on March 30, 1980.*

In the next two sentences, the **imparfait** is clearly the tense to use because the past occurrences took place on a regular basis, at unspecified times, and for an indefinite length of time.

Il **passait** tous les jours dans ma rue.	*He passed every day in my street.*
Mais il ne **savait** pas où **j'habitais**.	*But he did not know where I lived.*

However, there are instances when the speaker has to make a decision about which tense to use to express a unique perspective. Compare the following sets of sentences, and note the use of the **imparfait** for the verb **avoir** in the first sentence and the use of the **passé composé** for the same verb in the second sentence. Note that in the first sentence, the **imparfait** helps communicate a vague feeling (unspecified time or duration of the feeling), but in the second sentence, the **passé composé** helps communicate the sudden urge of the feeling supported by the use of the adverb **vraiment**.

J'avais envie de danser avec Patrick mais il ne voulait pas.	*I felt like dancing with Patrick, but he did not want to.*
J'ai eu vraiment envie de danser avec Patrick; alors je l'ai invité.	*I really felt like dancing with Patrick, so I invited him.*

Verbs indicating a feeling such as **aimer** (*to like/love*), a state of mind such as **penser** (*to think*), or a condition such as **être** (*to be*) will frequently be used in the **imparfait** because of their intangible nature and the difficulty one would have specifying for how long or at what moment someone thought something or something was a certain way. Here is a list of such verbs:

aimer	*to like/love*	avoir	*to have*
adorer	*to love/adore*	être	*to be*
détester	*to hate/detest*	avoir envie de	*to feel like*
croire	*to believe*	avoir besoin de	*to need*
penser	*to think*	avoir l'habitude de	*to be used to*
espérer	*to hope*	avoir l'impression de	*to feel like*
savoir	*to know*	avoir peur de	*to be afraid/scared of*
sembler	*to seem*	avoir sommeil	*to be sleepy*
pouvoir	*to be able to*	avoir tort/raison	*to be wrong/right*
vouloir	*to want*	avoir peur de	*to be afraid of*

Now look at the following examples:

Je ne **savais** pas qu'il y **avait** une fête chez Nicolas.	*I did not know there was a party at Nicolas's.*
Il **croyait** qu'on se rencontrait chez lui.	*He thought we were meeting at his house.*
Il **espérait** revoir tous nos copains.	*He was hoping he would meet all our friends.*
Tout le monde **était** chez moi.	*Everybody was at my house.*
Il y **avait** environ une dizaine de personnes.	*There were about 10 people.*
J'**avais** sommeil tout le matin.	*I was sleepy all morning long.*

Compare the following sets of sentences, and note the unique perspective the **imparfait** or the **passé composé** can give to what happened or was going on:

J'**avais** faim.	*I was hungry.*
J'**ai eu** faim.	*I got hungry.*
Nous **avions** peur.	*We were scared.*
Nous **avons eu** peur.	*We got scared.*
Je **connaissais** son secret.	*I knew his secret.*
J'**ai connu** son secret.	*I found out his secret.*

EXERCICE
11·10

Une matinée bien réussie. *A successful morning. Complete the following paragraph by writing each verb in parentheses in the appropriate past tense.*

La semaine dernière Emma 1. _____ (aller) en vacances. Le matin elle

2. _____ (avoir) l'habitude de se lever vers huit heures. D'abord elle

3. _____ (se laver) et 4. _____ (se brosser) les dents et

les cheveux. Ensuite elle 5. _____ (prendre) le petit déjeuner. Finalement

elle 6. _____ (faire) un long jogging ou une longue promenade. Mais

samedi matin, pendant qu'elle 7. _____ (se promener) au parc, elle

8. _____ (avoir) une énorme surprise. Eh oui! Elle

9. _____ (se trouver) nez à nez avec un beau chien roux. Le chien

10. _____ (s'approcher) d'elle. Il 11. _____ (être)

mignon et gentil et Emma 12. _____ (ne pas avoir peur) de lui. Son collier

13. _____ (indiquer) qu'il 14. _____ (s'appeler) Rex. Il y

15. _____ (avoir) aussi un numéro de téléphone sur son collier. Emma

16. _____ (téléphoner) à Jean, le maître de Rex. Jean

17. _____ (ne pas savoir) que son chien 18. _____ (être)

seul au parc. Quand il 19. _____ (entendre) la nouvelle, il

20. _____ (venir) le chercher tout de suite. Jean et Emma

21. _____ (devenir) de bons amis et Jean 22. _____

(offrir) un bébé de Rex à Emma.

EXERCICE
11·11

Une après-midi peu réussie. *A failed afternoon.* *Write the following sentences in French. Use your best judgment when choosing the* **passé composé** *or* **imparfait** *to express the past tense.*

1. Emma wanted to go to the pool yesterday afternoon, but she needed a new bathing suit.

_____

2. So she went to the store, and she bought a bikini.

_____

3. Later when she left her house, the sky was still blue.

_____

4. But when she arrived at the pool, it was starting to rain.

_____

5. Then she got scared when she heard thunder and saw lightning.

_____

6. She suddenly did not feel like swimming anymore.

_____

7. Emma returned to the bus station and took the bus.

_____

8. Finally she went back home and prepared dinner.

_____

Passé composé and imparfait in a sentence

There are instances when the **passé composé** and the **imparfait** will be used in the same sentence.

In the following sentence, note the use of the **imparfait** for the verb **aller** to express the progressive past tense (*was going*) and for the verb **devoir**, which expresses a general state of mind. Also note the use of the **passé composé** for the verb **se rappeler** to underline the instantaneous nature of the act of remembering and the specific time at which the act of remembering occurred.

Il **allait** quitter la maison mais il s'**est rappelé** qu'il **devait** d'abord fermer les fenêtres.	*He was going to leave the house, but he remembered that he had to close the windows first.*

A common type of sentence in which the **passé composé** and **imparfait** are found is a sentence in which an action was going on when another action interrupted the one in progress. The action that was in progress is expressed in the **imparfait** tense, while the interrupting action is expressed in the **passé composé** tense.

Les étudiants **écrivaient** une dissertation quand le nouvel étudiant **s'est présenté**.	*The students were writing a dissertation when the new student presented himself.*
Nous **avons regardé** un documentaire pendant que le professeur **corrigeait** nos devoirs.	*We watched a documentary while the teacher was correcting our homework.*
Le réveil **a sonné** alors que j'**étais** encore endormi.	*The alarm clock rang while I was still asleep.*

EXERCICE 11·12

Philippe et Chloé sont coquins. *Philippe and Chloé are rascals.* Write the letter of the best completion for each sentence on the line provided.

1. _____ Quand Philippe a vu Chloé pour la première fois,

2. _____ Quand il a dit bonjour à Chloé,

3. _____ Après que Philippe s'est présenté,

4. _____ Pendant que le prof enseignait,

5. _____ Alors que le prof parlait encore,

6. _____ Quand Chloé et Philippe étaient dehors,

7. _____ Chloé et Philippe riaient comme des fous,

8. _____ La copine de Chloé a demandé

a. elle a répondu salut.

b. Chloé et Philippe partaient en douce.

c. les étudiants prenaient des notes.

d. il a plu à Chloé.

e. c'était dans un cours de philosophie.

f. pourquoi ils riaient.

g. la cloche a sonné pour la fin du cours.

h. quand la copine de Chloé est arrivée.

Using the **imparfait** and **passé composé** in extended writing

In an extended piece of writing such as a journal page, a letter, an e-mail, or a story, **passé composé** and **imparfait** will alternate as necessary. Review the following paragraph in which descriptive elements such as the weather and the condition of the sky are expressed with **imparfait**, feelings such as *appreciating something* are expressed with **imparfait**, ongoing actions such as *walking* for an unspecified time are expressed with **imparfait**, but sequential occurrences taking place at specific moments of time such as a gunshot *erupting*, people *stopping* and *listening*, are expressed in the **passé composé**.

Il **faisait** un temps magnifique. Le ciel **était** bleu; il n'y **avait** pas un seul nuage à l'horizon. Nous **marchions** à petits pas dans la forêt. Les oiseaux **sifflaient** du haut des arbres et les branches des arbres **balançaient** doucement. Nous **appréciions** ces moments paisibles. Soudain un grand bruit **a interrompu** la tranquillité des lieux. **Nous nous sommes arrêtés** et **nous avons dressé** l'oreille. **Nous nous sommes** alors **dirigés** dans la direction du bruit et voilà que **nous nous sommes retrouvés** face à face avec un sanglier.

The weather was magnificent. The sky was blue; there was not a single cloud on the horizon. We were walking slowly in the forest. Birds were whistling from high up in the trees, and the branches of the trees were swinging gently. We were enjoying these peaceful moments. Suddenly a big noise interrupted the tranquillity of the place. We stopped and we listened. We then moved in the direction of the noise, and there we found ourselves face-to-face with a boar.

Here is a summary of key concepts to bear in mind when using the **passé composé** and **imparfait** tenses:

IMPARFAIT	PASSÉ COMPOSÉ
background and descriptive information such as dates and places	specific and completed occurrence
generic state of mind or feeling	sudden or instantaneous states of mind or feelings
progressive action without clear beginning or end	occurrence framed by clearly defined time
action interrupted by another action	occurrence that interrupted an action in progress
habitual action	occurrence that took place once or a specific number of times

---

VOCABULAIRE UTILE. *Useful vocabulary.*

Review this vocabulary before doing the upcoming exercise.

à ses pieds	*at his feet*
l'épée (*f.*)	*sword*
le bras	*arm*
le cavalier	*horseman*
le couteau	*knife*
le gentilhomme	*gentleman*
sur le coup	*immediately*

L'histoire de Barbe bleue. *Bluebeard's tale.* *Complete each sentence with the appropriate* **passé composé** *or* **imparfait** *form of the verb in parentheses.*

Le lendemain, Barbe bleue 1. _____ (venir) dans la tour chercher son

épouse pour la punir. Elle 2. _____ (se jeter) à ses pieds et une fois de plus,

elle 3. _____ (demander) pardon. Mais le cruel Barbe bleue

4. _____ (ne rien vouloir) entendre. Il 5. _____

(prendre) son couteau et 6. _____ (lever) le bras. Juste à ce moment-là,

deux cavaliers 7. _____ (entrer) dans le château. Ils 8.

_____ (être) armés d'épées. La jeune femme 9. _____

(reconnaître) ses frères. Ils 10. _____ (attraper) Barbe bleue qui

11. _____ (essayer) de fuir. Dans la bataille avec les deux cavaliers, Barbe

bleue 12. _____ (tomber) du haut d'une tour et il 13.

_____ (mourir) sur le coup. La jeune femme 14. _____

(se remarier) plus tard à un très honnête gentilhomme. Ils 15. _____ (avoir)

beaucoup d'enfants.

Adverbs and adverbial phrases

Adverbs have a variety of functions. However, the most common function of adverbs consists in modifying the meaning of a verb by telling how or in what way, how much or to what degree, when or how often, and where something is done. An adverb can be a single word such as **bien** (*well*) or a phrase such as **à toute allure** (*in a great hurry*).

The functions of adverbs

Look at the following lists of commonly used adverbs grouped as per function *How and where*, and note how these adverbs are used in the examples:

Comment et où *How and where*

ailleurs/partout	*elsewhere/everywhere*
bien/mal/mieux	*well/badly/better*
dehors/dedans	*outside/inside*
dessus/dessous	*on top/below*
devant/derrière	*in the front/in the back*
ensemble/seul	*together/alone*
ici/là	*here/there*
lentement/vite	*slowly/fast*

Je ne voudrais pas vivre **ailleurs**.	*I would not like to live elsewhere.*
Oh! Elle écrit **mal**!	*Oh! She writes badly!*
Le chien est **dehors**?	*Is the dog outside?*
Il est assis **derrière**.	*He is seated in the back.*

Beware that **bien** (*well*) and **mieux** (*better*) are adverbs that should not be confused with **bon** (*good*) and **meilleur** (*better*), which are adjectives. Compare the following sentences, and note that **bien** and **mieux** are invariable parts of speech that modify the meaning of the verb in the sentence.

Je **vais bien** aujourd'hui, **mieux** qu'hier.	*I am feeling fine today, better than yesterday.*
Elle **danse bien**, ta copine. Mais moi, je danse **mieux**.	*Your friend dances well. But I dance better.*

Note the irregular use of the adverb **bien** in the following examples. Although an adverb modifies an action verb (not the verb **être**), it is used after the verb **être** in these sentences:

123

Tu as gagné beaucoup d'argent? **C'est bien!**	*You earned a lot of money? That's nice!*
Elle a de bonnes notes? **C'est très bien!**	*She has good grades? That's very good!*

On the other hand, **bon** and **meilleur** are adjectives that describe a noun in the sentence and therefore agree in gender and number with that noun.

Cette **tarte** est **bonne, meilleure** que l'autre.	*This tart is good, better than the other one.*
Tu as de **bonnes idées**.	*You have good ideas.*

Similarly, remember that **mal** (*badly*) is an adverb that should not be confused with the adjective **mauvais** (*bad*). Compare the following sentences, and note that **mal** is an invariable part of speech that modifies the meaning of the verb in the sentence. On the other hand, **mauvais** is an adjective that describes a noun in the sentence and therefore agrees in gender and number with that noun.

Ce rasoir **marche mal**.	*This razor works badly.*
Mes gencives me **font mal**.	*My gums hurt.*
Quelle **mauvaise pièce**!	*What a bad play!*
Ce sont de **mauvaises plaisanteries**.	*These are bad jokes.*

Look at the following lists of commonly used adverbs grouped as per function *When or with which frequency*, and note how these adverbs are used in the examples:

Quand et avec quelle fréquence *When or with which frequency*

ainsi	*thus*	enfin	*finally*
alors	*then*	ensuite	*then*
après	*afterward*	maintenant	*now*
aujourd'hui	*today*	parfois	*sometimes*
autrefois	*formerly*	puis	*then*
avant	*before*	quelquefois	*sometimes*
déjà	*already*	soudain	*suddenly*
demain	*tomorrow*	souvent	*often*
donc	*so*	toujours	*always*
encore	*still*		

Tu termines **enfin** cette dissertation?	*Are you finally finishing this essay?*
Tu as **encore** faim?	*Are you still hungry?*
Nous faisons **toujours** attention.	*We always pay attention.*
Elle a **parfois** peur de conduire.	*She is sometimes afraid to drive.*
Il change **soudain** d'avis!	*He suddenly changes his mind!*

Look at the following lists of commonly used adverbs grouped as per function *To what degree*, and note how these adverbs are used in the examples:

Dans quelle mesure *To what degree*

assez	*enough/pretty much/fairly*	moins	*less*
aussi	*also*	peu	*little*
autant	*as much*	plus	*more*
beaucoup	*a lot*	presque	*almost*
comme	*as/like*	si	*so/such*
davantage	*more*	tellement	*so (much)*
environ	*approximately*	trop	*too much*
juste	*just*	vraiment	*really*
même	*even*		

Elle va **beaucoup** apprendre dans ce cours.	*She is going to learn a lot in this class.*
Ils parlent **peu**.	*They speak little.*
La ville est à **environ** deux kilomètres d'ici.	*The town is at approximately two kilometers from here.*
Il reste du café. Tu en veux **davantage**?	*There is coffee left. Do you want more?*
Tu vas **vraiment** vivre en Guadeloupe?	*Are you really going to live in Guadeloupe?*

Note that the adverb **aussi** (*also, in addition, moreover*) is never used at the beginning of a French sentence or clause. In the French sentence, it usually follows the verb.

Mireille est brune et mince; elle est **aussi** très jolie.	*Mireille is brown-haired and slim; she is also very pretty.*
Il est en France. Il voudrait **aussi** visiter le Canada.	*He is in France. He would also like to visit Canada.*
Apporte-moi un souvenir; rappelle-toi **aussi** ta tante.	*Bring me a souvenir; also remember your aunt.*

Note that the adverb **aussi** (*also, in addition, moreover*) may follow the stress pronoun in the French sentence.

Tu es gourmand! **Moi aussi.**	*You are fond of food! Me, too.*
Ils adorent jouer à cache-cache. **Nous aussi.**	*They love to play hide-and-seek. We do, too.*

Look at the following lists of commonly used adverbs grouped as per their affirmative function, and note how these adverbs are used in the examples. When the following adverbs are used to affirm or confirm a fact in a reply, they appear at the beginning of a sentence:

oui	*yes*
si	*yes (answer to negative question)*
volontiers	*gladly*
sûrement	*surely*
parfaitement	*of course*
bien sûr	*of course*
bien entendu	*of course*

Vous avez envie de boire un verre de vin? —**Volontiers!**	*Do you feel like having a glass of wine? —Gladly!*
Vous ne voulez pas d'eau? —**Si**, je voudrais un verre d'eau, s'il vous plaît.	*Don't you want any water? —Yes, I would like a glass of water, please.*

Look at the following lists of commonly used adverbs grouped as per their function of probability, and note how these adverbs are used in the examples:

peut-être	*maybe/perhaps*
probablement	*probably*
apparemment	*apparently*

J'irai **peut-être** au Maroc.	*I will perhaps go to Morocco.*
Il pleuvra **probablement** ce soir.	*It will probably rain tonight.*

When the following adverbs are used in a reply that does not include a verb, they appear at the beginning of a sentence:

Tu iras à la piscine? —**Peut-être!**	*Will you go to the pool? —Perhaps!*
Il va pleuvoir? —**Probablement!**	*Is it going to rain? —Probably!*

Look at the following lists of commonly used adverbs grouped as per their function of negativity, and note how these adverbs are used in the examples:

In negative sentences, the primary adverb of negation **ne** is accompanied by an auxiliary adverb of negation such as the following:

jamais	*never*
rien	*nothing*
guère	*not much/hardly*
pas	*not*
personne	*nobody*
plus	*no more/no longer/more*

These adverbs are placed after the conjugated verb in the sentence in the present, future, and near future tenses.

Cet ordinateur ne marche **guère**.	*This computer hardly works.*
Je ne referai **jamais** cette faute.	*I will never make this mistake again.*
Il ne va **plus** parler.	*He is not going to talk again.*

These adverbs are placed after the helping verb in the sentence in the **passé composé** except for **personne** (*nobody*) and **que** (*only*), which follow the past participle:

Elles n'ont **rien** fait.	*They did not do anything.*
Nous n'avons vu **personne**.	*We did not see anyone.*

Quel est le contraire? *What is the opposite?* *Write the letter of the opposite for each adverb on the line provided.*

1. _____ plus

2. _____ jamais

3. _____ peu

4. _____ quelquefois

5. _____ avant

6. _____ peut-être

7. _____ d'abord

8. _____ lentement

a. enfin

b. souvent

c. vite

d. toujours

e. sûrement

f. après

g. moins

h. beaucoup

Parlons de Jacques! *Let's talk about Jacques!* *Write in French. Use intonation structure for questions.*

1. Jacques really likes France. He wants to stay here a little longer.

_____

2. Of course! He has a lot to do and a lot to learn every day.

_____

3. He likes the French culture so much!

_____

4. So can he stay here for approximately a year?

_____

5. He is not ever going to go back home?

_____

6. Yes, of course! He will go back, but not yet.

_____

7. He can probably still stay one or two months.

_____

8. You are so pessimistic.

_____

Adverbs used before adjectives

Many previously seen adverbs are also found before adjectives; in that case, the adverb modifies the meaning of the adjective it precedes.

Ton arbre est **plus grand** cette année.	*Your tree is bigger this year.*
Ce tableau est vraiment **très beau**.	*This painting is really very beautiful.*
Oh non! Ta robe est **déjà sale**!	*Oh no! Your dress is already dirty!*
Elle a un **si joli** visage.	*She has such a pretty face.*
Ta mère est **si raisonnable**.	*Your mother is so reasonable.*
Cet argument est **assez logique**.	*This argument is pretty logical.*
Ton copain est **trop gentil**.	*Your friend is too nice.*
Toi aussi, tu es **tellement mignon**!	*You too are so cute!*
Ils sont **plutôt impatients**.	*They are rather impatient.*
Elle est **moins énergique** que toi.	*She is less energetic than you.*

Adverbs used before other adverbs

Some adverbs are also found before other adverbs; in that case, the first adverb modifies the meaning of the adverb it precedes.

Il me téléphone **assez souvent**.	*He calls me pretty often.*
Tu parles **trop fort**.	*You speak too loudly.*
Ce n'est **pas mal**.	*That's not bad.*
Je ne comprends **jamais rien**.	*I never understand anything.*
Elle est **presque toujours** présente.	*She is almost always present.*
Ça ne te plaît pas? Moi **non plus**.	*You don't like it? Me neither.*

Comment est cette personne? *How is this person?* *Complete each sentence according to the instructions in parentheses.*

1. Albert Einstein est _____! (*so intelligent*)

2. George Washington est _____. (*very admirable*)

3. Descartes est _____. (*so logical*)

4. Oprah Winfrey est _____. (*very rich*)

5. Bill Gates est _____. (*pretty generous*)

6. Angelina Jolie est _____. (*rather pretty*)

Comment font-ils les choses? *How do they do things?* *Complete each sentence according to the instructions in parentheses.*

1. Les enfants jouent _____. (*almost always*)

2. Les adultes travaillent _____. (*too hard*)

3. Les artistes créent _____. (*so spontaneously*)

4. Les paresseux ne font _____. (*never anything*)

5. Les gourmands mangent _____. (*really too much*)

6. Les chanteurs rock chantent _____. (*too loudly*)

7. Les mauvais professeurs enseignent _____. (*so badly*)

8. Les bons parents élèvent leurs enfants _____. (*rather well*)

Formation of adverbs derived from adjectives

Many adjectives can easily be changed into adverbs by adding the suffix **-ment** to their feminine form.

Adjectives that end in a consonant

When an adjective ends in a consonant, the suffix **-ment** is added to its feminine form.

MASCULINE ADJECTIVE	→ FEMININE ADJECTIVE	→ ADVERB
lent	lente	lentement
slow		*slowly*
seul	seule	seulement
alone		*only*
actuel	actuelle	actuellement
current		*currently*
cruel	cruelle	cruellement
cruel		*cruelly*
attentif	attentive	attentivement
attentive		*attentively*
naïf	naïve	naïvement
naïve		*naïvely*
cher	chère	chèrement
dear		*dearly*
fier	fière	fièrement
proud		*proudly*
heureux	heureuse	heureusement
happy		*fortunately*
malheureux	malheureuse	malheureusement
unhappy		*unfortunately*

Quelquefois on paie **chèrement** pour ses fautes.	*Sometimes one pays dearly for one's mistakes.*
Le journal sort **actuellement** une fois par semaine.	*The newspaper currently comes out once a week.*
Il pleut. **Heureusement**, j'ai mon parapluie.	*It is raining. Fortunately, I have my umbrella.*
Les étudiants ont **fièrement** reçu leurs diplômes.	*The students proudly received their diplomas.*

Adjectives that end in -e, -é, or -i

These can easily be changed into adverbs by adding the suffix **-ment** to their masculine form.

MASCULINE ADJECTIVE	→	ADVERB
raisonnable		raisonnablement
reasonable		*reasonably*
honnête		honnêtement
honest		*honestly*
instantané		instantanément
instantaneous		*instantaneously*
spontané		spontanément
spontaneous		*spontaneously*
poli		poliment
polite		*politely*
joli		joliment
pretty		*prettily*

Il vaut mieux se comporter **honnêtement** dans la vie.	*It is better to behave honestly in life.*
Il change d'avis **instantanément**.	*He changes his mind instantaneously.*
Il faut toujours parler **poliment**.	*We must always speak politely.*
Tu vas décorer la boîte **joliment**.	*You are going to decorate the box prettily.*

Adjectives that end in -ent or -ant

When these adjectives consist of more than one syllable, they can easily be changed into adverbs by substituting **-emment** to the **-ent** ending and **-amment** to the **-ant** ending.

ADJECTIVE	→	ADVERB
élég**ant**		élég**amment**
elegant		*elegantly*
fréqu**ent**		fréqu**emment**
frequent		*frequently*
pati**ent**		pati**emment**
patient		*patiently*
réc**ent**		réc**emment**
recent		*recently*

Habille-toi **élégamment** pour la fête ce soir.   *Dress elegantly for tonight's party.*
Attends-moi **patiemment**!   *Wait patiently for me!*
Récemment il y a des vols dans le quartier.   *Recently there are thefts in the neighborhood.*

Vous êtes **fréquemment** sur Facebook.   *You are frequently on Facebook.*

EXERCICE 12·5

Le portrait d'Alexandre. *Alexander's portrait.* *Complete each sentence with the adverb derived from the adjective in parentheses.*

1. Dès qu'il a un projet, il commence et finit _____. (rapide)

2. _____ il fait parfois des erreurs. (évident)

3. Mais ça arrive _____. (rare)

4. C'est le genre de personne qui peut travailler _____ mais vite. (patient)

5. C'est pourquoi le patron lui donne _____ les grands projets. (fréquent)

6. Il va _____ devenir superviseur un jour ou l'autre. (sûr)

7. _____ les gens trop ambitieux ne sont pas sympa. (général)

8. Mais ce n'est pas le cas. _____ Alexandre est gentil. (heureux)

9. Il n'est pas _____ gentil mais généreux. (seul)

10. Il aide volontiers et _____ tous ses collègues. (poli)

11. _____ c'est mon meilleur ami. (actuel)

Placement of adverbs

The most common position of an adverb in the French sentence is right after the conjugated verb in the sentence.

Note the placement of simple adverbs right after the verb in the following sentences when the verb is in a simple tense such as the present or simple future:

J'aime **beaucoup** les fraises.	*I like strawberries a lot.*
Tu iras **vite** au marché.	*You will quickly go to the market.*
Je t'entends **bien**.	*I hear you well.*

Note the placement of simple adverbs right after the auxiliary verb in the near future:

Ils vont **déjà** partir.	*They are already going to leave.*
Vous allez **aussi** refuser?	*Are you also going to refuse?*

Note the placement of simple adverbs right after the conjugated verb when the conjugated verb is followed by an infinitive:

Nous allons **souvent** chercher des fleurs.	*We often go get flowers.*
Ils veulent **toujours** manger.	*They always want to eat.*

Note that adverbs of time usually appear at the beginning or at the end of a sentence:

Demain, je vais me reposer.	*Tomorrow, I am going to rest.*
Je voudrais aller à la plage **maintenant**.	*I would like to go to the beach now.*

Note that adverbs of location usually appear at the end of a sentence:

Ne va pas **là-bas**!	*Do not go over there!*
Voilà mon livre. Mon cahier est **dessous**.	*There is my book. My notebook is under.*

Some adverbs such as **ainsi** (*thus*), **après** (*afterward*), **alors** (*then*), **puis** (*then*), and **ensuite** (*then*), because of their transitional function, are positioned at the beginning of a sentence or of a clause.

Tu vas prendre une douche. **Puis** tu vas te coucher.	*You are going to take a shower. Then you are going to go to bed.*
Tu as vingt et un ans; **donc** tu es majeur.	*You are twenty-one years old; so you are of legal age.*

EXERCICE
12·6

Comment je commence la journée. *How I start the day.* Write in French, being careful to place the adverb appropriately in the sentence.

1. First I wake up.

_____

2. Then I brush my teeth, and I take a shower.

_____

3. Afterward, I get dressed, and I brush my hair.

_____

4. Finally I eat breakfast.

_____

5. I usually go to the office around eight o'clock.

_____

6. So I have to take the bus at seven o'clock.

_____

7. At 7 A.M. there are already many people at the bus stop.

_____

8. When all goes well, I am at work at 7:45 A.M.

_____

Adverbial phrases

Adverbial phrases always modify the meaning of a verb. They come in a great variety of composite structures. Here are a few common ones:

Adverbial phrases introduced by a preposition

à bon marché	*for a good price*	de temps en temps	*from time to time*
à la mode	*in style*	en avance	*early*
à voix basse/hausse	*in a low/loud voice*	en général	*generally*
avec plaisir	*with pleasure*	en premier	*first*
d'abord	*first*	en retard	*late*
(bas/haut) de gamme	*(low/high) end*	par exemple	*for example*
de jour/de nuit	*during the day/ during the night*	sans cesse	*incessantly*
de préférence	*preferably*		

On vend cette maison **à bon marché**.	*They are selling this house for a good price.*
Je préfère arriver **en avance**.	*I prefer to arrive early.*
Cette petite fille bavarde **sans cesse**.	*This little girl talks incessantly.*
Je veux une télévision **de haut gamme**.	*I want a high-end television.*

Adverbial phrases introduced by tout

tout à coup	*suddenly*	tout de même	*anyway*
tout d'abord	*first of all*	tout à fait	*entirely*
tout de suite	*right away*	tout à l'heure	*in a little while*

Je veux sortir **tout à l'heure** mais **tout d'abord** je dois finir ma composition.	*I want to go out in a little while, but first of all I have to finish my composition.*
Tu veux être à la mode. C'est **tout à fait** normal.	*You want to be in style. That's quite normal.*

Adverbial phrases introduced by **d'un air** or **d'une manière**

d'un air arrogant	*arrogantly*
d'un air fâché	*angrily*

d'un air joyeux	*joyously*
d'un air ennuyé	*in a bored or annoyed manner*
d'une manière bizarre	*in a bizarre manner*
d'une manière efficace	*in an efficient manner*
d'une manière émouvante	*in a moving manner*
d'une manière satisfaisante	*in a satisfactory manner*

L'employé fait des efforts pour faire son travail **d'une manière satisfaisante**.	*The employee makes efforts to do his work satisfactorily.*
Papa est parti **d'un air fâché**.	*Dad left with an angry look.*
Maman a dit au revoir **d'un air ennuyé**.	*Mom said good-bye in an annoyed manner.*

EXERCICE
12·7

Comment Mme Tonie enseigne-t-elle? *How does Mrs. Tonie teach? Write in French, being careful to place the adverb appropriately in the sentence. Here are the verbs you will need to write your sentences.*

saluer	demander	aller	commencer
enseigner	présenter	surprendre	aimer
venir			

1. She greets students in an enthusiastic manner.

   _____

2. First of all, she asks students how they are.

   _____

3. Then she promptly starts the lesson.

   _____

4. She teaches in an efficient and interesting manner.

   _____

5. Sometimes she also presents lessons in a bizarre fashion.

   _____

6. Even when Mme Tonie surprises the students, they like her class.

   _____

7. For example, one day, she comes to class as the artist Monet.

   _____

Le bénévolat. *Volunteer work.* *Complete the following paragraph using the appropriate adverb from the list.*

au contraire	sûrement	peut-être	définitivement
surtout	déjà	attentivement	complètement
par exemple	gravement	aussi	immédiatement
régulièrement	même	jamais	

Si vous n'avez 1. _____ été bénévole, 2. _____ il

est temps aujourd'hui de vous engager dans une œuvre. Et 3. _____ si

vous avez 4. _____ été bénévole, vous allez 5. _____

trouver des possibilités de bénévolat sur notre site. Vous êtes 6. _____

ignorant des causes? Aucun problème! Ne vous inquiétez 7. _____ pas.

8. _____, étudiez 9. _____ les descriptions que nous

donnons sur notre site. Vous pouvez, 10. _____,

11. _____ rendre visite aux personnes âgées. Vous pouvez

12. _____ aider à divertir des enfants 13. _____

malades. Nous pouvons 14. _____ vous aider à trouver l'association et

l'action qui vous conviennent.

N'hésitez pas! Contactez-nous 15. _____!

Conditional sentences

Conditional sentences consist of an *if* clause and a result clause. Whereas the *if* clause serves to state a hypothesis, the result clause serves to state a consequence. Depending on the tenses used, this type of sentence may help predict what could still happen or state what could have happened.

Conditional sentences with the **imparfait** and present conditional

This type of sentence helps hypothesize what might happen in the present and the future. It includes an *if* clause introducing a condition to be realized (the verb in this clause is in the **imparfait**) and a result clause that would then ensue (the verb in this clause is in the conditional present).

> Si l'avion partait à l'heure, nous ne raterions pas notre correspondance.
>
> *If the plane left on time, we would not miss our connection.*

Use and formation of present conditional

The present tense of the conditional is used to express that something *would* hypothetically happen in the present or in the future under certain conditions. It is formed by using the future stem of the verb (see Chapter 9) and adding the endings of the **imparfait** tense: **-ais, -ais, -ait, -ions, -iez, -aient**.

Examine the following conjugations of regular verbs in this tense. Remember that the future stem of a regular verb is simply the infinitive form of the verb (minus the **-e** ending for **-re** verbs).

-er verbs	-ir verbs	-re verbs
. . . *would notice*	. . . *would choose*	. . . *would sell*
je remarquerais	je choisirais	je vendrais
tu remarquerais	tu choisirais	tu vendrais
il/elle/on remarquerait	il/elle/on choisirait	il/elle/on vendrait
nous remarquerions	nous choisirions	nous vendrions
vous remarqueriez	vous choisiriez	vous vendriez
ils/elles remarqueraient	ils/elles choisiraient	ils/elles vendraient

Now examine the following conjugations of irregular verbs in the present conditional:

aller	avoir	être	faire
. . . would go	*. . . would have*	*. . . would be*	*. . . would do/make*
j'irais	j'aurais	je serais	je ferais
tu irais	tu aurais	tu serais	tu ferais
il/elle/on irait	il/elle/on aurait	il/elle/on serait	il/elle/on ferait
nous irions	nous aurions	nous serions	nous ferions
vous iriez	vous auriez	vous seriez	vous feriez
ils/elles iraient	ils/elles auraient	ils/elles seraient	ils/elles feraient

The same spelling changes that occurred in the simple future tense (see Chapter 9) also appear in the present conditional.

e → è	l → ll	t → tt	y → i
acheter → j'achèterais	appeler → j'appellerais	jeter → je jetterais	payer → je paierais
to buy → I would buy	*to call → I would call*	*to throw → I would throw*	*to pay → I would pay*

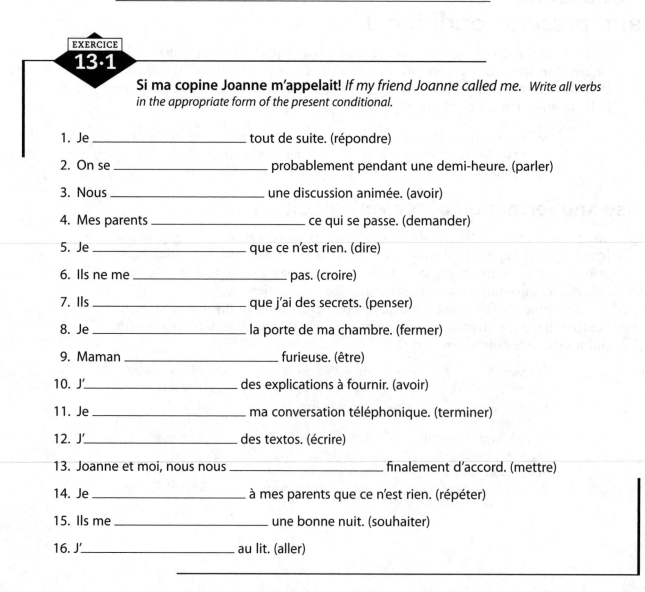

EXERCICE
13·1

Si ma copine Joanne m'appelait! *If my friend Joanne called me.* *Write all verbs in the appropriate form of the present conditional.*

1. Je _____ tout de suite. (répondre)

2. On se _____ probablement pendant une demi-heure. (parler)

3. Nous _____ une discussion animée. (avoir)

4. Mes parents _____ ce qui se passe. (demander)

5. Je _____ que ce n'est rien. (dire)

6. Ils ne me _____ pas. (croire)

7. Ils _____ que j'ai des secrets. (penser)

8. Je _____ la porte de ma chambre. (fermer)

9. Maman _____ furieuse. (être)

10. J'_____ des explications à fournir. (avoir)

11. Je _____ ma conversation téléphonique. (terminer)

12. J'_____ des textos. (écrire)

13. Joanne et moi, nous nous _____ finalement d'accord. (mettre)

14. Je _____ à mes parents que ce n'est rien. (répéter)

15. Ils me _____ une bonne nuit. (souhaiter)

16. J'_____ au lit. (aller)

Que ferais-je sans toi? *What would I do without you?* *Write the following sentences using verbs in the present conditional.*

1. I would often be alone.

   _____

2. I would not have a best friend.

   _____

3. I would not be able to share my feelings.

   _____

4. I would not have fun all the time.

   _____

5. I would be working all the time.

   _____

6. I would forget a lot of things.

   _____

Special meanings of aimer, vouloir, pouvoir, and devoir in the conditional present

The verbs **aimer** (*to like*), **vouloir** (*to want*), and **pouvoir** (*to be able to*) are often used in the present conditional to make a polite request.

Je **voudrais** une glace, s'il vous plaît.	*I would like an ice cream, please.*
J'**aimerais** essayer ce pantalon.	*I would like to try on these pants.*
Pourriez-vous me dire où se trouve la sortie?	*Could you tell me where the exit is?*
Ils **pourraient** écrire un texto s'ils avaient un téléphone ou un iPad.	*They could write a text message if they had a phone or an iPad.*

The verb **devoir** in the present conditional is used to express an obligation or a suggestion.

Tu **devrais** rendre visite à tes parents plus souvent.	*You ought to/should visit your parents more often.*
Nous **devrions** partir maintenant. Il est tard.	*We ought to/should leave now. It is late.*

Des achats! *Purchases!* *Write the following sentences in French to complete the dialogue between Gabriel and a salesperson.*

1. GABRIEL: Bonjour, monsieur. Je/J'_____ essayer cette paire de chaussures en pointure 10. (*I would like*)

2. VENDEUR: Bien, monsieur. Je vous cherche ces chaussures. Est-ce que vous les _____ en brun ou en noir? (*would you prefer*)

3. GABRIEL: Je les _____ en noir, s'il vous plaît. (*I would prefer*)

4. VENDEUR: Voilà, monsieur. Est-ce que vous _____ aussi essayer cette paire en noir? (*would like*)

5. GABRIEL: D'accord. Merci bien. Mais _____ -vous m'apporter cette autre paire aussi dans une pointure 10? (*could you*)

6. VENDEUR: Je suis à votre service, monsieur. Mais vous _____ acheter ces chaussures-ci. Elles sont très élégantes. (*you should*)

Using si clauses with the imparfait and result clauses with the conditional present

One of the most common uses of the present conditional is to express a result that is not guaranteed, because it is subject to certain conditions. In that case, it appears after a **si** (*if*) clause, which expresses the condition.

Look at the following sentences, and note that the verb in the **si** clause is in the **imparfait** tense and the verb in the result clause is in the present tense of the conditional mood:

Si j'avais le temps, **j'irais** au cinéma plus souvent.	*If I had the time, I would go to the movies more often.*
Si nous avions plus d'économies, nous **serions** plus à l'aise.	*If we had more savings, we would be more comfortable.*
Si vous gagniez la loterie, vous **auriez** de la chance.	*If you won the lottery, you would be lucky.*

In some cases, as in English, the condition for an opportunity to realize may be omitted and there is no **si** clause in the sentence.

Tu crois qu'il va faire beau? Ce **serait** bien!	*You think the weather will be good? That would be nice!*
Tu fais du saut à l'élastique? Moi, j'**aurais** une peur bleue.	*You go bungee jumping? I would be scared to death.*
Je ne sais pas où nous **irions** faire cela.	*I do not know where we would go to do this.*

Que d'hypothèses! *How many hypotheses! Finish each sentence with an appropriate hypothetical result. Write the letter of that result clause in the space provided.*

1. _____ Si j'étais un auteur célèbre,

2. _____ Si j'étais un oiseau tropical,

3. _____ Si personne ne m'aimait,

4. _____ S'il n'y avait pas de préjugés,

5. _____ S'il fallait renaître,

6. _____ Si je n'avais jamais faim,

7. _____ Si je buvais tout le temps du vin,

8. _____ Si j'habitais en France,

9. _____ Si j'avais des amis sénégalais,

10. _____ S'il y avait des habitants sur Mars,

a. je parlerais bien français.

b. je voudrais être artiste.

c. je serais alcoolique.

d. je serais plus mince.

e. je serais un perroquet.

f. il y aurait moins de conflits.

g. ce serait triste et déprimant.

h. je serais Shakespeare.

i. seraient-ils verts?

j. je visiterais l'Afrique.

Rêvons! *Let's dream! Write the following sentences in French using the **imparfait** and present conditional.*

1. If I lived near the beach, I would swim every day.

_____

2. If I had to live on an island, it would be Martinique.

_____

3. If I were an animal, I would be a dolphin.

_____

4. If I had to live with only one person, I would choose my best friend.

_____

5. If I could build a house, I would build a palace.

_____

6. If I bought a new car, I would buy a Tesla.

_____

Conditional sentences with the pluperfect and past conditional

This type of sentence helps hypothesize about the past. It includes an *if* clause introducing a condition that needed to be realized (the verb in this clause is in the pluperfect) and a result clause that would then have ensued in the past (the verb in this clause is in the past conditional).

Si l'avion était parti à l'heure, nous n'aurions pas raté notre correspondance.	*If the plane had left on time, we would not have missed our connection.*

Use and formation of the pluperfect

One of the uses of the pluperfect tense is to express that something **had already** happened prior to another past action. In the following sentence, note that while the action of going out (**sommes sortis**) is in the **passé composé**, the action of the rain stopping (**avait cessé**) preceded the action of going out and is therefore in the pluperfect:

Il **avait** déjà **cessé** de pleuvoir quand nous sommes sortis.	*It had already stopped raining when we went out.*

A common use of the pluperfect is in a **si** (*if*) clause to express the condition that had to be realized before a desired result could ensue.

J'aurais gardé ton secret **si tu m'avais demandé**.	*I would have kept your secret if you had asked me.*

The pluperfect is a compound tense similar to the **passé composé**. It is formed by using the appropriate auxiliary verb in the **imparfait** followed by the appropriate past participle (see Chapter 11). Examine the following conjugations of regular verbs in the pluperfect.

-er verbs	-ir verbs	-re verbs
. . . had eaten	*. . . had finished*	*. . . had lost*
j'avais mangé	j'avais fini	j'avais perdu
tu avais mangé	tu avais fini	tu avais perdu
il/elle/on avait mangé	il/elle/on avait fini	il/elle/on avait perdu
nous avions mangé	nous avions fini	nous avions perdu
vous aviez mangé	vous aviez fini	vous aviez perdu
ils/elles avaient mangé	ils/elles avaient fini	ils/elles avaient perdu

Now examine the following conjugations of irregular verbs in the pluperfect. Remember that the past participle of an **être** verb such **aller** (*to go*) agrees in gender and number with the subject of the verb.

aller	avoir	être
. . . had gone	*. . . had*	*. . . had been*
j'étais allé/allée	j'avais eu	j'avais été
tu étais allé/allée	tu avais eu	tu avais été
il/on était allé/elle était allée	il/elle/on avait eu	il/elle/on avait été
nous étions allés/allées	nous avions eu	nous avions été
vous étiez allé/allée/allés/allées	vous aviez eu	vous aviez été
ils étaient allés	ils/elles avaient eu	ils/elles avaient été
elles étaient allées		

EXERCICE 13·6

L'histoire des triplets. *The triplet story.* *Complete each sentence with the appropriate pluperfect form of the verb in parentheses.*

1. En septembre 2006 Serge _____ ses études. (commencer)

2. En décembre 2009 il _____ son diplôme. (recevoir)

3. En janvier 2010 il _____ en Afrique. (partir)

4. En juin 2011 il _____ aux États-Unis. (rentrer)

5. En juillet 2011 il _____ un emploi. (trouver)

6. En août 2011 il _____ (se marier).

7. En octobre 2011 sa femme _____ qu'ils allaient avoir un bébé. (annoncer)

8. Serge _____ des jumeaux. (vouloir)

Trois bébés sont nés au mois de mai!

Formation of the past conditional

The past tense of the conditional is used to express that something *would have* happened in the past under certain conditions. The past conditional is a compound tense formed by using the appropriate auxiliary verb in the present tense of the conditional followed by the appropriate past participle (see Chapter 11).

-er verbs	-ir verbs	-re verbs
. . . *would have noticed*	. . . *would have chosen*	. . . *would have sold*
j'aurais remarqué	j'aurais choisi	j'aurais vendu
tu aurais remarqué	tu aurais choisi	tu aurais vendu
il/elle/on aurait remarqué	il/elle/on aurait choisi	il/elle/on aurait vendu
nous aurions remarqué	nous aurions choisi	nous aurions vendu
vous auriez remarqué	vous auriez choisi	vous auriez vendu
ils/elles auraient remarqué	ils/elles auraient choisi	ils/elles auraient vendu

Now examine the following conjugations of irregular verbs in the past conditional. Remember that the past participle of an **être** verb such as **aller** (*to go*) agrees in gender and number with the subject of the verb.

aller	avoir	être
. . . *would have gone*	. . . *would have had*	. . . *would have been*
je serais allé/allée	j'aurais eu	j'aurais été
tu serais allé/allée	tu aurais eu	tu aurais été
il/on serait allé/elle serait allée	il/elle/on aurait eu	il/elle/on aurait été
nous serions allés/allées	nous aurions eu	nous aurions été
vous seriez allé/allée/allés/allées	vous auriez eu	vous auriez été
ils seraient allés/elles seraient allées	ils/elles auraient eu	ils/elles auraient été

EXERCICE
13·7

Suite de l'histoire des triplets. *The triplet story, continued. Complete each sentence with the appropriate past conditional form of the verb in parentheses.*

Si Serge et sa femme n'avaient pas eu de triplets...

1. They probably would have had twins. (**avoir des jumeaux**)

   _____

2. They would not have needed so many baby clothes. (**avoir besoin de vêtements de bébé**)

   _____

3. They would not have hired a nanny. (**engager une nounou**)

   _____

4. Serge would have gone back to work immediately. (**retourner au travail**)

   _____

5. They would not have received so many gifts. (**recevoir des cadeaux**)

   _____

6. They would have had less work. (**avoir moins de travail**)

   _____

7. They would have slept more. (**dormir davantage**)

   _____

8. They would not have been surprised. (**être surpris**)

   _____

Conditional sentences with pluperfect and past conditional

In this type of sentence, the **si** clause that introduces a condition that needed to be realized has a verb in the pluperfect; the clause that announces what could have happened as a result has a verb in the past conditional.

Si je n'**avais** pas **été** aussi pressée, je **n'aurais** pas **marché** dans la flaque.	*If I had not been in such a hurry, I would not have walked into the puddle.*
Si ma robe **avait été** sale, j'**aurais** sûrement **remarqué**.	*If my dress had been dirty, I would have surely noticed.*
Si le bus **était venu** tout de suite, je n'**aurais** pas **été** si mouillée.	*If the bus had come right away, I would not have been so wet.*
Si j'**avais su** que tu étais aussi en retard, je ne me **serais** pas **dépêchée**.	*If I had known that you were late too, I would not have hurried.*

Si Nathalie n'était pas partie... *If Nathalie had not left . . .* *Translate the following sentences into English.*

1. Si Nathalie n'était pas partie en France, elle n'aurait pas rencontré André.

   _____

2. Si elle n'avait pas rencontré André, elle ne serait pas restée en France.

   _____

3. Si elle n'était pas restée en France, elle ne se serait pas mariée.

   _____

4. Si elle ne s'était pas mariée, elle serait revenue aux États-Unis.

   _____

5. Si elle était revenue aux États-Unis, elle aurait travaillé avec son père.

   _____

6. Si elle avait travaillé avec son père, elle ne serait pas devenue aussi indépendante.

   _____

7. Si elle n'était pas devenue aussi indépendante, elle n'aurait pas pu devenir présidente-directrice-générale d'une grande société.

   _____

Object pronouns

Object pronouns are important because they allow you to efficiently refer to things or people previously mentioned without repeating nouns or noun phrases. In the following sentence, note how a considerable chunk of speech used in the question is replaced by the single pronoun **y** in the reply to the question:

Ils sont allés **à l'épicerie du coin**?
—Oui, ils **y** sont allés hier
après-midi.

*Did they go to the corner grocery
store? —Yes, they went there
yesterday afternoon.*

Review the various object pronouns in the following chart:

DIRECT/INDIRECT OBJECT PRONOUNS TO REPLACE PEOPLE ONLY		DIRECT OBJECT PRONOUNS TO REPLACE PEOPLE OR THINGS		INDIRECT OBJECT PRONOUNS TO REPLACE PEOPLE ONLY	
me (m')	*me/to me*	**le**	*him*	**lui**	*to him/to her*
te (t')	*you/to you (familiar)*	**la**	*her*	**leur**	*to them*
nous	*us/to us*	**l'**	*him/her (before vowel sound)*		
vous	*you/to you (formal-plural)*				
se (s')	*oneself/himself/ herself/themselves*	**les**	*them*		

Review the various object pronouns used to replace prepositional phrases except for à + person, in the following chart:

TO REPLACE **à** + THING OR PREPOSITIONAL PHRASE INDICATING LOCATION	TO REPLACE **de** + NOUN OR **de** + VERB
y (translations vary, but the pronoun can often mean *there* or *it*)	**en** (translations vary, but the pronoun can often mean *from there* or *from/of it*)

De grands concepts. *Big concepts.*

The first essential concept pertaining to object pronouns is that object pronouns receive the action of the verb directly (the noun or noun phrase receiving the action of the verb is not preceded by any preposition) or indirectly (the noun or noun phrase receiving the action of the verb represents one or several persons *and* is preceded by the preposition **à**).

In the following sentence, note that the noun replaced is **le panneau**. Because there is no preposition linking the verb **as vu** to the noun **le panneau**, the pronoun needed to replace **le panneau** is a *direct object pronoun*.

Tu as vu **le panneau**? —Oui, je l'ai vu.   *Did you see the sign? —Yes, I saw it.*

In the following sentence, note that the noun phrase replaced is **à ton copain**. Because the preposition **à** links the verb **as parlé** to the noun **copain**, the pronoun needed to replace **à ton copain** is an *indirect object pronoun*.

Tu as parlé **à ton copain**? —Oui,   *Did you speak to your friend? —Yes, I*
     je **lui** ai parlé ce matin.   *spoke to him this morning.*

Remember that an *indirect* object pronoun in the French language always replaces **à** + person(s). Look at the following examples of indirect object noun phrases:

à maman	*to Mom*
à cet ami	*to this friend*
à leurs parents	*to their parents*
au professeur	*to the teacher*
aux camarades de classe	*to the classmates*

The second essential concept pertaining to object pronouns is that direct object pronouns may replace persons, things, or phrases. One set of pronouns that may replace both people and things is the set of direct object pronouns: **le, la, l', les**. Look at the following questions and replies. All replies include the direct object pronoun **le** (or **l'** before a vowel sound).

Tu as vu **le panneau**? —Oui, je l'ai vu.   *Did you see the sign? —Yes, I saw it.*
Tu as vu **le panneau qui est à l'entrée de**   *Did you see the sign that is at the entrance of*
     la rue? —Oui, je l'ai vu.   *the street? —Yes, I saw it.*
Tu as vu **l'agent de police**? —Oui,   *Did you see the policeman? —Yes, I saw him.*
     je l'ai vu.

Position of object pronouns

Remember that the position of object pronouns in the French sentence is usually before the conjugated verb (before the conjugated auxiliary verb in compound tenses), unlike the position of the object pronoun after the verb in an English sentence. Compare the position of the object pronoun in the following French and English sentences:

Je **le** vois. *I see **him**.*   Je l'ai vu. *I saw **him**.*

In French sentences where two consecutive verbs have the same subject, the first verb is conjugated and the second verb is in the infinitive form. This syntactical format includes the near future. In that case, the object pronoun precedes the infinitive verb in the French sentence.

Le dernier film de Harry Potter? Elle   *The last Harry Potter movie? She would like*
     voudrait **le** voir. Nous, nous allons   *to see **it**. We are going to see **it** tonight.*
     le voir ce soir.

Tu vas faire ton projet? —Oui, je vais **le** faire tout de suite.	*Are you going to do your project? —Yes, I am going to do it right away.*

The only type of French sentence in which the object pronoun appears after the verb is an imperative affirmative structure.

Regarde-**le**!	*Watch him!*
Parle-**lui**!	*Speak to him!*

Beware that the object pronouns **me** and **te** become **moi** and **toi** in imperative affirmative structures.

Regarde-**moi**!	*Look at me!*
Retourne-**toi**!	*Turn (yourself) around!*

In negative sentences, the adverbs of negation (**ne... pas**, **ne... rien**, **ne... jamais**, etc.) "hug" the conjugated verb in simple tenses such as the present, the simple future, or the present conditional. They also "hug" the conjugated auxiliary verb in compound tenses such as the **passé composé**, pluperfect, or past conditional. But when an object pronoun appears, the position of the pronoun right before the conjugated verb overrides the position of **ne**. So **ne**, the primary adverb of negation, precedes the object pronoun that precedes the conjugated verb.

La chemise rouge? Je **ne la** veux **pas**.	*The red shirt? I do not want it.*
Du vin? Non, je **n'en** voulais **pas**.	*Wine? No, I did not want any.*
Ramona? Non, je **ne lui** ai **pas** encore téléphoné.	*Ramona? No, I have not called her yet.*
La France? Je **n'y** suis **jamais** allé.	*France? I never went there.*

In negative sentences with two consecutive verbs—this includes the near future—negative adverbs "hug" the conjugated verb. The pronoun precedes the infinitive verb.

Tu **ne** peux **pas nous** rendre visite aujourd'hui? Dommage!	*You cannot pay us a visit today? Too bad!*
La plage? Non, je **ne** vais **pas y** aller.	*The beach? No, I am not going to go there.*

Personal object pronouns **me, te, nous, vous,** and **se**

The pronouns **me/te/nous/vous/se** always replace people. They can be used as direct and indirect object pronouns. They are the indirect object when they are the object of a verb that is followed by the preposition **à** and a person. Here are some verbs followed by **à** + person:

apprendre à quelqu'un	*to teach to someone*	enseigner à quelqu'un	*to teach to someone*
conseiller à quelqu'un	*to advise someone*	parler à quelqu'un	*to speak to someone*
demander à quelqu'un	*to ask someone*	présenter à quelqu'un	*to present to someone*
dire à quelqu'un	*to tell (to) someone*	téléphoner à quelqu'un	*to call someone*
donner à quelqu'un	*to give to someone*		

In the following sentence, it is easy to identify the indirect object function of the pronoun **me** because it translates as *to me*:

Elle **me** parle.	*She talks to me.*

In the following sentence, even though the English translation of **me** is *for me*, it is important to understand that in the French sentence, the pronoun **me** is the direct object. Because in French, one says, **Je cherche Marie/Je cherche Paul/Je cherche mon amie**, one can conclude that the verb **chercher** is a transitive verb followed by a direct object.

Elle **me** cherche.	*She is looking for me.*

In the following sentence, even though the English translation of **me** is *me*, it is important to understand that in the French sentence, the pronoun **me** is the indirect object. Because in French, one says: **Je téléphone à Marie/Je téléphone à Paul/Je téléphone à mon amie**, one can infer that the verb **téléphoner** is followed by the preposition **à** + person (an indirect object).

Elle **me** téléphone.	*She calls me.*

Beware that the pronouns **me/te/nous/vous/se** are the same pronouns found in the conjugations of reflexive verbs. Review the present tense conjugation of the verb **s'appeler** (*to be called/named*) and of the verb **se dire** (*to tell oneself*). Look at the literal translation of each verbal form.

je m'appelle	*I call myself*
tu t'appelles	*you call yourself*
il/elle/on s'appelle	*he/she/one calls himself/herself/oneself*
nous nous appelons	*we call ourselves*
vous vous appelez	*you call yourselves*
ils/elles s'appellent	*they call themselves*

Once again, note **me/te/nous/vous/se** can be direct or indirect objects pronouns. They are direct objects in the conjugation of **s'appeler** because we say in French **appeler quelqu'un**. But they are indirect objects in the conjugation of the verb **se dire** because we say in French **dire à quelqu'un**.

je me dis	*I tell myself*
tu te dis	*you tell yourself*
il/elle/on se dit	*he/she/one tells himself/herself/oneself*
nous nous disons	*we tell ourselves*
vous vous dites	*you tell yourselves*
ils/elles se disent	*they tell themselves*

Les enfants **s'**amusent dehors.	*The children are having fun outside.*
Nous **nous** lavons chaque matin.	*We wash (ourselves) each morning.*
Tu **te** dépêcheras! D'accord?	*You will hurry! OK?*
Vous allez **vous** ennuyer.	*You are going to get bored.*
Ils **se** parlent souvent.	*They often talk to each other.*
Je **me** demande ce qu'ils disent.	*I ask myself (wonder) what they are saying.*

Note that the reflexive pronoun **se** is used in the following phrases where the subject is the impersonal pronoun **cela** (**ça** in its abbreviated form). In this case, **se** does not replace a person.

Cela (Ça) se voit.	*This is obvious.*
Cela (Ça) se comprend.	*This is understandable.*
Cela (Ça) ne se fait pas en France.	*This does not happen (is not done) in France.*

Remember that the pronoun follows the verb in the imperative affirmative syntactical structure and that the pronoun **te** becomes **toi** in that type of sentence.

Amuse-**toi**, Nicole!	*Have fun, Nicole!*
Dites-**vous** que c'est pour le mieux, mesdames!	*Tell yourselves that it's for the best, ladies!*
Arrêtons-**nous** ici!	*Let's stop here!*

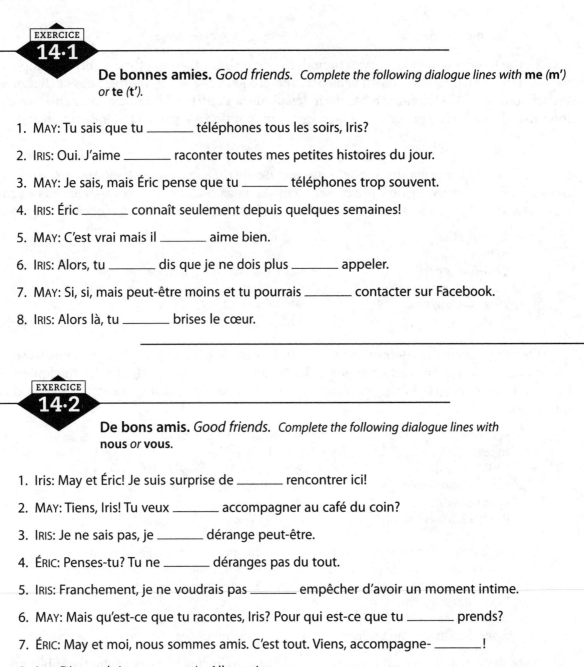

De bonnes amies. *Good friends.* *Complete the following dialogue lines with* **me (m')** *or* **te (t').**

1. MAY: Tu sais que tu _____ téléphones tous les soirs, Iris?

2. IRIS: Oui. J'aime _____ raconter toutes mes petites histoires du jour.

3. MAY: Je sais, mais Éric pense que tu _____ téléphones trop souvent.

4. IRIS: Éric _____ connaît seulement depuis quelques semaines!

5. MAY: C'est vrai mais il _____ aime bien.

6. IRIS: Alors, tu _____ dis que je ne dois plus _____ appeler.

7. MAY: Si, si, mais peut-être moins et tu pourrais _____ contacter sur Facebook.

8. IRIS: Alors là, tu _____ brises le cœur.

De bons amis. *Good friends.* *Complete the following dialogue lines with* **nous** *or* **vous.**

1. Iris: May et Éric! Je suis surprise de _____ rencontrer ici!

2. MAY: Tiens, Iris! Tu veux _____ accompagner au café du coin?

3. IRIS: Je ne sais pas, je _____ dérange peut-être.

4. ÉRIC: Penses-tu? Tu ne _____ déranges pas du tout.

5. IRIS: Franchement, je ne voudrais pas _____ empêcher d'avoir un moment intime.

6. MAY: Mais qu'est-ce que tu racontes, Iris? Pour qui est-ce que tu _____ prends?

7. ÉRIC: May et moi, nous sommes amis. C'est tout. Viens, accompagne- _____!

8. IRIS: D'accord. Je _____ suis. Allons-y!

Chez Éric. *At Éric's house.* *Write the following sentences in French. Take care to place the object pronouns appropriately and use the appropriate pronoun for you (familiar or plural).*

1. Mom, I present you my friends.

_____

2. (to Mom) Their names are Iris and May.

_____

3. (to Iris and May) I'm going to teach you to play the guitar.

_____

4. We are going to have fun.

_____

5. Mom will hear you; but do not worry!

_____

6. She is probably going to ask you to come back.

_____

7. I advise you to say yes.

_____

8. She will love you.

_____

Direct object pronouns le, la, l', and les

The pronouns **le**, **la**, **l'**, and **les** can replace people or things. They are used to replace direct object nouns or noun phrases. They can only replace a noun or noun phrase that does not include a preposition.

> Je dois nettoyer **le comptoir**? Bon, je **le** nettoie.
> Je dois nettoyer **la fenêtre**? Bon, je **la** nettoie.
> Je dois nettoyer **la table**? Non, je **l'**ignore.
> Je dois nettoyer **les verres**? Bon, je **les** nettoie.
> Est-ce que je vois **le cousin Henri**? Oui, je **le** vois.
> Est-ce que je vois **la cousine Henriette**? Non, je ne **la** vois pas.
> Est-ce que j'aime **la cousine Émilie**? Je ne **l'**aime pas.
> Est-ce que j'invite **les cousins Luc et Nicolas**? Oui, je **les** invite.

Note that in the following replies to questions, two object pronouns are used and that **me/te/nous/vous/se** precede the direct object pronouns **le/la/l'/les**.

> Tu crois que le prof va nous rendre nos examens? —Oui, je sais qu'il va **nous les** rendre.
>
> *Do you think that the teacher is going to return our exams to us? —Yes, I know that he is going to give them back to us.*
>
> Tu penses qu'il va te donner ta note? —Evidemment, il va **me la** donner.
>
> *Do you think he is going to give you your grade? —Of course, he is going to give it to me.*

Ma nouvelle voiture. *My new car. Complete the following dialogue lines with the appropriate object pronouns. Where two pronouns are required, remember to place* **me/te/ nous/vous** *before* **le/la/l'/les.**

1. PATRICE: Viens voir ma nouvelle voiture! Tu vas _____ adorer.

2. RÉMY: Oh! Quelle beauté! Je peux _____ conduire?

3. PATRICE: Je veux bien, mais attention. Si tu salis son bel extérieur, tu _____ nettoieras.

4. RÉMY: Ne t'inquiète pas, Patrice. Tes beaux sièges, je _____ nettoierai aussi volontiers.

5. PATRICE: Regarde tes jolies voisines là-bas. Je vais _____ inviter à faire un tour.

6. RÉMY: Laisse-moi faire ça. Je _____ connais bien.

7. PATRICE: Très bien. Tu _____ _____ présentes, alors?

8. RÉMY: Naturellement, je _____ _____ présenterai volontiers.

Indirect object pronouns lui and leur

The pronouns **lui** and **leur** can only replace a noun phrase consisting of **à** and a person (**lui**) or **à** and more than one person (**leur**).

Elle va rendre visite **à ses grands-parents**? —Oui, elle va **leur** rendre visite demain.	*Is she going to pay her grandparents a visit? —Yes, she is going to visit them tomorrow.*
Elle va apprendre **à Jeanine** à rouler en vélo? —Je crois qu'elle compte **lui** apprendre à faire du vélo bientôt.	*Is she going to teach Jeanine to ride the bike? —I think she intends to teach her to ride the bike soon.*
Elle a écrit **à son cousin** Jimmy? —Non, elle ne **lui** a pas encore écrit.	*Did she write her cousin Jimmy? —No, she did not write him yet.*
Elle rendra ce livre **au prof**? —Mais oui, elle **lui** rendra ce livre aujourd'hui.	*Will she return this book to the teacher? —Of course, she will return this book to him today.*

Note that in the following replies to questions, two object pronouns are used and that the direct object pronoun precedes the indirect object pronoun:

Tu crois que M. Cerise va expliquer **la leçon à Jojo**? —J'espère qu'il va **la lui** expliquer.	*Do you believe that Mr. Cerise is going to explain the lesson to Jojo? I hope that he is going to explain it to him.*
Il va demander **son argent aux parents de Jojo**? —Oui, il a dit qu'il allait **le leur** demander.	*Is he going to ask Jojo's parents for his money? Yes, he said that he is going to ask them for it.*

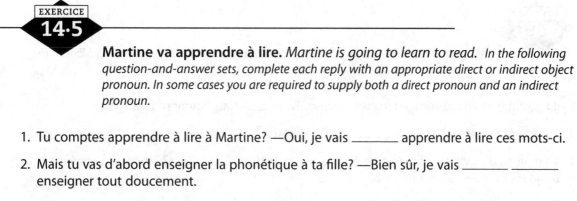

Martine va apprendre à lire. *Martine is going to learn to read.* *In the following question-and-answer sets, complete each reply with an appropriate direct or indirect object pronoun. In some cases you are required to supply both a direct pronoun and an indirect pronoun.*

1. Tu comptes apprendre à lire à Martine? —Oui, je vais _____ apprendre à lire ces mots-ci.

2. Mais tu vas d'abord enseigner la phonétique à ta fille? —Bien sûr, je vais _____ _____ enseigner tout doucement.

3. Et les plus petits? —Eh bien, je vais d'abord _____ apprendre à compter.

4. Est-ce qu'ils connaissent les nombres de 1 à 10? —Mais oui, ils _____ connaissent très bien.

5. Et les additions? —Ils savent _____ faire avec de petits nombres.

6. Tu pourrais leur donner ce livre. —Oui, tu as raison, je vais _____ _____ donner.

Object pronouns **y** and **en**

One use of the pronoun **y** is to replace a noun phrase including **à** and a thing.

Tu penses **aux devoirs de demain**? —Oui, c'est ça. J'**y** pense beaucoup.	*Do you think about tomorrow's homework? —Yes, I think about it a lot.*
Tu réponds souvent **aux questions du prof**? —Oui, j'**y** réponds tout le temps.	*Do you often answer the teacher's questions? —Yes, I answer them all the time.*

Another common use of the pronoun **y** is to replace a prepositional phrase indicating a location.

Tu vas **à la piscine**? —Non, je n'**y** vais pas aujourd'hui.	*Are you going to the pool? —No, I'm not going there today.*
La clé du bureau est **dans ton sac**? —Oui, elle **y** est.	*Is the office desk key in your purse? —Yes, it's there.*
Il est encore **en France**? —Oui, il **y** est toujours.	*Is he still in France? —Yes, he is still there.*

The object pronoun **en** is used to replace noun phrases or verbs that include the preposition **de** (*of, from*).

Tu as envie **d'une limonade**? —Non merci, je n'**en** ai pas envie.	*Do you want a lemonade? —No thanks, I do not want any.*
Tu reviens **du Canada**? —Oui, j'**en** suis revenue hier.	*Are you coming back from Canada? —Yes, I came back from there yesterday.*
Tu as envie **de manger du couscous**? —Oui, j'**en** ai vraiment envie.	*Do you feel like eating couscous? —Yes, I really feel like it.*

Note that, whereas **penser à** means to think about a thing or a person, **penser de** means to have an opinion of.

Qu'est-ce que tu **en** penses, de ce documentaire? —Il est très bien fait.	*What do you think of this documentary? —It is very well done.*

Des remarques et des conseils! *Comments and advice!* *Fill in each blank in the following sentences with the pronoun* **y** *or* **en**.

1. Il faut faire moins d'erreurs dans tes devoirs. Tu _____ fais vraiment beaucoup.

2. Tu dois faire des efforts. Tu n'_____ fais pas assez.

3. Tu reviens du gymnase? Qu'est-ce que tu fais quand tu _____ vas? Tu _____ reviens toujours fatigué.

4. Tu as envie d'un verre d'eau? Je t'_____ donne un.

5. Tu as envie de manger un sandwich? Ah non? Tu n'_____ as pas envie?

6. Tu ne sais pas la réponse à cette question? Ah! Je vois. Tu _____ penses.

7. Tu ne veux pas chercher la réponse dans ton livre? Elle _____ est certainement.

8. Où est la page des réponses? Ah! Tu vois! La réponse _____ est.

Bijou et Joujou. *Jewel and Toy.* *Complete the following paragraph with the appropriate object pronouns.*

J'ai deux chiens qui 1. _____ appellent Bijou et Joujou. Je 2. _____ adore. Leur jouet favori est une vieille balle rouge. Je 3. _____ lance la balle vingt ou trente fois par jour. Mes chiens ne 4. _____ fatiguent jamais. Ils courent et 5. _____ attrapent. Quelquefois la balle atterrit dans la rue. Alors je dois 6. _____ aller et 7. _____ ramasser. Il faudrait peut-être que j'achète une balle de plus. Nous 8. _____ avons besoin. Comme ça, je pourrais lancer deux balles, une pour Bijou et une pour Joujou. Je 9. _____ donne beaucoup d'exercice, n'est-ce pas? Qu' 10. _____ pensez-vous?

Past infinitive structures and agreement of past participles

·15·

The verbal structure that follows the preposition **après** when the subject of the verb in the **après** clause is the same as the subject of the main verb in the sentence is called the *past infinitive*. In the following example, the same subject (Alex) is the one who fed the dog and washed his hands.

Après avoir donné à manger au chien, Alex s'est lavé les mains.	*After feeding the dog, Alex washed his hands.*

Past infinitive structure of **avoir** verbs

Look at the following examples, and note that the past infinitive form of a verb is similar to the passé composé (see Chapter 11). However, the auxiliary verb is not conjugated.

Après avoir vu le film, nous avons eu une longue discussion.	*After watching the movie, we had a long discussion.*
Après avoir discuté les thèmes du film, nous avons écrit une dissertation.	*After discussing the themes of the movie, we wrote an essay.*
Après avoir relu ma composition, j'étais satisfait de mon travail.	*After rereading my composition, I was satisfied with my work.*

In the previous sentences, the verbs in the past infinitive form were **avoir** verbs, and the past participles in each verbal form remained in their original form regardless of the gender and number of the subject(s).

EXERCICE
15·1

Formons des passés de l'infinitif! *Let's form past infinitives! Write the phrases in parentheses in French. All verbs use the auxiliary* **avoir**.

1. (*after driving the car*—conduire la voiture)

_____

2. (*after seeing the accident*—voir l'accident)

_____

153

3. (*after calling the police*—appeler la police)

   _____

4. (*after describing the accident*—décrire l'accident)

   _____

5. (*after putting the car in the garage*—mettre la voiture au garage)

   _____

6. (*after telling the story*—raconter l'histoire)

   _____

Past infinitive structure of être verbs

Let's examine sentences in which the verbs in the past infinitive are **être** verbs. The past participle agrees in gender and number with the subject of the verb. Remember to add **-e** to the past participle to make it feminine, add **-s** to to make it plural, and add **-es** to make it feminine plural.

In the following example, **-es** is added to the past participle **sorti** to make it agree with the feminine plural subject **Danielle et Dara**:

Après être sorties de la salle de classe, Danielle et Dara ont échangé des idées.	*After leaving the classroom, Danielle and Dara exchanged ideas.*

In the following example, **-e** is added to the past participle **arrivé** to make it agree with the feminine singular subject **Dara**:

Après être arrivée chez elle, Dara s'est changée.	*After arriving home, Dara changed (clothes).*

In the following example, **-s** is added to the past participle **monté** to make it agree with the plural subjects **Alex et Dara**. The masculine form was used because among the subjects, there is at least one male.

Après être montés dans leurs chambres, Alex et Dara se sont préparés à aller dormir.	*After going up to their rooms, Alex and Dara prepared to go to sleep.*

In the following example, nothing is added to the past participle **allé** because the subject **Alex** is masculine singular.

Après être allé dire bonne nuit à ses parents, Alex s'est endormi.	*After saying good night to his parents, Alex fell asleep.*

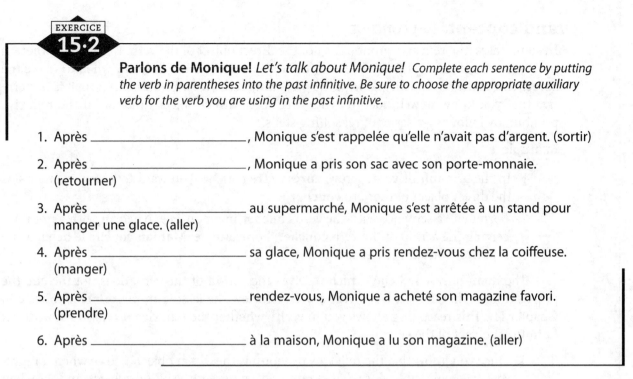

Parlons de Monique! *Let's talk about Monique!* *Complete each sentence by putting the verb in parentheses into the past infinitive. Be sure to choose the appropriate auxiliary verb for the verb you are using in the past infinitive.*

1. Après _____, Monique s'est rappelée qu'elle n'avait pas d'argent. (sortir)

2. Après _____, Monique a pris son sac avec son porte-monnaie. (retourner)

3. Après _____ au supermarché, Monique s'est arrêtée à un stand pour manger une glace. (aller)

4. Après _____ sa glace, Monique a pris rendez-vous chez la coiffeuse. (manger)

5. Après _____ rendez-vous, Monique a acheté son magazine favori. (prendre)

6. Après _____ à la maison, Monique a lu son magazine. (aller)

Past infinitive structure of reflexive verbs

Reflexive verbs use the auxiliary verb **être** in compound tenses and in the past infinitive form. However, the past participle of a reflexive verb agrees with the direct object of the verb when there is one placed before the verb. Often the reflexive pronoun is the direct object. Examine the following sentences. In each past infinitive form of the verb **se coucher** (*to go to bed*), the reflexive pronoun **s'** is the direct object of the verb **coucher** because it receives the action of the verb directly; in French, we say **coucher quelqu'un** for *to put someone to bed*.

When the reflexive pronoun represents Alex (male), nothing is added to the past participle **couché**.

> Après **s'**être couché, Alex a fait de beaux rêves.   *After going to bed, Alex had beautiful dreams.*

When the reflexive pronoun represents Dara (female), **-e** is added to the past participle **couché**.

> Après **s'**être couché**e**, Dara a fait de beaux rêves.   *After going to bed, Dara had beautiful dreams.*

When the reflexive pronoun represents Alex and Dara (a male and a female), **-s** is added to the past participle **couché**.

> Après **s'**être couché**s**, Alex et Dara ont fait de beaux rêves.   *After going to bed, Alex and Dara had beautiful dreams.*

When the reflexive pronoun represents Danielle and Dara (two females), **-es** is added to the past participle **couché**.

> Après **s'**être couché**es**, Danielle et Dara ont fait de beaux rêves.   *After going to bed, Danielle and Dara had beautiful dreams.*

Grand concept. *Big concept.*

In some cases, the reflexive pronoun is not the direct object of the verb. In that case, there is no agreement of the past participle with the reflexive pronoun. To know when to make the agreement of the past participle with the preceding reflexive pronoun of a verb, it is imperative that you know how to identify the direct or indirect object function of the reflexive pronoun by following a series of reasoning steps.

Example 1

1. In the past infinitive structure **après s'être couché**, you want to know whether **s'** is the direct object of the verb **coucher**.
2. Formulate a sentence with the verb **coucher** in a nonreflexive form with a noun receiving the action of the verb **coucher**. For example: **Maman couche le bébé.** *Mom is putting the baby to sleep.*

The noun phrase **le bébé**, which receives the action of the verb, does not include the preposition **à**. Therefore, it is a direct object. (Review the lesson on **me/te/nous/vous/se** in Chapter 14.) This reasoning allows you to verify whether the reflexive pronoun is the direct or indirect object of the verb.

3. Once you know that the reflexive pronoun is the direct object, add **-e** when it represents a female subject, **-s** when it represents a masculine plural subject, and **-es** when it represents a feminine plural subject.

Example 2

1. In the past infinitive structure, **Après s'être lavé les mains**, Dara... , you want to know whether **s'** is the direct object of the verb **laver**.
2. Ask yourself whether the subject washed herself (**s'**) *or* whether she washed her hands (**les mains**). Here **les mains** is the direct object that receives directly the action of the verb **laver** (**laver les mains**).

In the example **Après s'être lavé les mains**, Dara... , the reflexive pronoun **s'** has the function of indirect object because the subject washed her hands (direct object) *to herself* (**à quelqu'un** = indirect object).

3. Once you know that the reflexive pronoun is the indirect object, use the past participle in its original form without making it agree, regardless of the gender and number of the subject.

Après s'être **lavé** les mains, Dara...
Après s'être **lavé** les mains, Alex et Dara...
Après s'être **lavé** les mains, Dara et Danielle...

Example 3

1. In the past infinitive structure, **après s'être dit bonne nuit**, Alex et Dara... (*after saying good night to each other, Alex and Dara . . .*), you want to know whether **s'** (*to each other*) is the direct object of the verb **dire**.
2. Formulate a sentence using the verb **dire** followed by actual names of people. For example, **Alex dit bonne nuit à Dara.** *Alex says good night to Dara.* You realize that the pronoun **se** replacing **à Dara** or **à Alex** is an indirect object (**à** + person).
3. Once you know that the reflexive pronoun is the indirect object, use the past participle **dit** in its original form without making it agree, regardless of the gender and number of the subject.

Toujours après! *Always afterward!* *Using the reflexive verb in parentheses, translate each past infinitive phrase into French.*

1. After hurrying up, Michelle . . . (**se dépêcher**)

   _____

2. After getting angry, Michelle and Geneviève . . . (**se fâcher**)

   _____

3. After getting up, John . . . (**se lever**)

   _____

4. After bathing, the boys . . . (**se baigner**)

   _____

5. After washing their hands, the girls . . . (**se laver**)

   _____

6. After falling asleep, Mike and Lili . . . (**s'endormir**)

   _____

La routine de Mélanie. *Mélanie's routine.* *Complete each sentence by putting the verb in parentheses into the past infinitive. Be sure to choose the appropriate auxiliary verb for the verb you are using in the past infinitive.*

1. Après _____, Mélanie a pris une douche. (se lever)

2. Après _____, Mélanie est partie au travail. (se maquiller)

3. Après _____ au travail, Mélanie s'est fait un café. (arriver)

4. Après _____ un café, Mélanie a regardé son emploi du temps. (se faire)

5. Après _____ une idée du travail qu'elle doit faire, Mélanie a écrit son premier mémo. (se faire)

6. Après _____ de faire ce premier mémo, Mélanie a commencé à écrire un article. (se dépêcher)

7. Après _____ son article, Mélanie est allée aux toilettes. (finir)

8. Après _____ les mains et la figure, Mélanie est retournée au travail. (se laver)

Agreement of past participles in compound tenses

Review the following chart that summarizes the rules of agreement of past participles. These rules govern the past participle in past infinitive forms as well as the past participle in compound tenses such as the **passé composé**, the pluperfect, and the past conditional.

être VERBS	REFLEXIVE (être) VERBS	avoir VERBS
The past participle agrees with the subject of the verb.	The past participle agrees with the preceding direct object in the sentence (often the reflexive pronoun).	The past participle agrees with the preceding direct object when there is one.
Elle est sorti**e**. *She went out.*	**Elle** s'est fâché**e**. *She became angry.*	Je **l'**ai compris**e** (la leçon). *I understood it (the lesson).*
Ils sont sorti**s**. *They went out.*	**Ils** se sont fâché**s**. *They became angry.*	Je **les** ai vu**s** (les garçons). *I saw them (the boys).*
Elles sont sorti**es**. *They went out.*	**Elles** se sont fâché**es**. *They became angry.*	Je **les** ai appelé**es** (les filles). *I called them (the girls).*

You have already learned to make past participles agree with the subject of an **être** verb such as **aller** (*to go*) and **sortir** (*to go out*) in Chapter 11. In this chapter, you have learned to make past participles of reflexive verbs such as **se coucher** or **se fâcher** agree with the reflexive pronouns **me/te/nous/vous** when these are direct objects of the verb in past infinitive structures. The same concept applies to past participles in compound tenses.

In the following sentence, the past participle **fâchée** agrees with the preceding direct object, which is the reflexive pronoun **s'** representing **elle**:

Elle s'est fâché**e**.	*She got angry.*
Elle s'était fâché**e**.	*She had gotten angry.*
Elle se serait fâché**e**.	*She would have gotten angry.*

In the following sentence, the past participle **fâchés** agrees with the preceding direct object, which is the reflexive pronoun **s'** representing **ils**:

Ils se sont fâché**s**.	*They (m.) became angry.*
Ils s'étaient fâché**s**.	*They (m.) had become angry.*
Ils se seraient fâché**s**.	*They (m.) would have become angry.*

In the following sentence, the past participle **fâchées** agrees with the preceding direct object, which is the reflexive pronoun **s'** representing **elles**:

Elles se sont fâché**es**.	*They (f.) became angry.*
Elles s'étaient fâché**es**.	*They (f.) had become angry.*
Elles se seraient fâché**es**.	*They (f.) would have become angry.*

Beware of the following type of sentence in which the reflexive pronoun is not the direct object and the past participle does not agree with it. In the first sentence, **la main** receives the action of the verb directly and is the direct object of the verb. The reflexive pronoun is an indirect object (it answers the question *to whom*). In the second sentence, **la bise** receives the action of the verb directly and is the direct object of the verb. The reflexive pronoun is an indirect object (it answers the question *to whom*).

| Les deux hommes se sont **serré** la main. | *The two men shook hands.* |
| Les femmes se sont **fait** la bise sur la joue. | *The women kissed each other on the cheek.* |

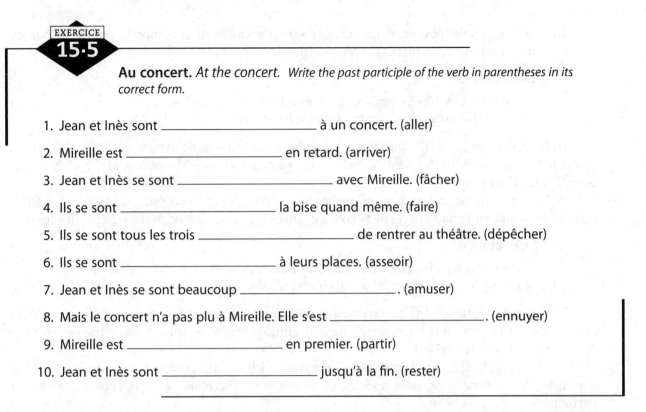

EXERCICE 15·5

Au concert. *At the concert.* *Write the past participle of the verb in parentheses in its correct form.*

1. Jean et Inès sont _____ à un concert. (aller)

2. Mireille est _____ en retard. (arriver)

3. Jean et Inès se sont _____ avec Mireille. (fâcher)

4. Ils se sont _____ la bise quand même. (faire)

5. Ils se sont tous les trois _____ de rentrer au théâtre. (dépêcher)

6. Ils se sont _____ à leurs places. (asseoir)

7. Jean et Inès se sont beaucoup _____. (amuser)

8. Mais le concert n'a pas plu à Mireille. Elle s'est _____. (ennuyer)

9. Mireille est _____ en premier. (partir)

10. Jean et Inès sont _____ jusqu'à la fin. (rester)

Agreement of the past participle with direct object pronouns le, la, l', and les

Now you will learn to make past participles of **avoir** verbs agree with the pronouns **le, la, l',** and **les**, which are by definition direct object pronouns, as well as with the pronouns **me/te/nous/ vous**, but only when they are direct objects of the verb.

When verbs are conjugated in a compound tense with the auxiliary verb **avoir**, you will make the past participle agree with the pronouns **le, la, l',** and **les** because they are direct objects of the verb preceding the verb.

Read and analyze the following series of mini-dialogues between Marc and Nathalie. Note that all verbs are in the **passé composé**.

DIALOGUE 1

NATHALIE: Dis, Marc, où est-ce que tu **as posé** le sac de provisions?

MARC: Je l'**ai posé** sur la table de la cuisine.

In Nathalie's sentence, the past participle **posé** remains unchanged because there is no direct object **before** the verb. In this sentence, the noun phrase receiving the action of the verb (direct object) is **le sac de provisions**.

In Marc's reply, the past participle **posé** agrees with the direct object pronoun **l'**, which is masculine singular because it replaces **le sac de provisions**. Therefore, its spelling remains unchanged.

DIALOGUE 2

NATHALIE: Dis, Marc, où est-ce que tu **as rangé** les fruits?

MARC: Je les **ai rangés** dans le frigo.

In Nathalie's sentence, the past participle **rangé** remains unchanged because there is no direct object **before** the verb. In this sentence, the noun phrase receiving the action of the verb (direct object) is **les fruits**.

Past infinitive structures and agreement of past participles   **159**

In Marc's reply, the past participle **rangés** agrees with the direct object pronoun **les**, which is masculine plural since it replaces **les fruits**. Therefore -**s** was added to the past participle.

DIALOGUE 3

NATHALIE: Dis, Marc, où est-ce que tu **as mis** la clé de la voiture?
MARC: Je l'**ai mise** sur le bureau comme d'habitude.

In Nathalie's sentence, the past participle **mis** remains unchanged because there is no direct object **before** the verb. In this sentence, the noun phrase receiving the action of the verb (direct object) is **la clé de la voiture**.

In Marc's reply, the past participle **mise** agrees with the direct object pronoun **la**, which is feminine singular since it replaces **la clé de la voiture**. Therefore -**e** was added to the past participle.

DIALOGUE 4

NATHALIE: Dis, Marc, où est-ce que tu **as mis** les clés de la maison?
MARC: Je les **ai mises** sur le bureau comme d'habitude.

In Nathalie's sentence, the past participle **mis** remains unchanged because there is no direct object **before** the verb. In this sentence, the noun phrase receiving the action of the verb (direct object) is **les clés de la maison**.

In Marc's reply, the past participle **mises** agrees with the direct object pronoun **les**, which is feminine plural since it replaces **les clés de la maison**. Therefore -**es** was added to the past participle.

EXERCICE 15·6

De retour de vacances. *Back from vacation.* *Write the past participle of the verb in parentheses in its correct form in each dialogue line.*

1. ÉRIC: Jasmine, où as-tu _____ le sac bleu? (mettre)

2. JASMINE: Je crois que je l'ai _____ au bas de l'escalier. (voir)

3. ÉRIC: Et où sont les deux valises? Je les avais _____ devant la porte. (poser)

4. JASMINE: Je les ai déjà _____ dans notre chambre. (monter)

5. ÉRIC: Franchement, tu es courageuse! Moi, j'aurais _____. (attendre)

6. JASMINE: J'étais pressée. Mais je n'ai pas encore _____ nos nouvelles cartes d'identité. (retrouver)

7. ÉRIC: Quoi! Tu les as toujours _____ dans ton sac à dos. (remettre)

8. JASMINE: Je sais bien! Ah! Les voilà! J'ai _____ peur! (avoir)

9. ÉRIC: Moi aussi. Tu te rappelles que j'avais _____ mon passeport une fois? (perdre)

10. JASMINE: Oui, tu l'avais si bien _____ que tu ne savais plus où. (ranger)

11. ÉRIC: Et ma carte de crédit! Je l'ai bien _____ dans mon portefeuille tout à l'heure. (voir)

12. JASMINE: Je l'ai _____ aussi, ta carte. Mais vérifie quand même! (voir)

Agreement of the past participle with direct object pronouns me/te/nous/vous

When verbs are conjugated in a compound tense with the auxiliary verb **avoir**, you will make the past participle agree with the pronouns **me**, **te**, **nous**, and **vous**, which necessarily appear before the verb but only when they are direct objects of the verb.

Read and analyze the following series of mini-dialogues between Marc and Nathalie. Note that all the verbs are in the **passé composé**.

DIALOGUE 1

NATHALIE: Dis, Marc, tu m'**as entendue**?
MARC: Non, pas du tout. Tu m'**as dit** quelque chose?

In Nathalie's sentence, the past participle **entendue** agrees with the pronoun **me**, which is feminine because it represents Nathalie. In this sentence, the pronoun **me** receives the action of the verb directly (direct object) because in French, the verb **entendre** is followed directly by the name or definition of the person (**entendre quelqu'un**).

In Marc's reply, the past participle **dit** does not agree with the direct object pronoun **m'**. The pronoun is an indirect object in this case because in French, the verb **dire** requires the preposition **à** before the name or definition of the person (**dire à quelqu'un**). Therefore, its spelling remains unchanged.

DIALOGUE 2

NATHALIE: Dis, Marc, tu m'**as écoutée**?
MARC: Mais oui, je t'**ai** bien **entendue**.

In Nathalie's sentence, the past participle **écoutée** agrees with the pronoun **m'**, which is feminine (it represents Nathalie). In this sentence, the pronoun **m'** receives the action of the verb directly (direct object) because in French, the verb **écouter** is followed directly by the name or definition of the person (**écouter quelqu'un**). Therefore, -**e** was added to the past participle **écouté**.

In Marc's reply, the past participle **entendue** agrees with the direct object pronoun **t'** (representing Nathalie). The pronoun is a direct object in this case because in French, the verb **entendre** is followed directly by the name or definition of the person (**entendre quelqu'un**). Therefore, -**e** was added to the past participle **entendu**.

DIALOGUE 3

NATHALIE: Dis, Marc, tes parents nous **ont invités**?
MARC: Mais oui, ils nous **ont invités** pour ce soir.

In Nathalie's and in Marc's sentences, the past participle **invités** agrees with the pronoun **nous**, which is masculine plural (it represents Nathalie and Marc). In this sentence, the pronoun **nous** receives the action of the verb directly (direct object) because in French, the verb **inviter** is followed directly by the name or definition of the person (**inviter quelqu'un**). Therefore, -**s** was added to the past participle **invité**.

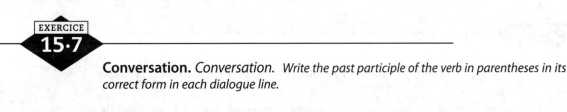

EXERCICE
15·7

Conversation. *Conversation. Write the past participle of the verb in parentheses in its correct form in each dialogue line.*

1. LISE: Tu m'as _____ ce joli bracelet, Yves! Que c'est gentil! (offrir)

2. YVES: Bien sûr! C'est la Saint Valentin aujourd'hui! Et toi, tu m'as _____ quelque chose? (acheter)

3. LISE: Je t'ai _____ ce beau dîner aux chandelles. Regarde! (préparer)

4. YVES: Mais, dis donc, est-ce que Bob et Marie ne nous ont pas _____? (inviter)

5. LISE: Si, ils nous ont _____ une invitation, mais pas pour aujourd'hui. (envoyer)

6. YVES: Tu ne m'avais pas _____ que c'était pour ce soir. (dire)

7. LISE: Écoute, Yves! Je t'ai simplement _____ de rentrer tôt ce soir. (demander)

8. YVES: Bon. Tant mieux. Je t'ai mal _____. C'est tout! (comprendre)

9. LISE: Aucun problème! Tu m'as _____ la bouteille de vin? (apporter)

10. YVES: Zut! Je ne t'ai pas _____ pour ça non plus! (entendre)

Agreement of past participles for verbs conjugated with either avoir or être

The following verbs are conjugated in the **passé composé** with the auxiliary verb **être** *only* when they do *not* have a direct object. The past participle agrees with the subject of the verb.

monter:	**Liliane** est montée en haut.	*Liliane went upstairs.*
descendre:	**Jeanine** est descendue en bas.	*Jeanine went downstairs.*
rentrer:	**Sophie** est rentrée.	*Sophie went home.*
sortir:	**Irène** est sortie.	*Irène went out.*
passer:	**Pascale** est passée.	*Pascale came by.*

The same verbs are conjugated with the auxiliary verb **avoir** when they have a direct object. Notice how the meaning of the verb changes when it has a direct object. The past participle agrees with the preceding direct object when there is one.

monter:	La valise? Marc l'a montée en haut.	*The suitcase? Marc took it upstairs.*
descendre:	La valise? Marc l'a descendue en bas.	*The suitcase? Marc took it downstairs.*
rentrer:	La voiture? Marc l'a rentrée.	*The car? Marc took it in.*
sortir:	La poubelle? Marc l'a sortie.	*The garbage? Marc took it out.*
passer:	L'épreuve? Marc l'a passée.	*The test? Marc took it.*

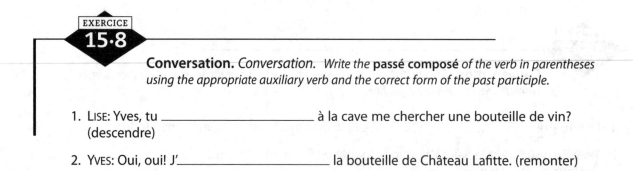

EXERCICE
15·8

Conversation. *Conversation. Write the* **passé composé** *of the verb in parentheses using the appropriate auxiliary verb and the correct form of the past participle.*

1. LISE: Yves, tu _____ à la cave me chercher une bouteille de vin? (descendre)

2. YVES: Oui, oui! J'_____ la bouteille de Château Lafitte. (remonter)

3. LISE: Tu l'_____? Très bien. (trouver)

4. YVES: Là où je l'_____ l'an dernier. (mettre)

5. LISE: Tu sais, Maryse _____ me voir ce matin. (passer)

6. YVES: Elle va bien? Elle _____ finalement _____ du Canada? (rentrer)

7. LISE: Oui, et elle _____ son examen de maîtrise. (passer)

8. YVES: Est-ce qu'elle a ses résultats? Elle _____? (réussir)

9. LISE: Elle ne sait pas encore, Yves! Elle n'_____ que quinze minutes. (rester)

10. YVES: Dommage. Ça fait longtemps que je ne l'_____. (ne pas voir)

VOCABULAIRE UTILE. *Useful vocabulary.*

Review this list of vocabulary before doing the next exercise.

la bêtise	*silliness*	crever	*to burst*
la grenouille	*frog*	respirer	*to breathe*
le ballon	*balloon*	retenir	*to hold back*
le bœuf	*ox*	s'enfler	*to swell up*
le souffle	*breath*		

EXERCICE 15·9

La grenouille qui voulait se faire aussi grosse que le bœuf. *The frog who wanted to be as big as the ox.* *Complete this version of the fable by writing either the* **passé composé** *or the past infinitive form of the verb in parentheses as appropriate.*

Un jour une grenouille 1. _____ (voir) un bœuf qui lui paraissait très

beau. Elle 2. _____ (se dire) qu'elle voudrait être grosse, elle aussi. Alors elle

3. _____ (respirer) et 4. _____ (retenir) son souffle

pendant très longtemps. Après l' 5. _____ (observer) pendant un certain

temps, le bœuf lui 6. _____ (dire) d'arrêter ces bêtises. «Tu ne seras jamais

aussi grosse que moi, petite grenouille. Tu 7. _____ (naître) petite. C'est ta

nature.» Mais la petite grenouille, obstinée, lui 8. _____ (répondre) qu'elle

ferait tout pour être aussi grosse que lui. Et elle 9. _____ (continuer) de

retenir son souffle. Malheureusement, après 10. _____ (s'enfler) comme un

ballon, la petite grenouille 11. _____ (crever) et elle

12. _____ (mourir). Que c'est triste!

Demonstrative, interrogative, and possessive pronouns

As previously seen, pronouns are used to allow for more efficient and less redundant communication. As speakers of a language become fluent, they increasingly rely on pronouns. Demonstrative pronouns are used to point something out that has been previously mentioned. Interrogative pronouns are used to ask questions about something previously mentioned.

Demonstrative pronouns

These pronouns are used to say *this/that one* and *these/those ones*. They reflect the gender (*m./f.*) and number (*sing./pl.*) of the noun they replace. Therefore, there are four forms of this pronoun:

MASCULINE SINGULAR	MASCULINE PLURAL	FEMININE SINGULAR	FEMININE PLURAL
celui	ceux	celle	celles
this/that one	*these/those*	*this/that one*	*these/those*

Quel essai est-ce que tu préfères? **Celui** de Simon ou **celui** d'Adeline?	*Which essay do you prefer? Simon's or Adeline's?*

Demonstrative pronouns are not used alone. They are followed:

- By **-ci** or **-là** to distinguish *this* one from *that* one

  Quel dessert veux-tu? **Celui-ci** ou **celui-là**?
  *What dessert do you want? Do you want **this one** or **that one**?*

- By a complement introduced by a preposition such as **de** (indicating possession or origin) or **en** (indicating the material or make)

Toutes ces voitures sont belles, mais **celle de** Jean-Jacques est ma favorite.	*All these cars are beautiful, but Jean-Jacques's is my favorite.*
Des accents que tu connais, tu aimes mieux **celui du** français ou **celui du** québécois?	*Of the accents that you know, do you prefer the French or Québécois?*
Il y a deux pantalons qui me plaisent, **celui en** laine et **celui en** lin.	*There are two pairs of pants that I like, the ones out of wool and the ones out of linen.*

◆ By a relative clause

Des deux pantalons, j'aime mieux **celui** qui coûte le plus cher.

*Of the two pairs of pants, I prefer **the ones** that cost the most.*

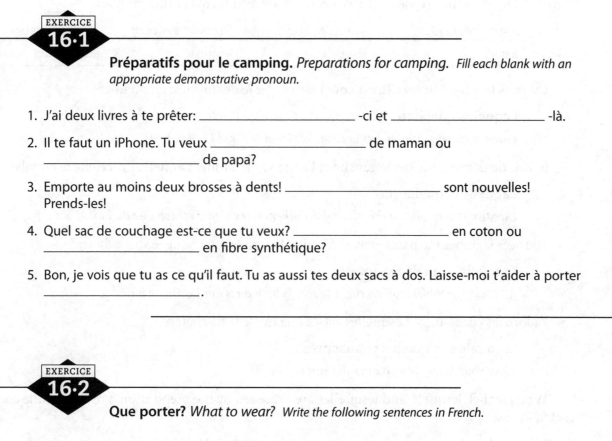

EXERCICE
16·1

Préparatifs pour le camping. *Preparations for camping. Fill each blank with an appropriate demonstrative pronoun.*

1. J'ai deux livres à te prêter: _____ -ci et _____ -là.

2. Il te faut un iPhone. Tu veux _____ de maman ou _____ de papa?

3. Emporte au moins deux brosses à dents! _____ sont nouvelles! Prends-les!

4. Quel sac de couchage est-ce que tu veux? _____ en coton ou _____ en fibre synthétique?

5. Bon, je vois que tu as ce qu'il faut. Tu as aussi tes deux sacs à dos. Laisse-moi t'aider à porter _____ .

EXERCICE
16·2

Que porter? *What to wear? Write the following sentences in French.*

1. I have a red T-shirt and a blue T-shirt. I think I'm going to wear this one.

   _____

2. Of all my shorts, I prefer that one.

   _____

3. Sometimes my sister lends me one of her dresses. Today I would like the cotton one.

   _____

4. Sometimes my mom offers to lend me one of her elegant dresses. But I prefer my sister's ones.

   _____

5. These brooches (**la broche**) are beautiful. Let (*familiar*) me try on this one and that one!

   _____

Demonstrative, interrogative, and possessive pronouns **165**

Interrogative pronouns lequel, laquelle, lesquels, and lesquelles

These pronouns are used to ask *which one(s)*. They reflect the gender (*m./f.*) and number (*singular/plural*) of the noun they replace. Therefore, there are four forms of this pronoun:

MASCULINE SINGULAR	MASCULINE PLURAL	FEMININE SINGULAR	FEMININE PLURAL
lequel	lesquels	laquelle	lesquelles

J'ai trois très bons livres à lire. **Lequel** est-ce que je devrais lire en premier?

Lequel = quel livre

*I have three very good books to read. **Which one** should I read first?*

Je vois deux rues, une sur la gauche et l'autre sur la droite. **Laquelle** est-ce que je prends?

Laquelle = quelle rue

*I see two streets, one on the left and the other on the right. **Which one** do I take?*

Tous ces légumes me paraissent excellents. **Lesquels** est-ce que je vais acheter?

Lesquels = quels légumes

*All these vegetables look excellent to me. **Which ones** am I going to buy?*

J'adore tes chaussures. **Lesquelles** est-ce que tu viens d'acheter?

Lesquelles = quelles chaussures

*I love your shoes. **Which ones** did you just buy?*

When **lequel**, **lesquels**, and **lesquelles** are preceded by the preposition **à** or **de**, use the contracted forms:

à + lequel = auquel	de + lequel = duquel
à + lesquels = auxquels	de + lesquels = desquels
à + lesquelles = auxquelles	de + lesquelles = desquelles

Il y a deux guichets de vente ici. **Auquel** est-ce qu'il faut aller?

auquel = à + lequel

*There are two sales booths here. **To which one** do I have to go?*

Je vois une dizaine de plages sur la carte. **Auxquelles** est-ce qu'on va aller?

auxquelles = à + lesquelles

*I see about ten beaches on the map. **To which ones** are we going to go?*

On parle de deux films dans cet article. **Duquel** est-ce que tu parlais?
*They speak about two movies in this article. **Which one** were you talking **about**?*

De tous ces animaux sauvages, **desquels** as-tu le plus peur?
Of all these wild animals, of which ones are you the most afraid?

VOCABULAIRE UTILE. *Useful vocabulary.*

Review this list of vocabulary before doing the next exercises.

l'argent (*m.*)	*silver*	le bracelet	*bracelet*
l'or (*m.*)	*gold*	le collier	*necklace*
la bague	*ring*	le diamant	*diamond*
la boucle d'oreille	*earring*	le médaillon	*locket*
la montre	*watch*		

EXERCICE
16·3

À la recherche d'un bijou. *Looking for jewelry. Fill in each blank with an appropriate form of **lequel**. The form of the verb will help you determine whether you need a singular or plural form of **lequel**.*

1. Voilà deux beaux colliers. _____ te plaît le mieux?

2. Voilà deux belles paires de boucles d'oreille. _____ te plaisent le mieux?

3. Regarde ces bagues en argent! _____ te plaisent le mieux?

4. Il y a aussi de beaux médaillons en or dans cette vitrine. _____ te plaît?

5. Cette montre en diamants est magnifique. Et l'autre aussi. _____ te plaît?

6. Il y a aussi ces beaux bracelets en or et en argent. _____ te plaît?

EXERCICE
16·4

Indécise. *Undecided. Write the following sentences in French using the appropriate demonstrative and interrogative pronouns. Practice using the verb **plaire** for to like.*

1. I like both necklaces. I do not know which one I like best.

   _____

2. I adore these two bracelets. I think I prefer the one out of gold.

   _____

3. These watches are magnificent. Which one do I prefer?

   _____

4. Look at these lockets. Which one do you like best, Jennie?

   _____

5. I like these three pairs of earrings. Which ones should I buy? These or those?

   _____

Possessive pronouns

These pronouns are used to express *mine, yours, his, hers, ours,* and *theirs.* The possessive pronoun reflects the gender (*masculine/feminine*) and number (*singular/plural*) of the noun it replaces—that is, *the object possessed, never the possessor.* Since the object can be masculine singular, masculine plural, feminine singular, or feminine plural, there are four forms for the pronoun *mine:*

MASCULINE SINGULAR	**Le** sac à dos? C'est **le mien.**		*The backpack? It is mine.*
MASCULINE PLURAL	**Les** draps? Ce sont **les miens.**		*The sheets? They are mine.*
FEMININE SINGULAR	**La** couverture? C'est **la mienne.**		*The blanket? It is mine.*
FEMININE PLURAL	**Les** serviettes? Ce sont **les miennes.**		*The towels? They are mine.*

	MASCULINE SINGULAR	MASCULINE PLURAL	FEMININE SINGULAR	FEMININE PLURAL
mine	le mien	les miens	la mienne	les miennes
yours	le tien	les tiens	la tienne	les tiennes
his/hers	les sien	les siens	la sienne	les siennes
ours	le nôtre	les nôtres	la nôtre	les nôtres
yours	le vôtre	les vôtres	la vôtre	les vôtres
theirs	le leur	les leurs	la leur	les leurs

Note that the French possessive pronoun is always preceded by an article (**le, la, les**), and if the preposition **à** or **de** precedes the article **le** or **les**, the contracted articles **au** and **aux** must be used.

Tu tiens **à** tes articles de toilette. Et moi, je tiens **aux miens.**

(aux miens = à les miens)

You value your toiletries. And I value **mine.**

Tu prends soin de tes affaires et moi, je prends soin des miennes.

(des miennes = de les miennes)

You take care of your things, and I take care of mine.

VOCABULAIRE UTILE. *Useful vocabulary.*

Review this list of vocabulary before doing the next exercises.

l'assiette (*f.*)	*plate*	la tente	*tent*
l'oreiller (*m.*)	*pillow*	le drap	*sheet*
la brosse à dents	*toothbrush*	le réveil	*alarm clock*
la serviette	*towel*	le tennis	*tennis shoe/sneaker*

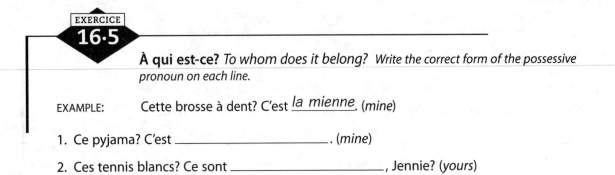

EXERCICE
16·5

À qui est-ce? *To whom does it belong? Write the correct form of the possessive pronoun on each line.*

EXAMPLE: Cette brosse à dent? C'est <u>*la mienne*</u>. (*mine*)

1. Ce pyjama? C'est _____. (*mine*)

2. Ces tennis blancs? Ce sont _____, Jennie? (*yours*)

3. Ces serviettes? Ce sont _____, à Jennie et à moi. (*ours*)

4. Ce drap? C'est _____. (*hers*)

5. Cette tente? C'est _____. (*hers*)

6. Ces assiettes blanches en plastique? Ce sont _____, Suzie et Marie? (*yours*)

7. Ces oreillers? Ce sont _____. (*theirs*)

8. Et ce réveil? C'est _____. (*theirs*)

Boucle d'or et les trois ours. *Goldilocks and the three bears. Write the correct form of the demonstrative, interrogative, or possessive pronoun in the blank spaces.*

Il y avait une fois une petite fille aux cheveux blonds et bouclés.

1. _____ s'appelait Boucle d'or. Un jour, alors qu'elle se promenait dans la forêt, elle est entrée dans la petite maison des trois ours (petit, moyen et grand). Ils étaient sortis. Boucle d'or a trouvé trois jolis bols de soupe sur la table. 2. _____ est-ce qu'elle devait boire? Elle a choisi 3. _____ du petit ours. Puis, elle a vu trois jolies chaises. 4. _____ est-ce qu'elle devait choisir pour s'asseoir? Elle a choisi 5. _____ du petit ours. Mais quand elle s'est assise, la chaise s'est cassée! Ensuite, Boucle d'or a monté l'escalier et dans la chambre à coucher, elle a trouvé trois jolis lits. 6. _____ est-ce qu'elle devait choisir pour se reposer? Elle a choisi 7. _____ du petit ours et elle s'est endormie dans ce lit.

À ce moment, les trois ours avaient fini leur promenade et sont rentrés chez eux. Ils ont vu que quelqu'un avait touché aux délicieuses soupes. Le petit ours a crié: « Où est 8. _____? » Puis, ils ont vu que quelqu'un avait déplacé les jolies chaises. Le petit ours a crié: « 9. _____ est cassée! » Alors, ils sont montés dans leur chambre à coucher et ils ont vu Boucle d'or couchée sur le lit du petit ours. Le grand ours et le moyen ours ont dit: « Cette fille est couchée sur un de nos lits! » Le petit ours a crié: « Oui, elle est naturellement sur 10. _____. » Boucle d'or s'est réveillée brusquement et a sauté par la fenêtre. Elle n'est jamais revenue parce qu'elle a eu si peur!

The subjunctive mood

In contrast with the indicative mood, which includes many tenses (present, past, and future), the subjunctive mood includes only two tenses that are used in real-life situations: present and past. In contrast also with the indicative mood, which indicates facts or certainty, the subjunctive mood indicates subjectivity and uncertainty. There are many opportunities to use the subjunctive mood in the French language.

Formation of present subjunctive

The present subjunctive is formed by adding -**e**, -**es**, -**e**, -**ions**, -**iez**, and -**ent** to the stem of the verb. The stem is obtained by dropping the -**ent** ending of the third-person plural in the present tense.

ils parlent	→	**parl**
ils finissent	→	**finiss**
ils vendent	→	**vend**

Note that the stems of regular -**er** verbs are the same in the present indicative and in the present subjunctive. In addition, present indicative and present subjunctive endings are the same except in the **nous** and **vous** forms. Therefore, the present indicative and present subjunctive conjugations of regular -**er** verbs are the same except in the **nous** and **vous** forms.

parler	finir	vendre
que je **parle**	que je **finisse**	que je **vende**
(*that I may speak*)	(*that I may finish*)	(*that I may sell*)
que tu **parles**	que tu **finisses**	que tu **vendes**
qu'il/elle/on **parle**	qu'il/elle/on **finisse**	qu'il/elle/on **vende**
que nous **parlions**	que nous **finissions**	que nous **vendions**
que vous **parliez**	que vous **finissiez**	que vous **vendiez**
qu'ils/elles **parlent**	qu'ils/elles **finissent**	qu'ils/elles **vendent**

Note: subjunctive endings are the same for all verbs except for **avoir** and **être**.

avoir	être
que j'aie	que je sois
(*that I may have*)	(*that I may be*)
que tu aies	que tu sois
qu'il/elle/on ait	qu'il/elle/on soit
que nous ayons	que nous soyons
que vous ayez	que vous soyez
qu'ils/elles aient	qu'ils/elles soient

Tu es triste **qu'on** ne **soit** pas dans le même cours?

Are you sad that we are not in the same class?

Vraiment! Tu doutes qu'**elle ait** sa maîtrise?

Really! You doubt that she has her master's?

Moi, j'aimerais bien qu'**elle explique** mieux.

I would like her to explain better.

Bon. Il vaut mieux que **nous finissions** cet exercice.

OK, we had better finish this exercise.

C'est bizarre que **ces deux prétendent** comprendre.

It's bizarre that these two pretend to understand.

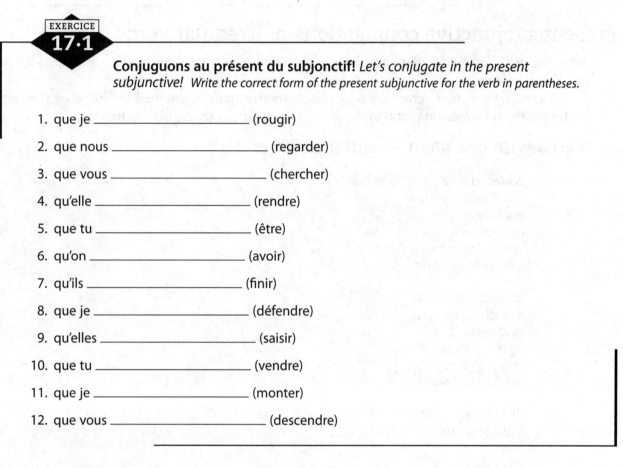

EXERCICE
17·1

Conjuguons au présent du subjonctif! *Let's conjugate in the present subjunctive! Write the correct form of the present subjunctive for the verb in parentheses.*

1. que je _____ (rougir)

2. que nous _____ (regarder)

3. que vous _____ (chercher)

4. qu'elle _____ (rendre)

5. que tu _____ (être)

6. qu'on _____ (avoir)

7. qu'ils _____ (finir)

8. que je _____ (défendre)

9. qu'elles _____ (saisir)

10. que tu _____ (vendre)

11. que je _____ (monter)

12. que vous _____ (descendre)

EXERCICE
17·2

Un excellent étudiant. *An excellent student. Complete the following lead-in phrases with the verb in parentheses conjugated in the appropriate form of the present subjunctive.*

Il faut qu'il...

1. _____ le professeur. (écouter)

2. _____ les devoirs. (avoir)

3. _____ son travail. (finir)

4. _____ aux discussions de classe. (participer)

5. _____ bien aux questions. (répondre)

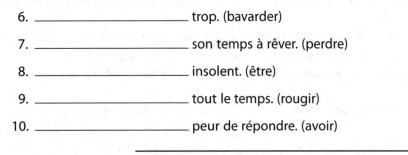

6. _____ trop. (bavarder)

7. _____ son temps à rêver. (perdre)

8. _____ insolent. (être)

9. _____ tout le temps. (rougir)

10. _____ peur de répondre. (avoir)

Present subjunctive conjugations of irregular verbs

Irregular verbs (except for **avoir** and **être**) have the subjunctive endings previously listed: **-e**, **-es**, **-e**, **-ions**, **-iez**, **-ent**.

For many irregular verbs, the present subjunctive stem is obtained by dropping the **-ent** ending of the third-person plural in the present tense, just as for regular verbs.

Verbs with one stem—regular endings

connaître (_to know/to be familiar_)
je/il/elle/on connaisse
tu connaisses
nous connaissions
vous connaissiez
ils/elles connaissent

craindre (_to fear_)
je/il/elle/on craigne
tu craignes
nous craignions
vous craigniez
ils/elles craignent

dire (_to say/to tell_)
je/il/elle/on dise
tu dises
nous disions
vous disiez
ils/elles disent

dormir (_to sleep_)
je/il/elle/on dorme
tu dormes
nous dormions
vous dormiez
ils/elles dorment

écrire (_to write_)
j'/il/elle/on écrive
tu écrives
nous écrivions
vous écriviez
ils/elles écrivent

faire (*to do, to make*)
je/il/elle/on fasse
tu fasses
nous fassions
vous fassiez
ils/elles fassent

lire (*to read*)
je/il/elle/on lise
tu lises
nous lisions
vous lisiez
ils/elles lisent

mettre (*to put/to put on*)
je/il/elle/on mette
tu mettes
nous mettions
vous mettiez
ils/elles mettent

plaire (*to please*)
je/il/elle/on plaise
tu plaises
nous plaisions
vous plaisiez
ils/elles plaisent

pouvoir (*to be able to/can*)
je/il/elle/on puisse
tu puisses
nous puissions
vous puissiez
ils/elles puissent

savoir (*to know*)
je/il/elle/on sache
tu saches
nous sachions
vous sachiez
ils/elles sachent

Il ne faut pas que **tu craignes** les chiens.

You must not fear dogs.

Il est bon qu'**on puisse** recycler.

It is good that we are able to recycle.

Tu veux que **je** te **fasse** un sandwich?

Do you want me to make you a sandwich?

Il est drôle que **cette fille** ne te **plaise** pas.

It is funny that you do not like this girl.

Ton prof est sûrement content que **tu lises** tout.

Your teacher is surely happy that you read everything.

C'est extraordinaire que **tu saches** toutes ces conjugaisons.

It's extraordinary that you know all those conjugations.

Il faut que **nous écrivions** nos cartes de remerciements.	*We have to write our thank-you cards.*
Elle ne voudrait pas qu'**il sorte** si tard.	*She would rather he did not go out so late.*

Verbs with two stems—regular endings

For the following irregular verbs, the present subjunctive stem is obtained by dropping the **-ent** ending of the third-person plural in the present tense for all forms except for **nous** and **vous**. In the following conjugations, note the distinctly different stem in the **nous** and **vous** forms. Also note that the **nous** and **vous** forms of those verbs are a duplication of the **imparfait** forms.

aller (*to go*)
j'/il/elle/on aille
tu ailles
nous **all**ions
vous **all**iez
ils/elles aillent

boire (*to drink*)
je/il/elle/on boive
tu boives
nous **buv**ions
vous **buv**iez
ils/elles boivent

croire (*to believe*)
je/il/elle/on croie
tu croies
nous **croy**ions
vous **croy**iez
ils/elles croient

devoir (*to have to/must*)
je/il/elle/on doive
tu doives
nous **dev**ions
vous **dev**iez
ils/elles doivent

prendre (*to take*)
je/il/elle/on prenne
tu prennes
nous **pren**ions
vous **pren**iez
ils/elles prennent

recevoir (*to receive*)
je/il/elle/on reçoive
tu reçoives
nous **recev**ions
vous **recev**iez
ils/elles reçoivent

tenir *(to hold)*
je/il/elle/on tienne
tu tiennes
nous **ten**ions
vous **ten**iez
ils/elles tiennent

venir *(to come)*
je/il/elle/on vienne
tu viennes
nous **ven**ions
vous **ven**iez
ils/elles viennent

voir *(to see)*
je/il/elle/on voie
tu voies
nous **voy**ions
vous **voy**iez
ils/elles voient

vouloir *(to want)*
je/il/elle/on veuille
tu veuilles
nous **voul**ions
vous **voul**iez
ils/elles veuillent

Papa insiste que **nous allions** à cette réunion.	*Dad insists that we go to this meeting.*
Il ne faut pas que **nous buvions**.	*We must not drink.*
Je voudrais vraiment que **tu viennes** avec moi.	*I would really like you to come with me.*
Je ne suis pas sûr que **tu veuilles** m'accompagner.	*I'm not sure that you want to accompany me.*
Je doute que **nous voyions** Arnold là-bas.	*I doubt that we will see Arnold over there.*

EXERCICE

17·3

Conjuguons au présent du subjonctif. *Let's conjugate in the present subjunctive.* *Write the correct forms of the present subjunctive of the verbs in parentheses.*

1. qu'elles _____ (aller)

2. qu'on _____ (boire)

3. que nous _____ (venir)

4. que je _____ (vouloir)

5. que nous _____ (pouvoir)

6. que tu _____ (tenir)

7. que je _____ (prendre)

8. qu'on _____ (recevoir)

9. que nous _____ (plaire)

10. que vous _____ (lire)

11. que j'_____ (écrire)

12. que tu _____ (craindre)

13. que je _____ (dormir)

14. qu'on _____ (faire)

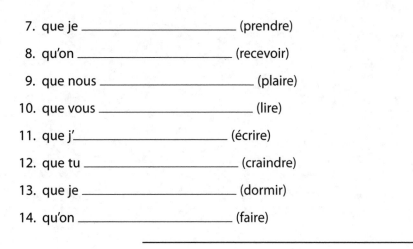

EXERCICE
17·4

Je voudrais que mes professeurs... *I would like my teachers to . . .* Complete the title phrase with the appropriate present subjunctive form of the verb in parentheses.

1. _____ indulgents avec nous. (être)

2. _____ que nous ne comprenons pas toujours. (voir)

3. _____ bien enseigner. (savoir)

4. _____ bien leurs étudiants. (connaître)

5. _____ en retard au cours. (ne pas venir)

6. _____ bien nous expliquer les choses une seconde fois. (vouloir)

7. _____ que nous pouvons tous apprendre. (croire)

8. _____ parole quand ils font des promesses. (tenir)

9. _____ à nos réunions d'étudiants. (venir)

10. _____ nos anxiétés. (comprendre)

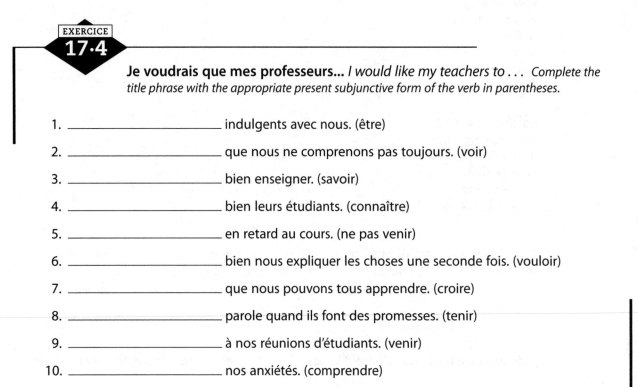

VOCABULAIRE UTILE. *Useful vocabulary.*

Review this list of vocabulary before doing the next exercise.

la limite de vitesse	*speed limit*	brûler	*to run (a light)*
la patience	*patience*	céder	*to yield*
la priorité	*right-of-way*	dépasser	*to exceed*
le feu rouge	*red light*	envoyer des textos	*to text message*
le permis de conduire	*driver's license*	porter	*to carry*
assuré	*insured*		

Comment devons-nous conduire? *How must we drive?* *Write the following sentences in French. Start each sentence with* **Il faut que nous...** *or* **Il ne faut pas que nous...**

1. We must be prudent.

_____

2. We must have a lot of patience.

_____

3. We must yield the right-of-way.

_____

4. We must carry our driver's license.

_____

5. We must be insured.

_____

6. We must not exceed the speed limit.

_____

7. We must not drink.

_____

8. We must not text message.

_____

9. We must not fall asleep.

_____

10. We must not run red lights.

_____

Uses of the present subjunctive

The present subjunctive is used to show that the action of the verb in the subordinate clause goes on at the same time as or later than the action expressed by the verb in the main clause.

In addition, the subject of the subordinate clause must differ from the subject of the main clause. Notice that the English equivalents are sometimes worded differently from the French. The word *that* (**que**) is not always used in English.

Il aimerait **que** <u>nous</u> achetions le nouvel iPad.   *He would like us to buy the new iPad.*
<u>Nous</u> sommes tristes **que** <u>vous</u> partiez.   *We are sad that you are leaving.*

Grands concepts. *Big concepts.*

Concept 1

Since the subjunctive is hardly ever used in English aside from set phrases such as, "**Be** it right, **be** it wrong . . .," translations from French to English will widely vary when the subjunctive is used in French. It is often impossible to translate literally. So you will have to use your own judgment about the best English equivalent for a French subjunctive verb.

> Il faut qu'on y aille.

> Literal translation: *It is necessary that we go there.*

> Preferable translation: *We have to go there.*

Concept 2

In addition, when translating from English to French, the structure in the French sentence will often be significantly different from the structure in the English sentence.

> Je ne veux pas / qu'il vienne.
> *I do not want / him to come.*

Concept 3

Do not use the subjunctive mood in an independent clause (stand-alone clause) or in a main clause (a stand-alone clause on which another clause depends).

This is an independent clause; it stands alone:

Je veux une glace.	*I want an ice cream.*

Examine the following sentence:

Je vais acheter une glace pendant que tu finis ton café.	*I am going to buy an ice cream while you are finishing your coffee.*

In the preceding sentence, there is a main clause, which stands alone and makes sense by itself: **Je vais acheter une glace.**

There is also a subordinate clause that only makes sense when linked to the main clause: **pendant que tu finis ton café.**

Only use the subjunctive in a dependent clause. The verb or the adjective used in the main clause or the conjunction introducing the dependent clause must trigger the use of subjunctive.

In the following sentence, the verb **Il faut** triggers the use of the subjunctive in the dependent clause.

Il faut / qu'il aille au cours.	*He must go to class.*

Present subjunctive after impersonal expressions of necessity or uncertainty

The following commonly used impersonal expressions are followed by the subjunctive:

Il est utile/inutile que	*It is useful/useless that*
Il est impensable que	*It is unthinkable that*
Il est important que	*It is important that*
Il est possible/impossible que	*It is possible/impossible that*
Il faut que	*It is necessary that/One must*
Il ne faut pas que	*One must not*

Il vaut mieux que	It is better that
Il est dommage que	It is a pity that
Il est rare que	It is rare that
Il est urgent que	It is urgent that

Il est rare que les gens n'**aiment** pas les vacances.	It is rare that people do not like vacations.
Il est important que les jeunes gens **aillent** à l'université.	It is important that young people go to university.
Il est possible qu'un étudiant brillant **reçoive** une bourse.	It is possible for a brilliant student to receive a scholarship.
Il est dommage que les examens **soient** parfois si difficiles.	It is too bad that exams are sometimes so difficult.

Note that impersonal expressions that express certainty are not followed by the subjunctive mood. In the following sentences, the simple future of the indicative mood is used after the expression **il est clair** and the **passé composé** of the indicative mood is used after **il est évident**.

Il est clair que **tu étudieras** la physique.	It is clear that you will study physics.
Il est évident que **nous avons fait** une faute.	It is evident that we made a mistake.

Also note the meaning of **il faut** changes in the negative form:

Il faut que vous arrêtiez de fumer.	**You have to** stop smoking.
Il ne faut pas que vous vous ruiniez la santé.	**You must not** ruin your health.

VOCABULAIRE UTILE. *Useful vocabulary.*

Review the following vocabulary before doing the next two exercises.

l'espèce (*f.*) en danger	*endangered species*	le préjugé	*prejudice*
la croyance	*belief*	le réchauffement	*warming*
la glace polaire	*polar ice*	le soleil	*sun*
la lune	*moon*	égal/égaux	*equal*

EXERCICE
17·6

L'environnement. *The environment. Checkmark the statements that appear to be true.*

1. _____ Il est possible que la lune tourne autour du soleil.

2. _____ Il est impossible que l'homme aille dans l'espace.

3. _____ Il est possible que les glaces polaires fondent.

4. _____ Il n'est pas urgent qu'on limite l'émission de CO_2.

5. _____ Il ne faut pas que nous protégions les espèces en danger.

6. _____ Il est inutile que nous recyclions le papier, le plastique et le verre.

7. _____ Il est juste que nous participions tous aux efforts de recyclage.

8. _____ Il ne faut pas que nous ignorions le réchauffement global.

9. _____ Il se peut qu'il y ait des galaxies qu'on n'a pas encore découvertes.

10. _____ Il est vrai qu'il y a des Martiens sur Mars.

EXERCICE
17·7

Les droits de l'homme. *Human rights.* *Complete the following statements by writing the verbs in parentheses in the present subjunctive.*

1. Il serait juste que tous les hommes _____ égaux. (être)

2. Il faut que tous les individus d'une nation _____ être représentés. (pouvoir)

3. Il est bon qu'une nation _____ toutes les croyances. (respecter)

4. Il ne faut pas qu'il y _____ des préjugés dans la société. (avoir)

5. Il est impératif qu'on _____ pour élire les membres du gouvernement. (voter)

6. Il est impensable que les femmes n'_____ pas les mêmes droits que les hommes. (avoir)

Present subjunctive after verbs or adjectives of advice, wishes, commands, doubts, and feelings

The present subjunctive is found in subordinate clauses introduced by verbs or adjectives expressing advice, wishes, commands, feelings, and doubts. Examine the following summary chart, which contains some examples of such verbs or phrases:

ADVICE	WISHES	COMMANDS	DOUBTS	FEELINGS
conseiller *to advise*	avoir envie *to feel like/want*	insister *to insist*	douter *to doubt*	être triste *to be sad*
recommander *to recommend*	désirer *to desire*	ordonner *to order*	ne pas être sûr(e) *to be uncertain*	être content(e) *to be happy*
proposer *to propose*	souhaiter *to wish*	défendre *to forbid*	ne pas être certain(e) *to be uncertain*	être désolé(e) *to be sorry*
suggérer *to suggest*	vouloir *to want*	interdire *to forbid*	être surpris *to be surprised*	regretter *to regret*

<u>Je recommande</u> que **vous fassiez** une demande. | *I recommend that you make a request.*

<u>Tu désires</u> que **je vienne**? | *Would you like me to come?*

<u>Il ordonne</u> que **nous restions**. | *He orders us to stay.*

<u>Je ne suis pas sûr</u> que **ce projet réussisse**. | *I'm not sure that this project will succeed.*

<u>Nous regrettons</u> que **vous ne puissiez pas** participer. | *We regret that you are unable to participate.*

Exprimez des opinions. *Express opinions. Write in French. Use* **vous** *for you in all the sentences, and use the verbs in parentheses.*

1. I recommend that you vote. (**voter**)

   _____

2. I wish that you would get involved. (**s'engager**)

   _____

3. I am not sure that you want to be involved. (**vouloir être engagés**)

   _____

4. I regret that you do not feel the need to participate. (**ne pas sentir le besoin de…**)

   _____

5. I suggest you get informed. (**se renseigner**)

   _____

6. I propose you take classes in political science. (**suivre des cours en sciences politiques**)

   _____

7. I insist that we all attend these classes. (**aller à…**)

   _____

8. I am surprised that you agree. (**être d'accord**)

   _____

Present subjunctive after specific conjunctions

The subjunctive is found in subordinate clauses introduced by conjunctions such as the following:

à moins que	*unless*
afin que/pour que	*in order that*
avant que	*before*
bien que/malgré que/quoique	*although*
de crainte que/de peur que	*for fear that*
jusqu'à ce que	*until*
pourvu que	*provided that*
sans que	*without*

Il faut payer la facture <u>à moins qu</u>'**il y ait** une erreur.	*We have to pay the bill unless there is an error.*
Prenez des parapluies <u>de peur qu</u>'**il ne pleuve** plus tard.	*Take umbrellas for fear that it may rain later.*
Attendez <u>jusqu'à ce que</u> **je finisse**.	*Wait until I finish.*

The subjunctive mood   **181**

L'histoire de Boucle d'or. *Goldilocks's story.* *Write the following sentences in French. Beware that the use of the subjunctive mood is not required in all dependent clauses.*

1. Goldilocks entered the bear's house before they came back home. (**entrer dans/rentrer**)

   _____

2. She tasted their soups until she found the best one. (**goûter/trouver**)

   _____

3. She broke a chair, although she did not mean to do it. (**casser/ne pas avoir l'intention**)

   _____

4. She chose the small bed because it looked cute. (**choisir/avoir l'air**)

   _____

5. She slept until the bears came up to their bedroom. (**dormir/monter à**)

   _____

6. When she woke up, she jumped through the window for fear that the bears would eat her. (**se réveiller/sauter/manger**)

   _____

Past subjunctive

The past subjunctive exists only in a dependent clause and must be introduced by the same verbs or adjectives previously mentioned for the present subjunctive. This tense is used when the action in the dependent clause precedes the action in the main clause. Note that in the following example, the action of consenting in the dependent clause took place before the action of being delighted in the main clause. First you consented, and then she was delighted.

<u>Elle est ravie</u> que **vous ayez consenti** à travailler avec elle.   *She is delighted that you consented to work with her.*

The past subjunctive is a compound tense formed with the appropriate auxiliary verb **avoir** or **être** in the present subjunctive and a past participle. You may review how to identify the correct auxiliary verb in Chapter 11 and how to make the agreement of past participles in Chapter 15.

Examine and compare the conjugation of an **avoir** verb (**parler**), an **être** verb (**arriver**), and a *reflexive* verb (**se lever**).

parler	arriver	se lever
que j'aie parlé	que je sois arrivé(e)	que je me sois levé(e)
(*that I spoke*)	(*that I arrived*)	(*that I got up*)
que tu aies parlé	que tu sois arrivé(e)	que tu te sois levé(e)
qu'il/elle/on ait parlé	qu'il/elle/on soit arrivé(e)	qu'il/elle/on se soit levé(e)
que nous ayons parlé	que nous soyons arrivé(e)s	que nous nous soyons levé(e)s
que vous ayez parlé	que vous soyez arrivé(e)(s)	que vous vous soyez levé(e)(s)
qu'ils/elles aient parlé	qu'ils/elles soient arrivé(e)s	qu'ils/elles se soient levé(e)s

The past subjunctive is used after the same expressions as the present subjunctive. It is used to show that the action or situation in the subordinate clause (after **que**) happened before the action or situation in the main clause.

Il est surpris que les étudiants **aient** tous **rendu** leurs devoirs.

He is surprised that the students all turned in their homework.

Je doute que mes camarades **soient arrivés** avant moi.

I doubt that my classmates arrived before me.

Note that when conjunctions such as **avant que** (*before*), **de peur que** (*for fear that*), and **sans que** (*without*) introduce a verb in the subjunctive, the adverb **ne** often appears before the verb. This is purely syntactical and should not be interpreted as giving the verb a negative meaning.

Je vais les réveiller à moins qu'**ils** _ne_ **se soient** déjà **levés**.

I am going to wake them up unless they have already gotten up.

EXERCICE
17·10

Feuilleton. *Soap opera. Write the past subjunctive form of each verb, using the subject provided for 1–12; then write the present subjunctive for numbers 13–18.*

1. (quitter) Je suis désolé que ta copine Marie t' _____, Christophe.

2. (rester) Ça m'étonne que vous _____ ensemble si longtemps.

3. (ne pas se marier) Je suis contente que vous _____.

4. (partir) Je veux bien te tenir compagnie à moins que tu ne _____ quelque part.

5. (être) Je regrette de te dire ça mais je doute que Marie t' _____ fidèle.

6. (écouter) Je ne suis pas sûre que tu m' _____ quand je t'avertissais.

7. (dire) Tu es fâché que j' _____ la vérité. Je comprends.

8. (être) Tu n'es pas content que j' _____ si franche.

9. (se faire) J'ai peur que tu _____ des illusions pendant le temps de ta liaison.

10. (faire) Bien qu'elle _____ des efforts pour être mon amie, je ne lui faisais pas confiance.

11. (tomber) Malgré que tu _____ amoureux d'elle, je suis restée ta meilleure amie.

12. (ne pas se rendre compte) Il est dommage que tu _____ que moi, je t'ai toujours aimé.

13. (ne pas sortir) Il est impensable que nous _____ ensemble. Nous sommes faits l'un pour l'autre!

14. (se dire) Je n'envoie pas ce texto de peur que tu _____ que je suis folle.

15. (ne pas comprendre) J'espère qu'un jour tu m'aimeras mais j'ai peur que tu
    _____ mes sentiments.

16. (être) Je voudrais te le dire mais je doute que ce _____ le bon
    moment.

17. (arriver) Alors je vais attendre jusqu'à ce que le bon moment _____.

18. (finir) Je ne veux pas que ce beau rêve _____.

Relative pronouns

·18·

Function of relative pronouns

Relative pronouns replace a noun called the antecedent; they introduce a new clause (subject, verb, and sometimes complement) that gives information about the antecedent.

The pronouns **qui** and **que**

The pronoun **qui** (*who, which,* or *that*) is the *subject of the verb in the relative clause* and can replace things or people. In the following sentence, **qui** is the relative pronoun that replaces **la prof**, and it is the subject of the verb **entre**.

> La prof **qui** <u>entre dans la salle de</u> <u>classe</u> est notre nouvelle prof.
>
> *The teacher **who** is entering our classroom is our new teacher.*

In the following sentence, **qui** is the relative pronoun that replaces **la réponse**, and it is the subject of the verb **est**.

> La réponse **qui** <u>est au tableau</u> semble correcte.
> *The answer **that** is on the board seems correct.*

The pronoun **que** (*whom, which, that*) is the *direct object of the verb in the relative clause* and can replace things or people. This pronoun is sometimes omitted in the English sentence. In the following sentence, **que** is the relative pronoun that replaces **la dame**, and it is the direct object of the verb **vois**.

> La dame **que** <u>tu vois là-bas</u> est la directrice.
> *The lady (whom) you see over there is the director.*

In the following sentence, **que** is the relative pronoun that replaces **l'ascenseur**, and it is the direct object of the verb **prends**.

> L'ascenseur **que** <u>je prends</u> mène au premier étage.
> *The elevator (that) I am taking leads to the first floor.*

Mon nouveau cours. *My new class.* *Write the appropriate relative pronoun* **qui** *or* **que (qu')** *in the space provided.*

1. Le cours _____ je suis ce semestre est assez difficile.

2. Le professeur _____ enseigne le cours est très jeune.

3. Les étudiants _____ s'inscrivent pour ce cours sont généralement très avancés.

4. Les devoirs _____ je devrai faire pour ce cours seront obligatoires.

5. J'ai déjà les livres _____ je dois utiliser.

6. Le syllabus _____ est sur le site web du professeur est celui de ce cours.

7. Cette fille là-bas est celle _____ s'est inscrite en même temps que moi.

8. Je me demande si ce cours est vraiment celui _____ elle voulait.

9. En tout cas, les études _____ nous allons faire me passionnent.

10. Et je ne suis pas le type de personne _____ s'intéresse à tout.

The pronouns qui and lequel

The pronoun **qui** is also used *after a preposition* to replace a person.

Le copain <u>à</u> **qui** tu as prêté ce CD est fiable.	*The friend <u>to</u> **whom** you lent this CD is reliable.*
La copine <u>pour</u> **qui** nous organisons cette fête est ma meilleure amie.	*The friend <u>for</u> **whom** we are organizing this party is my best friend.*

A form of **lequel** is used *after a preposition* to replace a thing. The form of **lequel** changes according to the gender and number of the noun it replaces. The four different forms of **lequel** are:

masculine singular	lequel	*masculine plural*	lesquels
feminine singular	laquelle	*feminine plural*	lesquelles

La moto sur <u>**laquelle**</u> tu es arrivé est neuve.	*The motorcycle on **which** you arrived is brand new.*
Le parking <u>dans</u> **lequel** tu as garé ta moto n'est pas gratuit.	*The parking lot in **which** you parked your motorcycle is not free.*

Remember to use the contracted forms of the prepositions **à** and **de** when they are followed by **lequel, lesquels,** and **lesquelles** (see the section on the interrogative pronoun **lequel** in Chapter 16).

à + lequel = auquel	de + lequel = duquel
à + lesquels = auxquels	de + lesquels = desquels
à + lesquelles = auxquelles	de + lesquelles = desquelles

In the following sentence, **auxquels** replaces the preposition **à** and the interrogative pronoun **lesquels** that replaces **les concerts** (masculine plural noun):

| Les concerts **auxquels** tu vas sont toujours très chers. | The concerts you attend are always expensive. |

Note that the pronoun **quoi** takes the place of **lequel** (or one of its forms) after a preposition when the antecedent is vague or when the antecedent is an entire idea.

| Je me demande **à quoi** tu penses. | I wonder **what** you are thinking about. |

EXERCICE
18·2

Mes professeurs et mes cours cette année. *My teachers and my classes this year. Write the appropriate relative pronoun **qui** or a form of **lequel** in the space provided.*

1. Le prof avec _____ tu parlais tout à l'heure, c'est mon prof de mathématiques.

2. La dame à _____ j'ai dit bonjour, c'est ma prof d'art.

3. Le monsieur derrière _____ nous marchons, c'est M. Rami, le prof de physique.

4. Les deux dames _____ bavardent en français, ce sont des profs de langue.

5. Ce laboratoire est celui dans _____ je vais apprendre l'informatique.

6. Cette salle de classe est celle dans _____ je vais suivre le cours d'anglais.

7. Voilà la liste de réunions _____ je devrai aller.

8. Voilà le prof de gymnastique. La salle dans _____ je vais faire du yoga est là, à droite.

The pronoun où

The pronoun **où** is used to say *where* and replace a location.

| Voilà la ville **où** auront lieu les prochains Jeux olympiques. | There is the city **where** the next Olympic Games will take place. |

The pronoun **où** is also used to say *when* in expressions like the following:

au moment où	at the moment when
le jour où	on the day when
l'année où	the year when
Il a su que ce film allait lui plaire **au moment où** il a commencé.	He knew he would like the movie from the moment when it started.

EXERCICE
18·3

Une année mémorable. *A memorable year.* *Translate each sentence into French.*

1. The year when I started college is memorable.

   _____

2. It was the year when I finished my high school studies.

   _____

3. I remember the day when I received my diploma.

   _____

4. The moment the diploma was in my hands, I knew that I was starting a new life.

   _____

5. The day when I started college, it was a new life.

   _____

The pronoun **dont**

The pronoun **dont** replaces **de qui** as well as **de** + form of **lequel**. It stands for things and people. It is often (but not always) translated into English as *of whom* and *whose*.

Examine the examples in the following table, and note that the pronoun **dont** is used to elaborate on relationships and possessions. Remember that noun phrases that define relationships and possessions require the preposition **de**. The pronoun **dont** is also used in clauses that include a verbal structure requiring the preposition **de**.

RELATIONSHIPS	POSSESSIONS	STRUCTURE IN RELATIVE CLAUSE INCLUDES THE PREPOSITION **de**
C'est le monsieur **dont** le fils est dans mon cours.	Regarde la pauvre fille **dont** le sac à dos a disparu.	Voilà l'ordinateur **dont** je me sers.
*It is the gentleman **whose** son is in my class.*	*Look at the poor girl **whose** backpack disappeared.*	*There is the computer I use.*
le fils **du** monsieur	le sac **de** la fille	se servir **de**...
C'est la fille **dont** le frère est dans ton équipe.	C'est la voisine **dont** le chien aboie toujours.	La chose **dont** j'ai besoin, c'est du papier.
*This is the girl **whose** brother is on your team.*	*This is the neighbor **whose** dog always barks.*	*The thing I need is paper.*
le frère **de** la fille	le chien **de** la voisine	avoir besoin **de**

Here is a list of expressions that are frequently found in relative clauses introduced by **dont**:

avoir besoin **de**	*to need*
avoir envie **de**	*to want/crave/desire*
avoir peur **de**	*to be afraid of*
rêver **de**	*to dream of*
parler **de**	*to talk about*
se servir **de**	*to use*
se souvenir **de**	*to remember*
être fier **de**	*to be proud of*

La ville **dont** je rêvais est Paris.	*The city I was dreaming about is Paris.*
Le pain **dont** j'avais le plus envie était le pain au chocolat.	*The bread I wanted the most was the chocolate croissant.*
Le jour **dont** je me souviens le mieux est le jour où nous sommes montés en haut de la Tour Eiffel.	*The day I remember the best is the day when we went up the Eiffel Tower.*

EXERCICE
18·4

Des vacances à Paris. *A vacation in Paris.* *Translate each of the following sentences into English. Beware of the varying translations for the pronoun* **dont**.

1. Mes vacances à Paris sont les vacances dont je me souviendrai toute ma vie.

   _____

2. L'incident avec le pickpocket à la cathédrale de Notre-Dame est le seul incident dont je n'ai pas un souvenir agréable.

   _____

3. La petite Smartcar, c'est la voiture dont beaucoup de gens se servaient.

   _____

4. Le métro était le transport dont le plus de gens avaient besoin.

   _____

5. La chose dont j'étais le plus fier, c'était de communiquer en français.

   _____

Les Jeux olympiques modernes. *Modern Olympic Games.* *Complete the following sentences with the appropriate relative pronoun* **qui**, **que**, **où**, **dont**, *or a form of* **lequel**.

C'est un français, Pierre de Coubertin, 1. _____ a fait revivre les jeux des Grecs de l'Antiquité. Les premiers Jeux olympiques 2. _____ ont eu lieu en 1896 à Athènes en Grèce sont devenus un événement sportif international majeur—un événement 3. _____ fascine les gens dans le monde entier. Les jeux comprennent les sports d'été et d'hiver 4. _____ des milliers d'athlètes participent à diverses compétitions. Les jeux se déplacent de pays en pays et il y a toujours une cérémonie d'ouverture et une cérémonie de clôture 5. _____ de nombreux athlètes participent. Les athlètes portent les drapeaux des pays 6. _____ ils représentent et 7. _____ ils sont fiers. Le pays 8. _____ ont lieu les jeux est responsable pour le bon déroulement des jeux et pour les cérémonies.

Answer key

1 Present tense and uses of regular and stem-changing verbs

1·1 1. cuisine 2. mange 3. débarrassent 4. lavent 5. regardent 6. réponds 7. téléphone 8. adore 9. bavarde 10. raccrocher

1·2 1. plaisante 2. raconte 3. écoute 4. attendons 5. réussit 6. éviter 7. travaille 8. accompagne 9. rentrer 10. choisit 11. arriver 12. prétend 13. passe 14. annonce 15. trompe 16. descend 17. éblouit 18. saisit 19. entends 20. grandit

1·3 J'ai une petite famille: une maman, un papa, un frère et une sœur. Nous mangeons ensemble chaque soir/tous les soirs. Ma mère et ma sœur Nina cuisinent. Pendant le dîner, papa parle/bavarde beaucoup et nous écoutons. Il est très drôle et adore/aime raconter des blagues/des plaisanteries.

Après le dîner, je nettoie la table; mon père et mon frère font la vaisselle. Ma sœur qui a beaucoup d'amis passe beaucoup de temps au téléphone. Ma mère reste dans sa chambre et répond aux e-mails/mèls.

1·4 1. possède 2. porte 3. rouspète 4. travailler 5. respectent 6. tutoient 7. vouvoie 8. habitent 9. envoie 10. sème 11. cèdent 12. aime

1·5 1. appelle 2. moquent 3. possède 4. rouspète 5. provoque 6. gagne 7. aime 8. préfère 9. cède 10. accepte 11. envoie 12. emmène 13. protéger 14. essaie 15. décède 16. enferme 17. révèle 18. décéder

1·6 Monsieur/M. et madame/Mme Duport ont une grande famille. Ils élèvent cinq enfants. Malheureusement, ils possèdent une petite maison. Alors les enfants partagent deux chambres (à coucher). Les Duport emmènent les enfants à l'école chaque jour/tous les jours. Les grands protègent les petits.

Pendant que le enfants passent la journée à l'école, Mme Duport travaille à son bureau et M. Duport nettoie la maison et cuisine.

La famille Duport espère posséder une grande maison un jour! Mais pour le moment, personne ne proteste.

1·7 1. Elle s'appelle Audrey Tautou. 2. Elle grandit dans une famille ordinaire. 3. Son père est chirurgien-dentiste. 4. Non, elle n'est pas enfant unique/Non, elle a un frère et deux sœurs. 5. Elle fait des films pour la télévision. 6. Elle gagne le césar du premier espoir féminin. 7. C'est un « Oscar ». 8. Les films *Le fabuleux destin d'Amélie Poulain*, *Coco avant Chanel* et *Da Vinci Code* la rendent célèbre.

2 Articles and genders

2·1 1. Qu'est-ce que tu veux, de la limonade ou de l'eau? —Un peu d'eau, s'il te plaît.

2. Tu prends du café le matin? —Oui, je prends toujours une tasse de café.

3. Tu as besoin de sucre dans ton café? —Oui, j'ai besoin de beaucoup de sucre.

4. Tu peux acheter une bouteille de vin pour le dîner? —Bien sûr, un dîner sans vin n'est pas un vrai dîner.

5. N'apporte pas de fleurs cette fois! —Pourquoi pas? Tu adores/aimes les fleurs.

6. Oui, mais j'ai beaucoup de roses du jardin. —(Est-ce que) Je peux apporter un dessert?

7. Non, merci. Nous avons des fruits comme dessert/pour le dessert. —Les fruits sont parfaits en été, tu as raison.

8. À ce soir! —Ou cet après-midi!

2·2 1. Est-ce que tu es étudiant? 2. Quelle est ta matière préférée cette année? 3. Qu'est-ce que tu veux faire dans dix ans? 4. Est-ce que tu veux être professeur, gérant d'hôtel, astronaute, acteur? 5. Qu'est-ce qui est important? L'argent, la célébrité, la fierté?

2·3 1. Les 2. la 3. nos 4. Les 5. les 6. leur 7. son 8. Notre 9. X 10. Un 11. ce 12. notre 13. l' 14. des 15. X 16. X

2·4 1. le ventre 2. la poitrine 3. les yeux 4. la main 5. la poitrine 6. le menton 7. la bouche 8. les dents 9. les pieds 10. les genoux

2·5 1. *done* 2. J'ai très mal à la jambe droite. Je ne peux pas marcher. 3. J'ai mal à l'orteil. Je crois qu'il est cassé. 4. J'ai mal au poignet. Je joue trop souvent au tennis. 5. J'ai mal au ventre. Je ne peux pas manger. 6. J'ai mal à la poitrine. Je dois avoir une bronchite. 7. J'ai mal au nez. J'ai un rhume. 8. J'ai mal aux dents. J'ai besoin d'un dentiste. 9. J'ai une griffure au visage/à la figure. 10. J'ai mal au coude.

3 The present tense and idiomatic uses of the irregular verbs aller, avoir, être, and faire

3·1 1. Salut, Johnny! Ça va/Tout va bien? 2. Ça va bien/Bien, merci. Et toi? 3. Bien. Ça va sans dire: je suis en vacances. 4. Allons à la pêche cet après-midi! 5. Cet après-midi, je vais chercher ma nouvelle robe. 6. La jolie robe qui va avec mon smoking? 7. Oui, pour samedi. Je vais bon train, n'est-ce pas? 8. Ça va de soi.

3·2 1. ai l'impression 2. avez raison 3. a de la chance. 4. ai hâte 5. a sommeil 6. a, ans 7. a honte 8. ont besoin 9. a envie 10. avons l'intention

3·3 1. Nous avons l'intention de 2. Tu as l'impression d' 3. Tu as sommeil? 4. Vous avez envie d' 5. Il a honte. 6. J'ai hâte 7. Nous avons l'habitude de manger 8. Ils ont de la malchance 9. a l'air 10. J'ai l'impression

3·4 Lolo et Lili sont des chiots et ils sont frère et sœur. Ils ont peur des bruits forts. Quand ils entendent un bruit, ils commencent à trembler. Les enfants Duport sont pleinement conscients de ça/cela. Ils ont l'habitude d'éviter les bruits. Malheureusement, leurs amis n'ont pas toujours envie d'être silencieux. Alors ils crient et les chiots ont besoin de réconfort. Ils ont confiance en la famille Duport. Vous pensez qu'ils ont de la chance d'avoir une famille sympa/gentille/agréable? Vous avez raison!

3·5 1. *done* 2. C'est, actrice 3. C'est un professeur 4. C'est tout 5. c'est à toi 6. Il est à moi 7. C'est samedi 8. suis à court 9. Ça m'est égal 10. sommes sur le point

3·6 1. C'est 2. C'est à moi 3. Je suis à court 4. est sur le point 5. Elle est d'accord 6. Elle est gentille/sympa 7. Ça y est, Irène est de retour 8. C'est formidable/chouette

3·7 1. h 2. e 3. g. 4. f 5. b 6. d 7. c 8. a

3·8 1. Mais j'ai envie de faire une promenade/un tour à bicyclette/en vélo. Il fait beau.

2. Ce beau temps me fait envie. C'est tout.

3. D'accord. Je fais les courses. Tu fais ton droit.

4. Ça fait combien de faire nettoyer la maison?

5. Ça ne fait rien. Je dois faire mon sport.

6. Bon. Je fais de mon mieux aujourd'hui.

3·9 1. est 2. habite 3. est 4. chante 5. a 6. envoie 7. adore 8. va 9. va 10. représente 11. fait

4 Adjectives and comparisons

4·1 1. Tous 2. tous 3. Tout 4. toute 5. Toute 6. Tous 7. toute 8. tous

4·2 1. Quel 2. quelle 3. Quel dommage 4. n'importe quel 5. peu importe 6. Quelle

4·3 1. j 2. g 3. h. 4. i 5. f 6. e 7. b 8. c 9. d 10. a

4·4 1. mon seul fils 2. un homme seul 3. son propre père 4. un certain charme 5. un jour certain 6. un pull propre 7. un mauvais dîner 8. un monsieur fâché 9. un livre lourd 10. son ancien copain

4·5 1. belle 2. petite 3. peureuse 4. inquiète 5. grosse 6. folle 7. sotte 8. américaine 9. active 10. cruelle

4·6 1. une salade fraîche 2. une personne folle 3. une laine douce 4. une robe chère 5. une mère fière 6. une garde-robe complète 7. une prière silencieuse 8. une brioche sèche 9. une démonstration publique 10. une voix basse

4·7 Suggested answers: 1. — 2. — 3. √ 4. √ 5. — 6. √ 7. √ 8. — 9. √

4·8 1. roses rouges 2. nouveaux livres 3. enfants actifs 4. chiens doux/gentils 5. bons dîners 6. beaux habits 7. vieilles voitures 8. bijoux chers 9. pommes fraîches 10. longues vacances 11. amis heureux 12. employés/travailleurs honnêtes

4·9 1. c 2. a 3. e 4. f 5. b 6. d

4·10 1. haute 2. audacieuse 3. populaire 4. entier 5. dix-neuvième 6. innombrables 7. techniques 8. grande 9. universelle 10. française 11. métallique 12. incroyable 13. chère 14. publique 15. remarquables 16. neuves 17. grands 18. hostiles 19. surpris/émerveillés 20. surpris/émerveillés 21. majestueuse 22. incroyable

5 The present tense of irregular verbs ending in -oir, -re, and -ir

5·1 Suggested answers: 1. — 2. — 3. √ 4. √ 5. — 6. √ 7. √ 8. √ 9. √ 10. —

5·2 1. Le soir, je dois étudier. 2. Mes parents savent que je suis un étudiant sérieux. 3. Mon frère John sait parler français. 4. Dans mon cours de français, nous devons faire des devoirs écrits après chaque classe. 5. Nous ne devons pas utiliser de traducteurs électroniques pour faire les devoirs. 6. Mon frère doit m'aider quelquefois. 7. Quelquefois je demande « Que veux-tu dire ? » parce qu'il sait plus que moi. 8. Sans le vouloir, il rend mon travail plus difficile.

5·3 1. Connaissez 2. est 3. perd 4. parcourt 5. secourt 6. décrit 7. écrit 8. connaissent 9. dit 10. prédit 11. annonce 12. écrit 13. décède 14. pillent 15. espèrent 16. découvrent 17. lisent 18. relisent 19. reconnaît 20. permettent

5·4 1. Ce beau tableau me plaît. Il te plaît aussi, Jeanine? 2. Et ces tableaux-ci? Ils te plaisent? 3. Regarde qui est là. Marc te plaît, Jeanine? 4. Il est beau. Il plaît à tout le monde. 5. Tu sais qu'il peint très bien? 6. Crois-moi! Il est excellent. 7. N'aie pas peur de lui parler! Il est gentil/sympa! 8. Oh! Ils éteignent les lumières. Il doit être l'heure de partir.

5·5 1. devient 2. retiens 3. parviens 4. viennent 5. proviennent 6. tiens 7. survient 8. tient 9. tenons 10. parvenons 11. Tiens 12. Tenez

5·6 1. dors 2. parcours 3. mens 4. sert 5. secours 6. sortons 7. pars 8. endorment 9. sert 10. ment

5·7 1. demande 2. dit 3. est 4. doit 5. est 6. met 7. tient 8. parcourt 9. tient 10. craint 11. dit 12. connaît 13. prend 14. nage 15. arrive 16. est 17. voit 18. revient 19. voit 20. court 21. dit 22. doit 23. va 24. dit 25. fait 26. boire 27. assure 28. vaut 29. rentrer 30. est 31. promet 32. peut

6 Prepositions, prepositional phrases, and verbal structures after prepositions

6·1 1. Nous allons à l'école vers huit heures du matin. 2. Nous avons cours chaque jour/tous les jours excepté/sauf le dimanche. 3. Mon premier cours le lundi est mon cours favori/préféré grâce au professeur. 4. Je suis assise entre mes bons amis Frank et Jerry. 5. Mon cours d'histoire aujourd'hui est à propos de la deuxième guerre mondiale. 6. Malgré Frank qui parle/bavarde pendant le cours, je suis très attentive. 7. Parfois/Quelquefois, à cause de lui, le professeur cesse de parler au milieu d'une phrase. 8. Devant moi, il y a une carte. 9. Sur la carte, nous pouvons voir tous les pays. 10. Pour moi, c'est un cours très intéressant.

6·2 1. Je vais au Luxembourg. La capitale du Luxembourg est Luxembourg. 2. Je vais au Québec. La capitale du Québec est la ville de Québec. 3. Je vais au Burundi. La capitale du Burundi est Bujumbura. 4. Je vais en Guyane française. La capitale de la Guyane française est Cayenne. 5. Je vais en Belgique. La capitale de la Belgique est Bruxelles. 6. Je vais en Martinique. La capitale de la Martinique est Fort-de-France. 7. Je vais au Cameroun. La capitale du Cameroun est Yaounde. 8. Je vais en France. La capitale de la France est Paris.

6·3 1. *done* 2. du Cameroun 3. du Sénégal 4. de Belgique 5. de Suisse 6. du Burundi 7. du Québec 8. de Louisiane 9. d'Algérie 10. du Mali

6·4 1. ouvert 2. acheté 3. créé 4. travaillé 5. continué

6·5 1. être allé 2. avoir fini 3. avoir réussi 4. être allée 5. avoir fait 6. avoir fini 7. être rentrée 8. être tombé 9. avoir épousé 10. avoir pris 11. avoir compris 12. avoir été 13. avoir attendu

6·6 1. au lieu de faire ses devoirs 2. au lieu de marcher 3. pour sortir jouer 4. sans demander permission 5. pour avoir désobéi

6·7 1. Je regrette de ne pas avoir ce livre. 2. Il regrette de ne pas pouvoir venir à cette fête. 3. Elle regrette d'être occupée aujourd'hui. 4. Nous regrettons d'avoir oublié d'apporter le gâteau. 5. Nos amis regrettent de ne pas avoir écrit. 6. Tu regrettes d'avoir vendu ta voiture, n'est-ce pas?

6·8 1. Je suis content(e) d'avoir beaucoup d'amis. 2. Il est content d'être en bonne santé. 3. Elle est ravie d'habiter en France. 4. Nous sommes tristes de partir bientôt. 5. Vous êtes jaloux de ne pas être riches. 6. Ils sont fâchés de devoir travailler ce weekend. 7. Je regrette de ne pas avoir fait de promenade avant la pluie. 8. Nous sommes malheureux de ne pas avoir réussi à cet examen. 9. Il est désolé d'avoir été en retard. 10. Elles sont fâchées de ne pas avoir d'invitation.

6·9 1. f 2. d 3. e 4. g 5. c 6. h 7. b 8. a

6·10 1. faire 2. organiser 3. escalader 4. faisant 5. avoir suivi 6. participer 7. avoir 8. accepter

7 Imperative, infinitive, and present participle structures

7·1 1. oublie 2. Rentre 3. Va, pars 4. Fais 5. Sois 6. regarde 7. Choisis 8. Mange 9. mets 10. Donne

7·2 1. Ouvrez 2. Élargissez 3. Devenez 4. Veuillez 5. oubliez 6. recevez 7. Soyez 8. Sachez 9. Explorez 10. discutez

7·3 1. E 2. F 3. C 4. A 5. I 6. H 7. B 8. D 9. G 10. J

7·4 1. Lire toute la journée, c'est mon hobby. 2. Répondre à mes questions est urgent. 3. Marcher seul dans les rues la nuit est dangereux. 4. Réussir à cet examen est mon seul but. 5. Acheter de nouveaux habits est amusant. 6. Aider les amis est naturel.

7·5 1. Jeannot, arrête de jouer à ce jeu! 2. Ne prétends pas faire les devoirs! 3. Tu oublies toujours d'écrire ce que tu dois faire. 4. Tu es capable d'avoir de bonnes notes. 5. Tu es sur le point de finir tes études de lycée. 6. Tu n'as pas honte d'être paresseux? 7. Tu as l'intention d' habiter/de vivre dans la rue? 8. Tu as de la chance d'avoir cette famille!

7·6 1. k 2. i 3. a 4. h 5. e 6. g 7. f 8. d 9. b 10. l 11. c 12. j

7·7   1. Gérard Depardieu grandit avec cinq frères et sœurs.   2. L'adolescent décide de voler des voitures.
3. C'est difficile à croire mais c'est vrai.   4. Il arrive à cesser de faire ça/cela.   5. Il commence à suivre des cours de comédie à Paris.   6. Le cinéma américain offre à Depardieu de jouer dans *Green Card*.
7. Depardieu apprend très vite à gagner beaucoup d'argent.   8. Il devient célèbre et riche et semble adorer/aimer les deux.

7·8   1. F   2. F   3. F   4. V   5. V   6. F   7. V   8. V   9. F   10. V

7·9   1. travailler   2. persévérer   3. facile   4. amusant   5. faut   6. être   7. dangereux   8. croire

7·10   1. e   2. f   3. g   4. h   5. a   6. b   7. c   8. d

7·11   1. En pratiquant beaucoup, apprendre une nouvelle langue devient facile.   2. En écoutant les nouvelles en français, je commence à comprendre plus/davantage.   3. En faisant des exercices de grammaire, je peux écrire le français plus correctement.   4. Mais quelquefois j'ai des difficultés en faisant mes devoirs.
5. On devient plus tolérant en comprenant les autres cultures.

7·12   1. It is dangerous to give in to your passions.   2. One has to have enough strength to listen to reason.
3. It is rare to find sincere politicians.   4. It is difficult to define love.   5. It is good to ask questions.
6. Hardship makes you stronger.

7·13   1. Dans   2. désolé   3. à   4. récolter   5. marcher   6. chercher   7. rendant   8. au   9. à
10. rencontrer   11. Sans   12. trouvé   13. enchanté   14. Quant au

8 Reflexive verbs

8·1   1. me réveille/me lève   2. me douche/me maquille   3. m'habille/me prépare   4. s'appelle/se coiffe
5. se souvient/s'excuse   6. m'endors/réveille   7. sèche/coiffe   8. me regarde/m'en vais

8·2   1a. Nous regardons un bon film.   1b. Nous nous regardons.

2a. La petite fille dit au revoir.   2b. Les petites filles se disent au revoir.

3a. J'aide mon cousin Maurice.   3b. Maurice et moi, nous nous aidons.

4a. Ils ne séparent pas les enfants.   4b. Les deux frères n'aiment pas se séparer.

5a. Il serre la main du monsieur.   5b. Les messieurs se serrent la main.

6a. Le/la secrétaire inscrit les étudiants.   6b. L'étudiant s'inscrit à un cours.

7a. Je rencontre Marianne.   7b. Marianne et moi, nous nous rencontrons aujourd'hui.

8a. Tu admires cette jolie dame.   8b. Tu t'admires dans le miroir.

8·3   1. PL   2. L   3. PL   4. PL   5. L   6. L   7. PL   8. PL   9. L   10. L

8·4   1. Dépêchez-vous!   2. Asseyez-vous!   3. Ne vous parlez pas!   4. Levez-vous!   5. Approchez-vous du tableau!   6. Ne vous inquiétez pas!   7. Rappelez-vous les réponses!   8. Parlez-vous!   9. Mettez-vous d'accord!

8·5   1. Le matin, Marie se lève, se lave la figure, se brosse les dents, se maquille et s'habille.

2. Jean-Marc se réveille, se rendort pour quelques minutes, se réveille de nouveau, se peigne les cheveux, se rase la figure, se lave, se sèche et s'habille.

3. Quand les hommes se rencontrent, ils se serrent la main et se disent bonjour.

4. Quand les femmes se rencontrent, elles se font la bise sur la joue et se font des compliments.

9 Future tenses

9·1   1. Tu vas venir à la fête ce soir?

2. Oui, mais je vais finir mes devoirs de math/mathématiques d'abord.

3. Bon. Je vais t'attendre chez moi.

4. Bon. Je vais te chercher vers sept heures.

5. Je vais porter ma nouvelle robe ce soir.

6. J'ai hâte d'aller à la fête. Ça va être amusant.

9·2   1. Tu t'habilles, Christophe?

       2. Oui, mais je veux me regarder dans le miroir. Attends!

       3. Oh! Tu es beau! Regarde-toi!

       4. Je me regarde. Pas mal!

       5. Regarde-moi maintenant!

       6. Tu es belle. Approche-toi!

9·3   1. sera   2. aura   3. créera   4. vivront   5. resteront   6. seront   7. feront   8. se promèneront
9. communiqueront   10. pourront

9·4   1. Il/Elle sera   2. Il/Elle portera   3. Il/Elle se transportera   4. Il/Elle se transformera   5. Il/Elle se battra   6. Il/Elle sauvera   7. Il/Elle n'aura   8. Il/Elle ne pourra pas   9. Il/Elle saura   10. Il/Elle obtiendra

9·5   1. me lèverai, prendrai   2. ferai, courrai   3. rentrerai, me ferai   4. me ferai, m'habillerai   5. me mettrai, enverrai   6. rejoindrai, bavarderai   7. irai, regarderai   8. m'assiérai/assoirai, boirai

9·6   Espérons qu'il ne pleuvra pas dimanche prochain. Juliette paraitra à l'église avec ses demoiselles d'honneur et ensuite Roméo arrivera. Le mariage aura lieu dehors. Il y aura 50 invités. Juliette et Roméo se regarderont tendrement. Ils feront leurs voeux. Ils s'embrasseront et tout le monde applaudira. Après la cérémonie, tous les invités iront au jardin.

9·7   1. Quand tu débarqueras de l'avion, appelle-moi! Je viendrai tout de suite.   2. Dès que/Aussitôt que tu arriveras, nous nous assiérons/assoirons pour manger.   3. Demain nous nous lèverons tôt et visiterons la ville.   4. Dimanche prochain, tu rencontreras mes amis.   5. La semaine prochaine, nous nous amuserons à regarder un grand match de basketball au stade.   6. Dans 10 jours, tu accompagneras ma famille à la Côte d'Azur.   7. J'espère qu'il ne pleuvra pas quand nous resterons à Nice.   8. S'il pleut, nous ne pourrons pas faire de la voile.   9. Il vaudra mieux aller au casino demain soir.   10. Le mois prochain, dès que/aussitôt que nous finirons nos vacances, je devrai commencer l'école.   11. À partir de demain nous ne nous parlerons qu'en français.   12. Bientôt tu parleras très bien français.

10   Negative and interrogative structures

10·1   1. jamais   2. personne   3. rien   4. Jamais personne   5. Ni l'un ni l'autre.   6. Jamais plus

10·2   1. f   2. e   3. d   4. c   5. b   6. a

10·3   1. Jeannot est capable de ne rien faire le weekend.   2. Il décide souvent de ne voir personne et de ne rien faire.   3. Il préfère ne plus aller à l'école.   4. Il ne veut plus rien étudier.   5. Il n'aime ni étudier ni travailler.   6. N'avoir rien à faire toute la journée semble ennuyeux!

10·4   1a. Est-ce que tu pars en voyage cet été?   1b. Pars-tu en voyage cet été?

       2a. Est-ce que Josette adore le Québec?   2b. Josette adore-t-elle le Québec?

       3a. Est-ce que nous pouvons passer le weekend dans votre chalet de montagne?   3b. Pouvons-nous passer le weekend dans votre chalet de montagne?

       4a. Est-ce que vous avez deux chiens là-bas?   4b. Avez-vous deux chiens là-bas?

       5a. Est-ce qu'ils sont méchants?   5b. Sont-ils méchants?

       6a. Est-ce que vos chiens sont des chiens de garde?   6b. Vos chiens sont-ils des chiens de garde?

10·5   1. Est-ce que tu organises le tour? C'est toi qui organises le tour.   2. Qui est-ce que tu invites?   3. Qui conduit?/Qui est-ce qui conduit?   4. Est-ce qu'on apporte tous à manger?   5. Quand est-ce qu'on part et à quelle heure?   6. Où est-ce qu'on reste pour la nuit?   7. Qu'est-ce qu'on va faire dimanche?   8. Pourquoi est-ce qu'on ne part pas aujourd'hui?   9. Comment est-ce que tu sais que les routes sont bonnes?   10. De combien de temps est-ce qu'on a besoin pour arriver?

10·6   1. Où est-ce que tu vas en vacances?   2. Avec qui est-ce que tu vas?   3. A côté de qui est-ce que tu es assis(e)?   4. Dans quel hôtel est-ce que tu restes?   5. Est-ce que ton hôtel est près ou loin de la plage?   6. Sur quelle plage est ton hôtel?   7. En face de quels autres hôtels est-ce qu'il est?   8. De quoi est-ce que tu as besoin?   9. Pour quels repas est-ce que tu paies à l'avance?   10. Pourquoi est-ce que tu ne restes pas plus longtemps?

10·7   1. d   2. h   3. e   4. a   5. c   6. g   7. f   8. b

10·8   1. Joey veut-il suivre des cours dans une université française?   2. Ses parents vont-ils payer les frais de scolarité?   3. Son professeur de français va-t-il écrire une lettre de recommandation pour Joey?   4. Joey va-t-il envoyer son dossier à l'université sans délai?   5. Le comité d'admission doit-il étudier son dossier?   6. Joey va-t-il recevoir une réponse au mois de mai?

10·9   1. Où et quand les Jeux olympiques vont-ils avoir lieu?   2. Qui va être le président du comité international?   3. Que doit-il organiser?   4. Pourquoi va-t-il être nécessaire de/Pourquoi va-t-il falloir/ exproprier des centaines de familles?   5. Que doit faire la ville de Rio ?

11   Imparfait and passé composé

11·1   1. était   2. avait   3. était   4. avait   5. avaient   6. voulait   7. avait   8. dormait   9. passait   10. était   11. priait   12. devait   13. avait   14. défendait   15. étaient   16. examinaient   17. voyaient   18. admiraient   19. pouvaient   20. était   21. avait   22. était   23. pouvait   24. avait   25. fallait   26. venaient

11·2   1. Je pleurais souvent.   2. Je voulais toujours ma maman.   3. Je mangeais des fruits tous les jours/chaque jour.   4. Je jouais quelquefois/parfois avec mon frère.   5. J'avais rarement des devoirs.   6. Quand il neigeait, mon école était fermée.   7. Je lisais de temps en temps.   8. D'habitude j'avais des amis à la maison l'après-midi.   9. Chaque fois que j'avais une nouvelle dent, je recevais un dollar.   10. Je n'étais jamais méchant(e).

11·3   1. était/était   2. allait   3. connaissait   4. adorait   5. avait   6. voyait   7. vendait   8. faisait

11·4   1. étiez   2. avions   3. donnaient   4. pouvions   5. réussissions   6. devions

11·5   1. a fait   2. a imaginé   3. a réussi   4. ont félicité   5. ont offert   6. ont prétendu   7. a ouvert   8. a plu   9. a invité   10. a dit

11·6   1. ont reçu   2. ont accepté   3. ont répondu   4. avons rendu   5. avons pris   6. avons mangé   7. ont fait   8. avons dansé   9. a plu   10. avons dû   11. a regardé   12. a joué

11·7   1. es allée   2. suis allée   3. es restée   4. suis restée   5. ne sont pas venus   6. sont rentrés   7. es revenue   8. suis allée   9. es tombée   10. suis sortie

11·8   1. me suis arrêté   2. t'es ennuyé   3. ne me suis pas amusé   4. nous sommes vus   5. t'es dépêchée   6. me suis amusée

11·9   1. a eu   2. a vu   3. a fermé   4. est remontée   5. a remarqué   6. n'a pas pu   7. est rentré   8. a vu   9. a demandé   10. a répondu   11. a confessé   12. a perdu   13. s'est fâché   14. a menacé   15. a demandé   16. est resté   17. a dit   18. est allée   19. a imploré   20. est montée

11·10   1. était   2. avait   3. se lavait   4. se brossait   5. prenait   6. faisait   7. se promenait   8. a eu   9. s'est trouvée   10. s'est approché   11. était   12. n'a pas eu peur/n'avait pas peur   13. indiquait   14. s'appelait   15. avait   16. a téléphoné   17. ne savait pas   18. était   19. a entendu   20. est venu   21. sont devenus   22. a offert

11·11   1. Emma voulait aller à la piscine hier après-midi mais elle avait besoin d'un nouveau maillot de bain.   2. Alors elle est allée au magasin et elle a acheté un bikini.   3. Plus tard quand elle a quitté sa maison, le ciel était encore bleu.   4. Mais quand elle est arrivée à la piscine, il commençait à pleuvoir.   5. Alors elle a eu peur quand elle a entendu le tonnerre et vu des éclairs.   6. Soudain elle n'avait plus envie de nager.   7. Emma est retournée à l'arrêt d'autobus/de bus et a pris l'autobus/le bus.   8. Finalement elle est rentrée chez elle/à la maison et a préparé le dîner.

11·12   1. e   2. a   3. d   4. c   5. b   6. g   7. h   8. f

11·13   1. est venu   2. s'est jetée   3. a demandé   4. ne voulait rien   5. a pris   6. a levé   7. sont entrés   8. étaient   9. a reconnu   10. ont attrapé   11. essayait   12. est tombé   13. est mort   14. s'est remariée   15. ont eu/avaient

12 Adverbs and adverbial phrases

12·1 1. g 2. d 3. h 4. b 5. f 6. e 7. a 8. c

12·2 1. Jacques aime vraiment la France. Il veut rester ici un peu plus longtemps. 2. Bien sûr! Il a beaucoup à faire et beaucoup à apprendre tous les jours/chaque jour. 3. Il aime tellement la culture française! 4. Alors il peut rester ici pour environ une année/un an? 5. Il ne va jamais rentrer chez lui/à la maison? 6. Mais si, bien sûr! Il va rentrer mais pas encore. 7. Il peut probablement encore rester un mois ou deux. 8. Tu es si pessimiste.

12·3 1. si intelligent 2. très admirable 3. si logique 4. très riche 5. assez généreux 6. assez jolie

12·4 1. presque toujours 2. trop dur 3. si spontanément 4. jamais rien 5. vraiment trop 6. trop fort 7. si mal 8. plutôt bien

12·5 1. rapidement 2. Évidemment 3. rarement 4. patiemment 5. fréquemment 6. sûrement 7. Généralement 8. Heureusement 9. seulement 10. poliment 11. Actuellement

12·6 1. D'abord je me lève. 2. Alors/Ensuite/Puis je me brosse les dents et je prends une douche. 3. Après je m'habille et je me brosse les cheveux. 4. Finalement/Enfin je prends le petit déjeuner. 5. D'habitude je vais au bureau vers huit heures. 6. Alors je dois prendre le bus à sept heures. 7. À sept heures du matin, il y a déjà beaucoup de monde à l'arrêt d'autobus/de bus. 8. Quand tout va bien, je suis au travail à 7h45.

12·7 1. Elle salue les étudiants d'une manière enthousiaste. 2. Tout d'abord elle demande aux étudiants comment ils vont. 3. Alors/Ensuite/Puis elle commence la leçon promptement. 4. Elle enseigne d'une manière efficace et intéressante. 5. Quelquefois/Parfois elle présente aussi les leçons d'une manière bizarre. 6. Même quand Mme Tonie surprend les étudiants, ils aiment son cours. 7. Par exemple, un jour, elle vient en cours en tant que l'artiste Monet.

12·8 1. jamais 2. peut-être 3. même 4. déjà 5. définitivement 6. complètement 7. surtout 8. Au contraire 9. attentivement 10. par exemple 11. régulièrement 12. aussi 13. gravement 14. sûrement 15. immédiatement

13 Conditional sentences

13·1 1. répondrais 2. parlerait 3. aurions 4. demanderaient 5. dirais 6. croiraient 7. penseraient 8. fermerais 9. serait 10. aurais 11. terminerais 12. écrirais 13. mettrions 14. répéterais 15. souhaiteraient 16. irais

13·2 1. Je serais souvent seul(e). 2. Je n'aurais pas de meilleur ami. 3. Je ne pourrais pas partager mes sentiments. 4. Je ne m'amuserais pas tout le temps. 5. Je travaillerais tout le temps. 6. J'oublierais beaucoup de choses.

13·3 1. voudrais/aimerais 2. préféreriez 3. préférerais 4. voudriez/aimeriez 5. pourriez 6. devriez

13·4 1. h 2. e 3. g 4. f 5. b 6. d 7. c 8. a 9. j 10. i

13·5 1. Si j'habitais près de la plage, je nagerais chaque jour/tous les jours. 2. Si je devais vivre/habiter sur une île, ce serait la Martinique. 3. Si j'étais un animal, je serais un dauphin. 4. Si je devais vivre/habiter avec une seule personne, je choisirais mon/ma meilleur(e) ami(e). 5. Si je pouvais construire une maison, je construirais un palais. 6. Si j'achetais une nouvelle voiture, j'achèterais une Tesla.

13·6 1. avait commencé 2. avait reçu 3. était parti 4. était rentré 5. avait trouvé 6. s'était marié 7. avait annoncé 8. avait voulu

13·7 1. Ils auraient probablement eu des jumeaux. 2. Ils n'auraient pas eu besoin de tant de vêtements de bébé. 3. Ils n'auraient pas engagé de nounou. 4. Serge serait retourné au travail immédiatement. 5. Ils n'auraient pas reçu tant de cadeaux. 6. Ils auraient eu moins de travail. 7. Ils auraient dormi davantage. 8. Ils n'auraient pas été surpris.

13·8 1. If Nathalie had not gone to France, she would not have met André. 2. If she had not met André, she would not have stayed in France. 3. If she had not stayed in France, she would not have married. 4. If she had not married, she would have come back to the United States. 5. If she had come back to the United States, she would have worked with her father. 6. If she had worked with her father, she would not have become as independent. 7. If she had not become as independent, she could not have become CEO of a big company.

14 Object pronouns

14·1 1. me 2. te 3. me 4. te 5. m' 6. me, t' 7. me 8. me

14·2 1. vous 2. nous 3. vous 4. nous 5. vous 6. nous 7. nous 8. vous

14·3 1. Maman, je te présente mes amies. 2. Elles s'appellent Iris et May. 3. Je vais vous apprendre à jouer de la guitare. 4. Nous allons nous amuser. 5. Maman va vous entendre; mais ne vous inquiétez pas! 6. Elle va probablement vous demander de revenir. 7. Je vous conseille de dire oui. 8. Elle vous aimera/ adorera.

14·4 1. l' 2. la 3. la 4. les 5. les 6. les 7. me les 8. te les

14·5 1. lui 2. la lui 3. leur 4. les 5. les 6. le leur

14·6 1. en 2. en 3. y, en 4. en 5. en 6. y 7. y 8. y

14·7 1. s' 2. les 3. leur 4. se 5. l' 6. y 7. la 8. en 9. leur 10. en

15 Past infinitive structures and agreement of past participles

15·1 1. après avoir conduit la voiture 2. après avoir vu l'accident 3. après avoir appelé la police 4. après avoir décrit l'accident 5. après avoir mis la voiture au garage 6. après avoir raconté l'histoire

15·2 1. être sortie 2. être retournée 3. être allée 4. avoir mangé 5. avoir pris 6. être allée

15·3 1. Après s'être dépêchée 2. Après s'être fâchées 3. Après s'être levé 4. Après s'être baigné 5. Après s'être lavé les mains 6. Après s'être endormis

15·4 1. s'être levée 2. s'être maquillée 3. être arrivée 4. s'être fait 5. s'être fait 6. s'être dépêchée 7. avoir fini 8. s'être lavé

15·5 1. allés 2. arrivée 3. fâchés 4. fait 5. dépêchés 6. assis 7. amusés 8. ennuyée 9. partie 10. restés

15·6 1. mis 2. vu 3. posées 4. montées 5. attendu 6. retrouvé 7. remises 8. eu 9. perdu 10. rangé 11. vue 12. vue

15·7 1. offert 2. acheté 3. préparé 4. invités 5. envoyé 6. dit 7. demandé 8. comprise 9. apporté 10. entendue

15·8 1. es descendu 2. ai remonté 3. as trouvée 4. ai mise 5. est passée 6. est rentrée 7. a passé 8. a réussi 9. est restée 10. ai pas vue

15·9 1. a vu 2. s'est dit 3. a respiré 4. a retenu 5. avoir observée 6. a dit 7. es née 8. a répondu 9. a continué 10. s'être enflée 11. a crevé 12. est morte

16 Demonstrative, interrogative, and possessive pronouns

16·1 1. celui, celui 2. celui, celui 3. Celles-ci/Celles-là 4. Celui, celui 5. celui-ci/celui-là

16·2 1. J'ai un tee-shirt rouge et un tee-shirt bleu. Je crois/pense que je vais porter celui-ci. 2. De tous mes shorts, je préfère celui-là. 3. Quelquefois/Parfois ma sœur me prête une de ses robes. Aujourd'hui je voudrais celle en coton. 4. Quelquefois/Parfois ma mère offre de me prêter une de ses robes élégantes. Mais je préfère celles de ma sœur. 5. Ces broches sont belles. Laisse-moi essayer celle-ci et celle-là!

16·3 1. Lequel 2. Lesquelles 3. Lesquelles 4. Lequel 5. Laquelle 6. Lequel

16·4 1. J'aime les deux colliers. Je ne sais pas lequel j'aime le mieux. 2. J'adore ces deux bracelets. Je crois/pense que je préfère celui en or. 3. Ces montres sont magnifiques. Laquelle est-ce que je préfère? 4. Regarde ces médaillons! Lequel est-ce que tu aimes le mieux, Jennie? 5. J'aime ces trois paires de boucles d'oreille. Lesquelles est-ce que je devrais acheter? Celles-ci ou celles-là?

16·5 1. le mien 2. les tiens 3. les nôtres 4. le sien 5. la sienne 6. les vôtres 7. les leurs 8. le leur

16·6 1. Celle-ci 2. Duquel 3. celui 4. Laquelle 5. celle 6. Lequel 7. celui 8. la mienne 9. La mienne 10. le mien

17 The subjunctive mood

17·1   1. rougisse   2. regardions   3. cherchiez   4. rende   5. sois   6. ait   7. finissent   8. défende   9. saisissent   10. vendes   11. monte   12. descendiez

17·2   1. écoute   2. ait   3. finisse   4. participe   5. réponde   6. bavarde   7. perde   8. soit   9. rougisse   10. ait

17·3   1. aillent   2. boive   3. venions   4. veuille   5. puissions   6. tiennes   7. prenne   8. reçoive   9. plaisions   10. lisiez   11. écrive   12. craignes   13. dorme   14. fasse

17·4   1. soient   2. voient   3. sachent   4. connaissent   5. ne viennent pas   6. veuillent   7. croient   8. tiennent   9. viennent   10. comprennent

17·5   1. Il faut que nous soyons prudents.   2. Il faut que nous ayons beaucoup de patience.   3. Il faut que nous cédions la priorité.   4. Il faut que nous portions notre permis de conduire.   5. Il faut que nous soyons assurés.   6. Il ne faut pas que nous dépassions la limite de vitesse.   7. Il ne faut pas que nous buvions.   8. Il ne faut pas que nous envoyions des textos.   9. Il ne faut pas que nous nous endormions.   10. Il ne faut pas que nous brûlions des feux rouges.

17·6   1. √   2. —   3. √   4. —   5. —   6. —   7. √   8. √   9. √   10. —

17·7   1. soient   2. puissent   3. respecte   4. ait   5. vote   6. aient

17·8   1. Je recommande que vous votiez.   2. Je souhaite que vous vous engagiez.   3. Je ne suis pas sûr(e) que vous vouliez être engagés.   4. Je regrette que vous ne sentiez pas le besoin de participer.   5. Je suggère que vous vous renseigniez.   6. Je propose que vous suiviez des cours en sciences politiques.   7. J'insiste que nous allions tous à ces cours.   8. Je suis surpris(e) que vous soyez d'accord.

17·9   1. Boucle d'or est entrée dans la maison des ours avant qu'ils ne rentrent.   2. Elle a goûté leurs soupes jusqu'à ce qu'elle trouve la meilleure.   3. Elle a cassé une chaise bien qu'elle n'ait pas l'intention de faire ça/cela.   4. Elle a choisi le petit lit parce qu'il avait l'air mignon.   5. Elle a dormi jusqu'à ce que les ours montent à leur chambre (à coucher).   6. Quand elle s'est réveillée, elle a sauté par la fenêtre de peur/de crainte que les ours la mangent.

17·10   1. ait quitté   2. soyez restés   3. ne vous soyez pas mariés   4. sois parti   5. ait été   6. aies écoutée   7. aie dit   8. aie été   9. te sois fait   10. ait fait   11. sois tombé   12. ne te sois pas rendu compte   13. ne sortions pas   14. te dises   15. ne comprennes pas   16. soit   17. arrive   18. finisse

18 Relative pronouns

18·1   1. que   2. qui   3. qui   4. que   5. que   6. qui   7. qui   8. qu'   9. que   10. qui

18·2   1. qui   2. qui   3. qui   4. qui   5. lequel   6. laquelle   7. auxquelles   8. laquelle

18·3   1. L'année où j'ai commencé l'université est mémorable.   2. C'était l'année où j'ai terminé/fini mes études de lycée.   3. Je me rappelle le/Je me souviens du jour où j'ai reçu mon diplôme.   4. Au moment où le diplôme était dans mes mains, j'ai su que je commençais une nouvelle vie.   5. Le jour où j'ai commencé l'université, c'était une nouvelle vie.

18·4   1. My vacation in Paris is the vacation I will remember all my life.   2. The incident with a pickpocket at Notre-Dame is the only incident that I do not have a pleasant memory of.   3. The little Smartcar is the car a lot of people used.   4. The subway was the transportation that most people needed.   5. What I was the most proud of was communicating in French.

18·5   1. qui   2. qui   3. qui   4. où   5. auxquelles   6. qu'   7. dont   8. où